Mass Media and Drug Prevention:

Classic and Contemporary Theories and Research

THE CLAREMONT SYMPOSIUM
ON APPLIED SOCIAL PSYCHOLOGY

This series of volumes highlights important new developments on the leading edge of applied social psychology. Each volume focuses on one area in which social psychological knowledge is being applied to the resolution of social problems. Within that area, a distinguished group of authorities present chapters summarizing recent theoretical views and empirical findings, including the results of their own research and applied activities. An introductory chapter frames the material, pointing out common themes and varied areas of practical applications. Thus each volume brings together trenchant new social psychological ideas, research results, and fruitful applications bearing on an area of current social interest. The volumes will be of value not only to practitioners and researchers, but also to students and lay people interested in this vital and expanding area of psychology.

Series books published by Lawrence Erlbaum Associates:

• *Reducing Prejudice and Discrimination*, edited by Stuart Oskamp (2000).

• *Mass Media and Drug Prevention: Classic and Contemporary Theories and Research*, edited by William D. Crano and Michael Burgoon (2002).

Mass Media and Drug Prevention:

Classic and Contemporary Theories and Research

Edited by

William D. Crano
Claremont Graduate University

Michael Burgoon
University of Arizona

The Claremont Symposium on
Applied Social Psychology

LAWRENCE ERLBAUM ASSOCIATES, PUBLISHERS
2002 Mahwah, New Jersey   London

Camera ready copy for this book was provided by the editors.

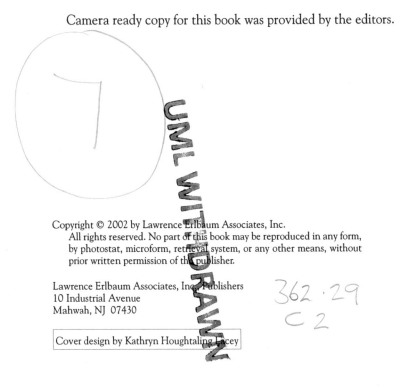

Lawrence Erlbaum Associates, Inc., Publishers
10 Industrial Avenue
Mahwah, NJ 07430

Cover design by Kathryn Houghtaling Lacey

Library of Congress Cataloging-in-Publication Data

Mass media and drug prevention : classic and contemporary theories and
research / edited by William D. Crano, Michael Burgoon
        p. cm.
    Includes bibliographical references and index.
    ISBN 0-8058-3477-X (cloth : alk. paper) — ISBN 0-8058-3478-8 (pbk. :
alk. paper)
    1. Drugs and mass media–United States. 2. Drug abuse–United
States–Prevention. I. Crano, William D., 1942- II. Burgoon, Michael.
    HV5825 >M254 2002
    362.29'17'0973—dc21   2001040408
                                                              CIP

Books published by Lawrence Erlbaum Associates are printed on acid-free
paper, and their bindings are chosen for strength and durability.

Printed in the United States of America

10 9 8 7 6 5 4 3 2 1

DEDICATION

This book reports the results of the 17th Claremont Symposium on Applied Social Psychology. The founder of the Claremont Symposium, and the Director of the first 16 meetings of the symposium series, is Dr. Stuart Oskamp, who, over the years, patiently and persistently nurtured this Symposium. Without Stu Oskamp's constant help and encouragement, the 17th Symposium never would have occurred. It is fitting, therefore, that this volume is dedicated respectfully to

Dr. Stuart Oskamp

Professor of Psychology (Emeritus)

Claremont Graduate University

CONTENTS

Foreword

Alan I. Leshner

National Institute on Drug Abuse

The mass media have been used extensively for communicating drug abuse prevention messages to the public throughout the history of the drug abuse problem in the United States. With its rather checkered history—the "reefer madness" of the 1930s and the "scare tactics" of the 1970s—the mass media have not always met expectations as effective prevention tools. In fact, research on the drug information campaigns of the 1970s found little evidence of media effectiveness in preventing drug abuse. Indeed, some were concerned that these campaigns might have been counter-productive; they hypothesized that the campaigns inadvertently might have introduced children to information about drugs long before they would encounter them in their lives, and suggested much greater usage than was actually true. Indeed, as is shown in this volume, a major thrust in many drug prevention efforts today is to inform adolescents of the nonnormative nature of drug use in their age group.

With the limited exposure provided by public service advertising campaigns, and the challenging methodological problems that all mass media research entails, many of which are described in this volume (e.g., see Flay & Sobel, 1983, on attempting to control for external influences, and the proper interpretation of media-based research results), there was little to encourage research in this area. In the 1990s, however, there was a resurgence in research interest in media effects, and attention turned to how best to design campaigns and measure the impact of media in preventing substance abuse behaviors. Based on rigorous research paradigms similar to those used in school- and family-based prevention intervention research, and despite daunting methodological and logistical problems, some successful research models in substance abuse campaigns emerged (e.g., Donohew, Lorch, & Palmgreen, 1991; Flynn et al., 1994; Palmgreen, Donohew, & Lorch, 1995). These studies, in turn, have served as models for considerable research today. Although the logistical problems have not gone away, the methodological sophistication of current media researchers has enabled us to gain considerable insight into methods of drug abuse prevention that may prove efficacious.

When NIDA was asked to undertake the evaluation of the Office of National Drug Control Policy (ONDCP) National Youth Anti-drug Media Campaign in 1997, we were pleased with the opportunity to expand our plans to establish a communications research program on the use of mass media for drug abuse prevention. We understood that new research in this important area would not only contribute to the science, but would also help to improve communications practice by providing guidance on the development of concepts and messages for public health campaigns in the future.

NIDA's communications research portfolio grew from one grant before 1997 to nine grants this past year. Several of our initial grantees have written articles on their research for this volume, as have scientists working in related areas. This publication provides an overview of the history of communications research and the applicatio of communication theories to youth drug use; a meta-analysis of the substance abuse communications literature; innovative methods to improve message development for teens; and the results of the recent field testing of the sensation-seeking antidrug campaign model that has guided the ONDCP campaign and other efforts to address this high-risk audience.

This important publication will provide researchers and practitioners a compendium of the state-of-the-art literature to guide the development of future research and the design and implementation of science-based prevention practice in many public health fields.

REFERENCES

Donohew, L., Lorch, E., & Palmgreen, P. (1991). Sensation seeking and targeting of televised antidrug PSAs. In L. Donohew, H. Sypher, & W. J. Bukoski (Eds.), *Persuasive communication and drug abuse prevention* (pp. 209-226). Hillsdale, NJ: Lawrence Erlbaum Associates.

Flay, B. R., & Sobel, J. L. (1983). The role of mass media in preventing adolescent substance abuse. *National Institute on Drug Abuse Research Monograph Series, 47,* 5-35.

Flynn, B. S., Worden, J. K., Secker-Walker, R. H., Pirie, P. L., Badger, G. J., Carpenter, J. H., & Geller, B. M. (1994). Mass media and school interventions for cigarette smoking prevention: Effects 2 years after completion. *American Journal of Public Health, 84,* 1148-1150.

Palmgreen, P., Donohew, L., & Lorch, E. (1995). Reaching at-risk populations in a mass media drug abuse prevention campaign. Sensation seeking as a targeting variable. *Drugs and Society, 8,* 27-45.

Preface

We designed this book to tell the story of the mass media's potential in the war against drug abuse. The story is based on scientific evidence that has been gathered from the early 1920s to the present day. In the more than 80 years of scientific scrutiny, social scientists have learned much about the use of media in health promotion and disease prevention. The story is not one of uniform success. As in most fields of scientific endeavor, failure is a constant bedfellow, but the successes, when they occur, often help us forget earlier disappointments. The successes reported here are important, as is their potential application. Those interested in using the media for positive purposes or in learning about the media's potential in the war on drugs may find this book useful and informative.

Today, in the early days of the 21st century, we are witnessing one of the country's most intense exercises in the use of the mass media for the public good. The National Youth Anti-drug Media Campaign has as its goal the elimination or minimization of illicit drug use in our young adolescents. Whether this immense campaign succeeds or fails rests, in part, on past knowledge and its current usage. As the authors of this book's many chapters will show, we know much about the effective use of mass media in persuasion—and it is persuasion on which most hopes for success in the antidrug media campaign rest. Every chapter provides information that the conscientious practitioner may use to maximize the persuasive effects of a presentation. We believe that the intelligent use of this information could have a material impact on the success of the antidrug campaign. This success will stand as an important service to the country as a whole, and will encourage social psychologists and communication scientists to engage in further prosocial applications of their trade. The potential use of this book is enormous, and we hope that the information it presents will be used as a foundation for further contributions to the society at large.

We describe the chapter contents of the book in detail in the introductory chapter. For the moment, let us consider the broad sections into which the text is divided to provide an initial picture of what is covered. In the first section (*Introduction, Early Theories and Research*), our authors discuss the early history of mass-media theory and research, and detail the many regularities that have been found in media-influence research. Approaches and variables that work, and those that do not, are cogently described in this section.

In the second section of the book (*Contemporary Theories and Research*), the authors discuss promising theoretical approaches, and the research that has given rise to their optimistic evaluations. The chapters in this section show that the media can succeed in motivating healthy behavior, but there are many pitfalls that must be avoided.

The final section of this book (*Summing Up*) contains chapters that do just that—sum up. When treatments in the field are delivered via the mass media, evaluating their effects can be problematic. In different ways, the chapters in this section illustrate the validity of this observation, while suggesting how evaluations can be made with greater fidelity. The first chapter of Section III is focused on variations of evaluative models used in applied social research. The proper choice of evaluative approach is essential if we are to extract valid inferences from the obtained results. The second chapter in this section quantitatively integrates previous findings from earlier media research. This meta-analysis provides one of the most comprehensive evaluations of the effects of the mass media on substance abuse. The results will prove surprising to many, as will the extent of detail the meta-analysis makes available. The final chapter of the book summarizes an evaluation of scientific attempts to exploit the media from the standpoint of the media professional. The worm turns in this final chapter—now the evaluators are being evaluated. There is much to learn from those whose professional lives are conjoined with the mass media. This chapter supplies considerable advice to the researcher seeking to maximize media impact in the service of a prosocial outcome.

We hope this brief description will whet the reader's appetite for all that follows in this volume. Social scientists whose research purview includes persuasion and the media, practitioners who would use the media to present their message, intelligent readers who wish to understand the society in which they live, and in which the mass media have played so important a role—all of these individuals will find something of value here. We hope you will avail yourself of the riches contained here. The information you will take from the works described here will surely prove worth the time and effort taken to dissect each chapter thoroughly and thoughtfully.

ACKNOWLEDGMENTS

Developing a monograph of this scope requires the help and cooperation of a host of people and organizational entities, and we are happy to acknowledge them here. First and foremost, we express our sincere gratitude to the contributors to this book. With very little inducement other than the love of the work, they painted thoughtful, stimulating, and incisive pictures of the ways in which the mass media have been, and can be, used to combat a critical social problem. The contributors to this monograph have reviewed classic and contemporary theories relating media to persuasion, discussed new methods and research results in media-based persuasion, examined issues of evaluation and assessment of media effects, and supplied evaluations of media-prevention practices from the perspective of evaluation scientists and media professionals themselves. We believe the contributions of these chapters will materially enhance our understanding of the role of the possible role the mass media may play in mitigating a major social problem, drug abuse, and are grateful to our authors for sharing their insights and allowing us to gather them in one central text.

We also are happy to acknowledge the continuing support and involvement of Claremont Graduate University in the Symposium. From supplying student support to help with arrangements, organization, and planning, to arranging for appropriate venues, mailings, reservations, and all the other details involved in dealing with such an endeavor, the Graduate University has proved a capable and willing facilitator of our work. Our sister colleges in the Claremont Colleges system also deserve our thanks. As in previous years, they have provided encouragement and often other, more tangible support in our endeavors, and we acknowledge their support and hope that we can count on its continuance in the future: to Claremont McKenna College, Harvey Mudd College, Pitzer College, Pomona College, and Scripps, the Women's College at Claremont, we offer our thanks.

In addition to their financial support, the facilitative social climate of the Claremont schools and the Graduate University also deserves mention. When this year's symposium was in its initial planning stage, one of us (WDC) received a telephone call from the President of the Claremont Graduate University, Dr. Steadman Upham. He expressed his hope that we would be able to assemble the speakers and their guests for a reception and dinner at his house on the night of the Symposium. These kinds of phone calls are not a common feature of our collective university experience. Indeed, it is the first such call that either of us ever received. To

Peggy and Stead Upham, our sincere thanks for your warmth and hospitality. Claremont indeed is a special place.

The topic of this year's Symposium, mass media and drug prevention, fits perfectly with a currently ongoing national effort, the National Youth Anti-drug Media Campaign, which was designed and developed to mobilize the mass media to combat drug abuse, one of this country's most significant and enduring social problems. The National Institute on Drug Abuse (NIDA) has played a major role in this effort, helping to determine the best ways to evaluate this complex program in a scientifically credible and creditable manner, and informing current advertising approaches with the most recent advances in psychological and communication-based theories of social influence. In fostering this advisory role, NIDA has supported the work of social influence, persuasion, and media researchers in their attempts to bring their particular expertise to bear in the fight against drug abuse. The work of many of those who have received such support for their research endeavors appears on the pages of this monograph. NIDA deserves our sincere thanks for its farsighted vision in fostering research that will play an important role in the country's future. We are particularly grateful to Dr. Alan Leshner, the Director of NIDA, who has written a thoughtful foreword to this volume, and to Susan David, who has helped coordinate extramural research on mass media and prevention at NIDA, and who has been most helpful in supporting our efforts, and the efforts of many of the contributors to this volume.

Claremont Graduate University students have played a pivotal role over the long history of the Symposium series. This year was no exception. Without your help this year, the Symposium would not been nearly as enjoyable. In fact, it probably would not have occurred. Although almost the entire corps of graduate students was involved in the 17th Symposium, we particularly want to acknowledge Christy Ballweber and Michael Dobbs for their help in all phases of the Symposium's arrangement, and in this monograph's production.

Finally, it is fair to say that without Stuart Oskamp's help and guidance, this endeavor might have become an unpleasant chore, rather than the rewarding intellectual experience that it was. We are grateful to Stu for his constant amiability and willingness to help, his encouragement, and his good sense. In large part, this is as much Stu Oskamp's book as anyone's.

—William D. Crano and Michael Burgoon

I

INTRODUCTION, EARLY THEORIES, AND RESEARCH

1

Introduction

William D. Crano

Claremont Graduate University

The backstory of the 2000 Claremont Symposium on Applied Social Psychology, the 17th such meeting, began in 1997, when at the call of the President and both houses of Congress the Office of National Drug Control Policy (ONDCP) launched the National Youth Anti-Drug Media Campaign. The Campaign is one of the country's most ambitious social intervention programs, and certainly one of the most massive and expensive drug-abuse prevention efforts. Using the mass media, the ONDCP is attempting to reach as many youth as possible, across the length and breadth of the land, along with their parents, to inform them of the dangers of drug abuse and encourage and facilitate their rejection of illicit drugs.

The need for an ameliorative campaign of this kind became increasingly evident as the 1990s progressed. In the prior decade, drug use by adolescents had declined substantially, and more or less steadily (*Monitoring the Future*, 1997). In 1991, however, the decline reversed itself, and drug use began to rise—and continued to do so into the late 1990s. Even more worrisome was the finding that upsurge in drug use was not confined to advanced adolescents—eighth graders were showing the same pattern as their older brothers and sisters. Obviously, something had to be done, but the most optimal response to this dangerous predicament was not entirely obvious. To be sure, science has identified many factors associated with adolescent drug use, but clear causal linkages between these factors and usage have yet to be established. In some ways, the decline in usage evident in the 1980s inadvertently might have retarded scientific progress. When things are going well, there is little motivation to discover what to do if the tide shifts. As the *Monitoring the Future* (1997) report showed, drug usage declined steadily in the 1980s.

What it did not show was *why* it was declining. At the time, however, the felt need to understand the causal dynamics underlying the good news was not strong. Thus, when the tide shifted in the early 1990s, the prevention community was not prepared to provide solid advice regarding possible solutions. Just as we did not know why things had gotten better in the 1980s, we did not know why things had gotten so much worse in the 1990s. The media campaign is designed to reverse the tide of drug abuse in the adolescent population. There is good evidence that by doing so, we will have a positive effect on the entire life cycle of drug abuse. By delaying the onset of drug use, we may be able to persuade some potential users never to begin abusing drugs, and others to progress much more slowly, if at all, through increasingly dangerous stages of drug abuse (see Hawkins et al., 1997). The media campaign is meant to play an ameliorative role in this process by educating youth and providing them with the knowledge to reject drugs; by preventing them from initiating use of drugs, especially inhalants and marijuana, the so-called gateway drugs; and, by convincing the occasional user to stop using drugs altogether (see McCaffrey, 1999).

In collaboration with the Partnership for a Drug-Free America, the ongoing Campaign is multidimensional: It makes use of newspapers, television, radio, magazines, in-theatre video ads, school-based materials, billboards, an Internet Web site, brochures for parents, and other, less conventional media (e.g., basketball backboards, book covers), to spread the anti-drug message. The Campaign is unique in that it does not rely solely on the goodwill of the media to disseminate the anti-drug message. Half of all media use is purchased by public funds; an equal pro bono match is provided by the media corporations. In this way, twice as much material is disseminated. Inasmuch as the advertising is being bought, it is not relegated to the usual public service announcement slot, generally some time in the wee hours of the morning when most of the intended audience—and the rest of the world—is fast asleep. As will be shown (see Selnow, chap. 12, this volume), this partnership of government and private media corporations sometimes proved awkward, but the general goal of the Campaign to reach all of the nation's youth is proceeding inexorably.

Coincident with the media Campaign is a massive evaluation effort organized and coordinated by the National Institute on Drug Abuse (NIDA). It is designed to assess the effects of this intensive Campaign on adolescent drug abuse. The Campaign poses extraordinarily difficult problems for evaluation scientists. First, there is no untreated control group against which to compare the effect of the media Campaign. The Campaign is meant to reach into every home in the country, immediately, so there is no obvious way in which a control comparison can be mounted. Indeed, an untreated comparison group would have been antithetical to the central vision of the Campaign. In addition, it probably would have proven politically difficult, perhaps unfeasible, to deny communities the projected ameliorative effects of the Campaign. Imagine the response of the mayor of a large city who is informed that the Campaign, and all its potential benefits, was slated to skip his or her city for purposes of scientific comparison. For these reasons, a comparison group was not part of the Campaign design.

In addition to lacking a control group, the Campaign evaluators have no pretest data against which to infer change. The Campaign was put in the field so rapidly that there was no time to develop the instruments to test pretreatment levels of drug awareness, knowledge of dangers, attitudes, intentions, and so on. Overcoming these constraints in designing an evaluation of a major social intervention is a formidable challenge, but the quality of the team that NIDA has helped assemble for this undertaking seems up to the task. Although the Campaign is still in its infancy, there are hopeful signs of its success. The very early field evaluations of the program suggest that it has raised awareness about drugs and their harmful effects, and more recent surveys suggest that this awareness is being transformed into more highly valenced anti-drug attitudes.[1] Whether these attitudes will result in positive behavior change remains to be seen, but without the Campaign, there would be little reason even to hope for positive changes in adolescents' attitudes toward drugs, and the effects of these attitudes on subsequent drug use.

The lessons learned in the early phases of this campaign, ranging from the desirability of involving parents, to avoiding schools as the primary data gathering venue, to recognizing the importance of media monitoring data to help interpret the cost-benefit ratio of Campaign productions, will help to modify current approaches and facilitate creation of more powerful persuasive effects in the coming years (McCaffrey, 1999). There is little doubt that the Campaign has made an impact on knowledge and attitudes; whether the impact translates into a reduction of drug abuse now and in the future, and an attendant reduction of the terrible costs of later addiction, is not yet answerable (see Sloboda & David, 1997). However, the signs are favorable that the Campaign will contribute measurably to the well being of the youth of the nation and, by extension, to the well being of the nation itself.

---

[1] An updated web site for information on the Campaign is found at www.media-campaign.org

At the same time that the fundamental design and evaluation of the program was underway, NIDA was actively involving the scientific community in basic research on applied communication and persuasion, seeking to identify variables and establish theory that could be taken into the field to combat drug abuse. Many of the scientists involved in this NIDA-supported enterprise are represented on the pages of this book. As will be seen from the quality of their work, NIDA's investment appears wise and well justified.

THE PLAN OF THIS VOLUME

We conceived and produced this book within the historical context outlined here. The work is meant to help synthesize our knowledge, and in so doing, to guide our efforts into the future. Considerable knowledge is contained in the pages of this volume. Past approaches, successes and failures alike, may help enlighten future programs of research and practice. We believe in the cyclical nature of progress in social research, in which our laboratory successes supply the insights necessary to succeed in the field, and, in a similar manner, our field research informs future theory building (see Crano & Brewer, in press). In our view, in the pages of this volume there is considerable advice, implicit and explicit, about the logical next steps we must take in using the mass media to help alleviate the crisis of drug abuse the country is experiencing. We hope through the efforts of the many researchers represented here that those next steps will contribute to a solution to the drug problem, or at a minimum that they will begin to attenuate its ferocity.

The logical ordering of the chapters in this book is meant to facilitate understanding and to help readers develop a comprehensive picture of mass media and drug prevention, including where we have been, where we are at this moment, and where we might be in the next decade. We began the volume with a foreword by Dr. Alan Leshner, Director of the National Institute on Drug Abuse, to set the stage and situate the book historically and scientifically. Leshner's foreword presents a brief view of the Campaign in particular, and the state of the art in general, from the vantage point of a person who is singularly qualified to comment on these issues. Given the nature of his position as director of the country's most important drug prevention agency, his unvarying commitment to the solution of drug abuse in this country through the application of science-based knowledge, and his superb scientific credentials, Alan Leshner's views deserve our closest attention. The current view of the Director, that the media have a potentially significant role to play in drug prevention, is particularly heartening. His stress on the necessity for work in the field to contribute to science is in keeping with traditional NIDA values, and is well taken. Preventative media practices based on scientific evidence have a greater chance of continued success and contribution than practices that, although creative, may have little or no scientific basis. We have seen too much of this latter approach that, even when successful, provides little insight into why a promising technique worked, or why one that appeared equally promising failed. Leshner's hope that the research his agency has funded will "improve communications practice by providing guidance on the development of concepts and messages for public health campaigns in the future" clearly emphasizes his view of the necessity for a scientific basis of media-based prevention work, and this is precisely what this volume is about.

Section I: Early Theories and Research

Having thus set the stage, we move to a consideration of the early history of theory and research on media effects, ably presented by Drs. Ellen Wartella and Patricia Stout. The evolution of theories on the effects of mass media is interesting and heuristic. In their chapter, Wartella and Stout trace the ebb and flow of scientific opinion regarding the potential of the mass media to effect behavior change. The early days of the discipline were marked by a decided optimism. Lasswell's (1948) *hypodermic needle model* of media effects, a direct effects model, reflects this rosy view. It suggests a straightforward cause-effect process, in which the mass media inject the appropriate attitude into the general populace, as a doctor injects a drug via hypodermic needle, and the injected substance then has its effect on the recipient(s). Contrary to expectations of the direct effects approach, media influence did not seem to operate in this simple and straightforward manner, and predictive failures gave rise to alternative models. Katz and Lazarsfeld (1995) advanced a particularly influential model, which held that the effects of the mass media were carried to the general populace via opinion leaders. This movement from a main effects orientation to a more interactionist view represents a common progression in the development of theory in social science. The model also converged on results of earlier media research by Peterson and Thurstone (1933), who, years earlier, had shown that the data of their intricate and sophisticated media effects quasi-experiment did not map onto a simple direct cause-effect model. This complexity of media effects on attitudes and actions was mirrored in later research of great importance for public health, the Stanford Heart Disease Prevention Program (Farquhar et al., 1990) and the Minnesota Heart Health Program (Luepker et al., 1994), but let's allow Wartella and Stout to describe the historic movement of scientific advance and retreat in mass media research. The wise reader will take from this chapter not only past theoretical failures, which are well documented here, but also promising directions for future research, which the information in this chapter points to and helps organize.

We follow this chapter with Dr. Charles Atkin's comprehensive review of successful and unsuccessful media health campaign design, and his discussion of best practice principles and strategies that appear most likely to have their intended impacts. In his chapter, Atkin considers the effects of a host of social influence variables, as they were implemented in the field, and suggests ways in which they might be used effectively in future mass media health campaigns. Like Wartella and Stout, he counsels caution and realism in developing expectations of media effects. Short-term massive attitude and behavior change is not the likely outcome of most media campaigns. A long-haul orientation, in which small gains are built-on, and constantly reinforced, seem to be the lot of the mass media practitioner (Derzon & Lipsey, chap. 11, this volume, sound a similar note). These modest gains can be augmented by *message multipliers,* which stimulate message receivers to seek out more information on the issue, sensitize targets to it, and so on. *Indirect influence* also is implicated in Atkin's presentation. This concept, which now is receiving increased scientific scrutiny, has to do with the effects on attitudes that are *related* to the issue under persuasive attack, but not identical to it. For example, Pérez and Mugny (1987) found that under carefully defined and prescribed circumstances, persuasive messages on abortion reform affected targets' beliefs on the acceptability of contraception, even in the complete absence of change on the focal attitude, abortion.[2] Recent research has shown that linked attitudes that do not on the surface appear remotely related to the focal issue, and between which even the influence targets themselves do not perceive a relationship, may be affected under appropriate circumstances (Crano & Alvaro, 1998a, 1998b; Crano & Chen, 1998; Wood, Lundgren, Ouellette, Busceme, & Blackstone, 1994). These indirect changes, in turn, may result in later focal change. This research suggests that a frontal attack on a given attitude object may not always be the best approach and, furthermore, that focal attitude change, when it occurs, may be delayed (see Moscovici, 1985).

---

[2] It is interesting and important to note that Pérez and Mugny's (1987) peruasive message never mentioned contraception.

In addition to multipliers and indirect change effects, Atkin also anticipates pseudo-normative influence effects by warning against the use of tactics that indicate that a proscribed behavior is common; such approaches, as Leshner implied in the foreword to this volume, may encourage message recipients to climb on the bandwagon. In the case of drug abuse, this response is counterproductive in the extreme. The largest portion of Atkin's chapter applies basic persuasion theory to health communication, to demonstrate the utility of our hard-won laboratory-based understandings to real world problems. It is undeniable that more focused attention on these recommendations by the advertising-media community would pay great dividends, and it is our hope that the advisors to the Campaign will make use of the information and recommendations contained in this chapter, and those that follow in this volume. We have suffered long enough from the effects of advertising copy that relies solely on creative intuition. Although communications created in blissful ignorance of well-established relationships tempered by laboratory and field research may be charming, they are just as likely to harm as to help. We do not argue that private enterprises should not support such approaches—It's their money—but to use public monies on ill-informed communication tactics seems an intolerable waste, a betrayal of the public trust. Atkin's wide-ranging survey of strategies and tactics demonstrates that solid research-based advice is available to facilitate and enhance almost any form of persuasive technique that is envisioned. All that is needed is the motivation to read and understand the available research. This chapter provides an excellent guide to that information.

Section II: Contemporary Theories and Research

Section II of the volume is concerned with theories and research results specifically relevant to mass media prevention campaigns. This section is focused principally on theoretical approaches that may prove, or have proved, relevant in mass-mediated persuasion, and the empirical outcomes of the tests of these theories. The section begins with a chapter by Dr. Michael Burgoon and his colleagues, which describes the use of interactive media in prevention research. There are at least three features of this important chapter that deserve close scrutiny. The first is their strong review of the persuasive potential of interactive media in past research. As Michael Burgoon and his colleagues show, interactive media offer a host of advantages to the practitioner. By interactive media, the authors follow Street and Rimal's (1997) view, which embraces computer-based approaches that provide users with information access while simultaneously controlling the manner in which the information is presented, and the kinds of responses that are made to the queries of the user. A second noteworthy feature of the chapter is the authors' review of their own work using reactance theory to help account for, and minimize, resistance to health-related persuasive communications. This theory is based on the idea that people resent attempts to impinge on their freedom. A persuasive message may be perceived as such, and thus may be resisted. Reactive responses of this type are especially probable in adolescents, who as a class are generally sensitive to issues of independence. The third important feature of this chapter involves Burgoon and his colleagues' description of two major studies designed to alleviate reactance, and thereby amplify the impact of their interactive media-based persuasion campaign. These studies contain important guidance for future studies and applications.

This chapter is followed by a summary of work undertaken and reported by Dr. Martin Fishbein and his colleagues. Over the years, Fishbein and Ajzen's (1975) theory of reasoned action (TRA) has stimulated constant research in communication and social psychology, and more recently in applied attempts to modify attitudes and actions (e.g., Fishbein, Middlestadt, & Hitchcock, 1991). The TRA has shown impressive staying power, and is being used across a broad spectrum of research on important social issues, from AIDS prevention to weight loss. In their chapter, Fishbein and colleagues discuss the TRA along with other important theories of behavioral prediction, and show that all of them appear to triangulate on four central factors that affect intentions and actions. With this understanding, the authors construct a new integrated model of high applicability to social influence in applied field settings. The model simultaneously points to the most likely route to successful persuasion, while acknowledging the many factors that may serve to block positive behavior (or intention) change. Applying this model to the work of the National Youth Antidrug Media Campaign uncovers a host of potential factors that may have important implications for the campaign's success or failure, and for the appropriate interpretation of any results derived from this research. This chapter suggests that it may be critical to distinguish between regular marijuana users and those who have tried the drug only once or twice. Different predictions flow from this distinction, and different persuasive approaches are likely to succeed or fail as a function of the target audience's usage patterns.

Dr. Louis Donohew and his colleagues reinforce the potential importance of individual differences is in their chapter. For many years, Donohew's work has focused on the individual difference variable of sensation seeking (Zuckerman, 1988). The present chapter reviews this work, and seeks to develop a more precise understanding of the dynamics of sensation seeking in persuasion. Variations in attention to novel stimuli are centrally implicated in considerable earlier work, and Donohew and colleagues link this variable to sensation seeking. Attention to novelty, they suggest, may be a trait with evolutionary survival relevance. As such, it is an important feature of our genetic make-up, having important motivational features: Darwin (1859) himself, for example, observed, "It is human nature to value any novelty" (p. 33). If this is so, then understanding sensation seeking may have important implications for media-based prevention. In this chapter, Donohew and his colleagues present a model of attention and sensation seeking, and review the results of a series of critically important prevention studies that have given rise to the model and provided information useful in its refinement and development. The research of Donohew's group is widely acknowledged as one of prevention's major success stories (see Leshner in the Foreword of the present volume). Those who would understand the role of the media in disease prevention must be familiar with the important body of work summarized here.

Dr. Joseph Priester describes a program of research of much shorter duration than Donohew's, but nonetheless of high potential application to media-based health persuasion. Priester's work, performed in collaboration with Richard Petty, is concerned with attitudinal ambivalence and its effects on susceptibility to attitude change and persistence (e.g., Priester & Petty, 1996, 2001). A central insight of this approach is that some attitude objects may stimulate *both* approach *and* avoidance, positive *and* negative affect. For example, almost all smokers have negative attitudes toward smoking, but nonetheless, many persist in their habit. Most standard theories of attitude structure and change are hard-put to explain this common contradiction. The "evaluative tension" that characterizes ambivalent attitudes results in some unusual, but predictable, outcomes, and Priester's chapter represents a promising approach to understanding this process and capitalizing on it in the practice of media-based health persuasion efforts.

The penultimate chapter of Section II, by Drs. Jason Siegel and Judee Burgoon, reviews three theories of high potential relevance to prevention research: expectancy states theory, expectancy violations theory, and language expectancy theory. At the heart of all three theories is the presumption that a violation of expectations causes some form of attentional response. In this sense, the expectancy theories reviewed here dovetail nicely with research reviewed earlier (see Donohew et al., chap.6, this volume). Depending on the particular form of violation, we can expect on the basis of prior research to observe heightened or attenuated susceptibility to media-based persuasive messages. To make use of these approaches, we must know what our targets expect to see and hear. Armed with this information, we can then use these theories to guide our production of presentations that violate expectations, and thus stimulate greater attention to the persuasive communication. The expectancy violation method has been used in only a limited number of prevention applications, but the results of such studies have been very encouraging (e.g., see Buller, Borland, & Burgoon, 1998; Burgoon & Burgoon, 1990; Klingle & Burgoon, 1995).

The apparent failure of two major national campaigns, *D.A.R.E.* and *Here's Looking at You 2000*, to curb drug use in school-age children forms the backdrop of the final chapter of the central section of this volume. In his chapter, Dr. Marvin Eisen discusses the possible reasons underlying the failure, and then describes an alternative curricular approach, the Lions-Quest *Skills for Adolescence* (SFA) curriculum (Laird, 1992). This prevention model is considerably more involved than the standard approaches, requiring more than 20 drug education units, which are embedded in a 103-session life-skills curriculum, along with the active cooperation of students, teachers, school administrators, and parents. The curriculum must be purchased, and requires extensive teacher training. Some powerful social psychological theories require commitment of this nature to help ensure behavior change (e.g., Cooper & Fazio, 1984; Festinger, 1957), and the design of the SFA appears to recognize this fact. The outcome of this high level of commitment to the SFA curriculum is examined in a large-scale evaluation, whose parameters and initial results are described in Eisen's chapter. This program appears to offer "the first empirical evidence that a widely used commercially available drug prevention curriculum produces salutary primary or secondary prevention effects on students' substance use behaviors" (from Eisen, chap. 9, this volume). Those who create or evaluate media-based social interventions should examine the factors that differentiate this approach from others, which have not proved so successful in past, careful, evaluations.

Section III: Summing-Up

Evaluating social interventions, especially interventions based on the mass media, is difficult. Research on studies of this sort is almost inevitably quasi-experimental, and as such, subject to a host of influences that are beyond the capacity of the researcher to control (Cook & Campbell, 1979; Crano & Brewer, in press). We consider three different features of evaluation in the chapters of Section III. In the first chapter of this section, Stewart Donaldson discusses the various forms of evaluation that can be used in the assessment of social intervention effects, and argues that the distinction has much to do with many past failures. In part, this sad state of affairs arises because social intervention effects typically are mediated via other variables—target characteristics, social context, and so on. The trick, as Donaldson suggests, is to identify these high-potential mediators—to discover the settings in which, the populations on which, and the conditions under which, a treatment effect is most likely to occur.

This idea is an interesting extension of classic discussions of construct validity, which played so important a role in the methodological and theoretical growth of psychology. By implication, the high-potential mediator model argues that we must have some understanding of the network of variables that impinge on the critical outcome (e.g., cessation of marijuana use). Understanding this network, Donaldson argues, puts us in a better position to construct social interventions that operate as we wish them to operate. The idea of the high-potential mediator is a construct of high potential utility.

The second chapter of Section III, by Drs. James Derzon and Mark Lipsey, presents a comprehensive quantitative summary of research conducted on media effects on youth substance knowledge, attitudes, and behaviors. This meta-analysis is one of the most comprehensive available today, summarizing and combining the effects of more than 70 studies, across 123 distinct participant samples. The results of this analysis speak for themselves, and so will not be summarized here; it is important to note, however, that the analysis reveals that earlier pessimism regarding the role of the mass media on substance-related beliefs and behaviors might have been misplaced. The combination of results from many prior studies suggests that the media do have an impact, and deserve a place in any comprehensive, community-wide effort to reduce drug-abuse in adolescents. The details of this research, the decisions that make or break any meta-analysis, are presented clearly and compellingly by the authors of this chapter. This work deserves to play an important part in the planning of any future effort that involves the use of the mass media to attenuate drug-abuse. The findings are complicated, but clear, and their implications deserve our close attention.

It is true that the results do not suggest that the mass media represent the magic bullet, which, used properly, will end drug-abuse in adolescents once and for all. The sizes of the media effects disclosed in this chapter are not enormous. However, two facts are is important to understand in framing these findings. First, most media researchers today recognize that the media alone are not likely to turn the tide of drug abuse in this country. The mass media are better viewed as part of an arsenal of weapons that may be directed at the problem. The National Youth Anti-drug Media Campaign implicitly recognizes this view in its multifaceted attack on adolescent drug-abuse. The second fact that should be kept in mind when assessing media impact has to do with the cost-benefit ratio of media use to drug-abuse. When generalized to the population at large, the savings made available by even small effects are sizeable. Taken in this light, Derzon and Lipsey's results suggest that the media represent an extremely cost-efficient method to minimize the effects of illicit drug use.

The final chapter of this volume presents an evaluation, with a unique twist. Generally when we speak of evaluations in this field, we are concerned with the effects of a program (as Eisen presented in chap.10, this volume) or, less frequently, of the effects of a host of programs (as in Derzon & Lipsey, chap. 11, this volume). Dr. Gary Selnow turns the tables in his chapter. Rather than evaluate the media, he has asked media professionals to evaluate the researcher/evaluators engaged in the fight against drug-abuse. Learning how our close associates view us can be painful sometimes, and at points in Selnow's chapter, some painful observations are made, but their utility in the long run clearly is well worth the suffering. This chapter can be useful to any planning to use the media in social intervention research. The observations of media professionals are on target, and clearly identify aspects of researchers' actions that might be profitably modified. The media and action-oriented researchers often find themseves in a symbiotic relationship. Clearly, we researchers often need the media to foster our agendas. Just as clearly, the media need researchers to provide grist for the media mill. Understanding this mutual dependency is profitable for both sides of this coin, and Selnow provides the basis for this understanding. The view from the professional's desk is refreshing, timely, and informative. Let's hope it will impinge on those of us who make use of the media to foster antidrug sentiments and actions.

The individual chapters of this volume make a noteworthy contribution to our understanding of the mass media, and the means by which the media may contribute to the solution of a vexing social problem. We recognize that the problem of adolescent drug abuse is not likely to be solved any time soon, and certainly not by a single volume of work. Nonetheless, the ideas contained in this volume provide the basis for important advances. We have learned much over years of research on the media, and it is time we use this knowledge instrumentally to help solve one of this country's most vexing challenges. It is in this spirit that our authors present their work in this book.

REFERENCES

Buller, D. B., Borland, R., & Burgoon, M. (1998). Impact of behavioral intention on effectiveness of message features: Evidence from the Family Sun Safety Project. *Human Communication Research, 24,* 433-453.

Burgoon, M., & Burgoon, J. K. (1990). Compliance-gaining and health care. In J. P. Dillard (Ed.), *Seeking compliance: The production of interpersonal influence messages* (pp. 161-188). Scottsdale, AZ: Gorsuch Scarisbrick.

Cook, T. D., & Campbell, D. T. (1979). *Quasi-experimentation: Design and analysis issues for field settings.* Boston: Houghton Mifflin.

Cooper, J., & Fazio, R. (1984). A new look at dissonance theory. In L. Berkowitz (Ed.), *Advances in experimental social psychology* (Vol 17, pp. 229-266). Orlando, FL: Academic Press.

Crano, W. D., & Alvaro, W. D. (1998a). Indirect minority influence: The leniency contract revisited. *Group Process and Intergroup Relations, 1,* 99-115.

Crano, W. D., & Alvaro, E. M. (1998b). The context/comparison model of social influence: Mechanisms, structure, and linkages that underlie indirect attitude change (Vol. 8, pp. 175-202). In W. Stroebe & M. Hewstone (Eds.), *European review of social psychology.* Chichester: Wiley.

Crano, W. D., & Brewer, M. B. (in press). *Principles and methods of social research* (2nd ed.). Mahwah, NJ: Lawrence Erlbaum Associates.

Crano, W. D., & Chen, X. (1998). The leniency contract and persistence of majority and minority influence. *Journal of Personality and Social Psychology, 74,* 1437-1450.

Darwin, C. (1859). *The origin of the species by natural selection.* New York: A. L. Burt.

Farquhar, J. W., Fortmann, S. P., Flora, J. A., Taylor, B., Haskell, W. L., Williams, P. T., Maccoby, N., & Wood, P. D. (1990). Effects of community wide education on cardiovascular disease risk factors: The Stanford five-city project. *Journal of the American Medical Association, 264,* 359-365.

Festinger, L. (1957*). A theory of cognitive dissonance.* Stanford, CA: Stanford University Press.

Fishbein, M., & Ajzen, I. (1975*). Belief, attitude, intention and behavior: An introduction to theory and research.* Reading, MA: Addison-Wesley.

Fishbein, M., Middlestadt, S. E., & Hitchcock, P. J. (1991). Using information to change sexually transmitted disease-related behaviors: An analysis based on the theory of reasoned action. In J. N. Wasserheit, S. O. Aral, & K. K. Holmes (Eds.), *Research issues in human behavior and sexually transmitted diseases in the AIDS era* (pp. 243-257). Washington, DC: American Society for Microbiology.

Hawkins, J. D., Graham, J. W., Maguin, B., Abbot, R., Hill, K. G., & Catalano, R. (1997). Exploring the effects of age of alcohol use initiation and psychosocial risk factors on subsequent alcohol misuse. *Journal of Studies on Alcohol, 58,* 280-290.

Katz, E., & Lazarsfeld, P.F. (1955). *Personal influence: The part played by people in the flow of mass communications*. Glencoe, IL: The Free Press.

Klingle, R. S., & Burgoon, M. (1995). Patient compliance and satisfaction with physician influence attempts: A reinforcement expectancy approach to compliance-gaining over time. *Communication Research, 22*, 148-187.

Laird, M. (1992). *Evaluation of Lions-Quest Skills for Adolescence program: An analysis of student's attitudes, use patterns, and knowledge about harmful drugs. Final report*. Newark, OH: Quest International.

Lasswell, H. D. (1948). The structure and function of communication in society. In L. Bryson (Ed.), *Communication of ideas* (pp. 37-51). New York: Harper & Row.

Luepker, R. V., Murray, D. M., Jacobs, D. R., Jr., Mittelmark, M. B., Bracht, N., Carlaw, R., Crow, R., Elmer, P., Finnegan, J., & Folsom, A. R. (1994). Community education for cardiovascular disease prevention: Risk factor changes in the Minnesota Heart Health Program. *American Journal of Public Health, 84*, 1383-1393.

McCaffrey, B. R. (1999). Investing in our nation's youth. National Youth Anti-Drug Media Campaign: Phase II (Final Report). Available on the Internet at the following address: http://www.mediacampaign.org/publications/phaseii/index.html

Monitoring the Future Study. (1997). Rockville, MD: National Institute on Drug Abuse.

Moscovici, S. (1985). Social influence and conformity. In G. Lindzey & E. Aronson (Eds.), *The handbook of social psychology* (Vol. 2, 3rd ed., pp. 347-412). New York: Random House.

Pérez, J. A., & Mugny, G. (1987). Paradoxical effects of categorization in minority influence: When being an out-group is an advantage. *European Journal of Social Psychology, 17*, 157-169.

Peterson, R. C., & Thurstone, L. L. (1933). *Motion pictures and the social attitudes of children*. New York: Macmillan.

Priester, J. R., & Petty, R. E. (1996). The gradual threshold model of ambivalence: Relating the positive and negative bases of attitudes to subjective ambivalence. *Journal of Personality and Social Psychology, 71*, 431-449.

Priester, J. R., & Petty, R. E. (2001). Extending the bases of subjective attitudinal ambivalence: Interpersonal and intrapersonal antecedents of evaluative tension. *Journal of Personality and Social Psychology, 80*, 19-34.

Sloboda, Z., & David, S. L. (1997). *Preventing drug use among children and adolescents: A research-based guide*. Rockville, MD: National Institute on Drug Abuse.

Wood, W., Lundgren, S., Ouellette, J. A., Busceme, S., & Blackstone, T. (1994). Minority influence: A meta-analytic review of social influence processes. *Psychological Bulletin, 115*, 323-345.

Street, R. L. & Rimal, R. N. (1997). Health promotion and interactive technology: A conceptual foundation. In R. L. Street, W. R. Gold, & T. Manning (Eds.), *Health promotion and interactive technology: Theoretical applications and future directions* (pp. 103-120). Mahwah, NJ: Lawrence Erlbaum Associates.

Zuckerman, M. (1988). Behavior and biology: Research on sensation seeking and reactions to the media. In L. Donohew, H. E. Sypher, & E. T. Higgins (Eds.), *Communication, social cognition, and affect* (pp. 173-194). Hillsdale, NJ: Lawrence Erlbaum Associates.

2

The Evolution of Mass Media and Health Persuasion Models

Ellen A. Wartella and Patricia A. Stout

University of Texas at Austin

Over the past 25 years there has been an enormous growth of interest in the role of the mass media in promoting healthy behavior through persuasive media campaigns. Within communication research, this specialty is today called *health communication*. Health communication is a multifaceted and complex area. Topics include client/provider communication, issues related to developmental communication, media coverage of health issues and media content, campaign message design issues and their relationship to social values, information, and power, among others. Although these topics in health communication are of obvious relevance to the promotion of health behavior, they are beyond the scope of this chapter and are not reviewed here.

In this chapter, we look instead at the recent development of approaches to the study of mass media in health campaigns through a historical lens, placing the recent growth of health communication study in historical context. Although health communication as a subspecialty of communication research is fairly young, the study of media's role in persuasion and health campaigns is much older and goes back at least to the early 20th century. We review the role of earlier studies of communication campaigns for their impact on the study of and use of mass media in the promotion of health behavior. All of this is intended to set the stage for an overview of the current characteristics of successful health communication campaigns, some of which are described and evaluated in the chapters that follow in this volume.

The argument we make is simple: A reconsideration of the power of mass media to influence audiences occurred in the 1970s and, when coupled with several important demonstrations of the power of well-defined and orchestrated public health campaigns, led to a burgeoning of research interest and funding for media and health communication. This is now a very vibrant area of research in communication, and it is a research area that has reinvigorated interdisciplinary study of communication. In some ways, it has brought communication study back to its interdisciplinary roots in the early 20th century, by combining social psychological theories of attitudes and behavior changes with notions of how to shape and target media messages.

EARLY STUDIES OF MASS MEDIA AND PERSUASION

It is no longer easy to write the history of theories of mass media effects on audiences. There are several competing views of what constituted American study of the power of the mass media and its ability to influence American audiences during the first half of the 20th century. And it's safe to say there is no one theory of media effects today. During the 1980s and early 1990s there was considerable interest in the field of communication research in the history of American communication research study. Articles and book chapters (Chaffee & Hochheimer, 1985; Delia, 1987; Katz, 1987; 1988; Rogers, 1982; Sproule, 1983), special seminars and conferences (Gannett Center for Media Studies seminar from 1986-1994, as cited in Dennis & Wartella, 1996), and books (Dennis & Wartella, 1996; Rogers, 1994) were devoted to the examination of the roots of American communication study and the institutionalization of that study within the academy. Much of this work seemed to be directed at either dismissing or defending the notion of the "received history" of the field as perpetuated by Katz and Lazarsfeld's (1955) classic, *Personal Influence*. That history privileged the role of four founding fathers (Kurt Lewin, Harold Lasswell, Carol Hovland, and Paul Lazarsfeld) in establishing a social science perspective for studying the effects of mass media on audiences in American culture. In that received history, some of the early public information campaigns directed at political and health issues figured prominently in developing a view of the "limited power" of mass media to influence audiences.

The received history regarding the study of American media during the first half of the 20th century goes something like this: The first three decades of the 20th century brought enormous changes in the means of communication, with first film and then radio broadcasting. Coupled with the reach of newspapers, magazines, and books, the mass media of the early 20th century were a focus of public debate and commentary. The political scientist Harold Lasswell is said to have coined the phrase *the hypodermic needle model of media impact*, which captures the then dominant view about media's influence on audiences as having "direct effects." The effectiveness of the World War I propaganda campaigns (as studied by Lasswell, 1948), along with the rise of public relations during the first two decades of the century, with their ability to influence what newspapers printed about individuals and the ability of media to create the "pictures in our heads" as Walter Lippmann (1922) put it, created a sense of the enormous power of the mass media to directly influence their audiences. The observations about the powerful mass media's ability to directly influence audiences were gradually put to empirical test by social scientists, primarily in the 1930s and 1940s, with special importance given to the work of sociologist Paul Lazarsfeld and his colleagues at the Columbia University Bureau of Applied Social Research. They demonstrated that rather than having direct, undifferentiated, and powerful effects on audiences, media effects are highly limited, indirect, operating through "opinion leaders," and subject to processes of psychological and social mediation within the audience (Katz & Lazarsfeld, 1955). Thus, by the 1950s, social scientists had dispelled the notion of powerful media effects and had empirically demonstrated the "limited effects" of media's influence on voting in political elections, and preferences in fashion, movie attendance, or product choices. Subsequent to these groundbreaking studies of information campaigns, communication research became institutionalized in the American university in the 1950s in departments of communication and in communication research institutes, most notably with the founding of programs at Illinois and Stanford by Wilbur Schramm, who helped establish a tradition of communication research study within the academy.

Criticisms of this received history have focused on the fact that it ignores the contributions of earlier traditions of communication scholarship such as that of the critical/cultural tradition, which is now popular in media studies (see Sproule, 1983); that it privileges equating the study of mass media with the study of the effects of messages on individual audience members and with the quantitative methods of the social sciences; and that it exaggerates the contributions of the four "founding fathers" while undervaluing the work of others (for instance, the Payne Fund researchers in the early 1930s and other theorists about media and society at the University of Chicago in the first third of the 20th century). These critiques offer a historical opening to justify the current diversity of theoretical approaches (and in particular the cultural studies tradition) within contemporary communication study, and the expansion of communication research to the study of media institutions, media policy, and larger cultural and media trends and practices. They are not particularly helpful to understanding the shifting interest and models of the role of the mass media in persuasive information campaigns in particular health campaigns. The received history did capture the trajectory of much of the research and theorizing about the role of the mass media in persuading audiences and influencing their behavior. For indeed, during the first half of the 20th century there were several studies of the impact of media messages and, in particular, public information campaigns about health and public issues, which demonstrated that media influence is limited. One could show a move in theory from a "direct effects" model to a "limited effects" model.

For instance, during the period of 1900 to the mid-1930s (what McGuire, 1996, called the first stage of attitude change research) there were several large-scale investigations of media campaigns to influence audiences that are somewhat representative of the "direct effects" model. For instance, one of the earliest studies of a health campaign is the 1922 study by K. S. Lashley and J. B. Watson (the John B. Watson of behaviorist psychology). They investigated the effects of a film campaign on venereal disease in producing short-term changes in the audience's knowledge of the causes of venereal disease, attitudes toward venereal disease, and subsequent use of contraceptives and treatment for venereal disease. This study is a classic experimental investigation of how exposure to a film's message can directly impact an audience's knowledge, attitude, and behavior. Interestingly, Lashley and Watson found the film's effects to be most pronounced in changing the audience's knowledge about the disease, and less effective in producing the expected attitude or behavioral change. In short, the venereal disease campaign was not as successful as a powerful media effects view would lead one to believe.

Similarly, the 1933 study by social psychologists Ruth C. Peterson and L. L. Thurstone is illustrative of the more complicated view of media effects on audiences that was current by the 1930s and the empirical paradigm to be followed in succeeding generations of studies of media's influence on audiences' attitudes and behaviors. Yet it too privileged as an effect of mass media the ability of films to "change" children's and adolescents' attitudes. Peterson and Thurstone conducted a series of attitude change studies as part of the Payne Fund investigation of the influence of film on youth. They designed a series of pretest-posttest experiments with children and adolescents utilizing a variety of Hollywood-made motion pictures that were thought to influence children's attitudes toward various ethnic groups, racial groups, and social classes (including the controversial *Birth of a Nation* and the anti-war film *All Quiet on the Western Front*).

Children's attitudes were measured through paper-and-pencil tests in their classrooms and then they were given free tickets to attend a local movie 2 weeks later. The day after moviegoing, the children were tested in their classrooms again. To measure the influence of the films on the audience's attitudes, Peterson and Thurstone developed and elaborated the Thurstone Equal Appearing Interval Scale for measuring attitudes. In all, they conducted two dozen studies, some of them on the effect of a single film, others on the cumulative effects of two or three pictures on the same theme, and they examined the persistence of attitude changes produced 2 to 19 months after moviegoing. The results of these studies did not support a powerful, direct effects model of media influence, but they did demonstrate that movies could produce attitude changes. The results were greater for younger children than for older ones, and seeing two or three movies treating the same topic in the same way achieved greater results than seeing only one film. Further, Peterson and Thurstone demonstrated that the effects of the movies on attitudes were more likely to appear when the children had no firsthand knowledge about the people or ideas presented: That is, when the media do not have to compete with the children's already formed opinions on the topic, media's influence is greatest. And in at least one study, attitude change was shown to persist for as long as 19 months.

In many ways this 1933 study by Peterson and Thurstone demonstrated a paradigmatic approach to studying media effects: the use of a field experiment to examine the short-term effects of mass media information messages on producing short-term attitude change. However, it took another 10 or so years before researchers articulated a theory of the relative inability of the media to change audience attitudes and behaviors.

It was during the late 1940s and early 1950s that the work of Paul Lazarsfeld and his colleagues at Columbia and Carl Hovland and his colleagues at Yale became important both to the "received history" of communication research study and to the demonstration of the limited role of the media in any intentional public information campaign.

The two paradigmatic studies by Lazarsfeld are *The People's Choice* (Lazaarsfeld, Berelson & Gaudet, 1948) and *Personal Influence* (Katz & Lazarsfeld, 1955). The first is a study of the effects of radio and newspapers on voting patterns among residents of Erie County Ohio in the presidential campaign of 1940, and the second is a study of the role of "opinion leaders" relative to the mass media in shaping the preferences of a sample of Decatur, Illinois, women in moviegoing, fashion, grocery shopping, and public affairs issues. These two field surveys used self-report queries to examine the power of the mass media to influence respondents' attitudes and behaviors. They found that radio and print media or newspapers and magazines were relatively ineffective in converting respondents' attitudes or in directly affecting their behavior, either voting behavior or product purchases. Rather, the media tended to be better at reinforcing respondents' already held attitudes. Reinforcement results from a combination of selectively attending to material in the mass media with which they already agreed and selectively retaining what they attend to, such that the audience's memory of the material is consistent with its attitudes toward the subject matter. In the second study, the mass media were shown to have limited effects, which operate through "opinion leaders" who, though they themselves might be influenced by the mass media, are only a small fraction of the mass audience, and it is these opinion leaders who more directly influence the larger mass of audience members.

These large-scale sociological studies of media's limited influence were reinforced by the publication of Hovland, Lumsdaine, and Sheffield's 1949 book, *Experiments in Mass Communication*. It reported a series of social psychological studies carried out during World War II of the effects of the *Why We Fight* film series on soldiers' attitudes toward the war. These classic studies found few effects of the training films on soldiers' attitudes toward the war or their motivation to serve as soldiers, the ultimate objective of the films. Indeed, the findings from these studies were somewhat complicated: They found, for instance, a sleeper effect such that 9 weeks after initially seeing the films, soldiers forgot much of the information in the films but their opinions changed even more compared to the changes that were observed immediately after having seen the films.

These two major empirical studies of media campaigns seemed to suggest that the mass media were not influential in changing audience attitudes directly. These studies, when coupled with a field study by Star and Hughes (1950), which demonstrated the failure of a planned information campaign about the United Nations to influence community attitude toward the UN, crystallized the view that mass media alone could not change people's attitudes directly—and attitude change until the late 1960s was the criterion variable for demonstrating an effect of public communication campaigns. Scholars like Klapper (1960) in *The Effects of Mass Communication* questioned the efficacy of using mass media in persuasive communication campaigns. During the same period of the 1950s and 1960s, according to McGuire (1985), social psychologists theorizing about persuasion and attitude change also became frustrated primarily over the difficulty of demonstrating that attitude measures could predict behavior change (Wicker, 1969).

Thus, by the 1960s, there was sufficient evidence to argue for a limited role for mass media in persuading audiences about politics or health issues. The failure of large-scale field surveys and experimental studies to demonstrate that planned media information campaigns could change audience attitudes or behavior led to disenchantment with such campaign research. Scholars of the mass media moved away from conceptualizing public information campaign effects in terms of the ability to influence attitude changes. Indeed, by the early 1970s, media researchers who studied the short-term effects of media messages on audiences faced a quandary: Common sense and the wider public suggested that the mass media, and in particular television, could hold great power over viewers, yet social science research suggested more limited effects. By the 1970s, it became clear that no one grand theory of either direct or limited media effects was available or likely to help us understand the complexity of media's role in individual, social, and cultural life.

Communication researchers—and other social scientists interested in social problems like violence in America—shifted their research strategies to looking at the role of media messages in shaping a particular topic or problem domain. For example, the agenda-setting effect of news media accounts for how news coverage of issues influences audience perceptions of the public importance of these issues. On the other hand, social learning theory has been used to account for the effects of violent portrayals in entertainment television and film on audience's learning of aggressive behaviors. Thus, today, there are no overarching grand theories of media effects, but there is a growing body of empirical research on how targeted media messages can influence audiences (e.g., Selnow & Crano, 1987).

COMMUNITY-WIDE HEALTH COMMUNICATION CAMPAIGNS IN THE 1970S

The quandary over the role and effectiveness of mass media was evident in efforts in the 1970s to address societal health problems through large-scale community campaigns. Could media be helpful in health persuasion campaigns? And under what conditions? Some projects, notably the Stanford Heart Disease Prevention Program Three Community Study (SHDPP) and the Minnesota Heart Health Program (MHHP), examined directly the effectiveness of mass media by designing different methods of message delivery in different communities under study. Thus the intervention to a community might include no use of mass media, use of mass media alone, or use of mass media in combination with interpersonal communication.

The SHDPP (Farquhar et al., 1990) used a quasi-experimental approach to assess the effectiveness of media on changes in information, attitudes, and risk-related behaviors for heart disease by comparing different media treatments on 3 matched communities. Mass media consisted of a variety of media, including some 50 television spots, three hours of television programming, more than 100 radio spots, several hours of radio programming, weekly newspaper columns, newspaper advertisements and stories, billboards, direct mail, and other assorted materials. The campaign ran for nearly 18 months during 1973 and 1974. The high-risk audience in the media-only community showed less general improvement relative to the media plus intensive face-to-face instruction community (while the no-treatment community fared least well of all). However, for certain kinds of behavior associated with risk reduction, mass media efforts were found to be quite successful, even in the absence of supplemental interpersonal communication. Researchers concluded that other behaviors, like cigarette smoking cessation, require a "constellation of media events which contain a considerable amount of skills training" (Maccoby & Solomon, 1981, p. 115). The success of the Three Community Study prompted creation of the Five City Study in 1978, which drew on much from the original design while enlarging the scope of the project.

The campaign strategy of mixing mass media and supplemental interpersonal communication did not always result in such positive outcomes. The Minnesota Heart Health Program involved an intervention in 6 communities in the upper Midwest over nearly a 6-year period (Luepker et al., 1994). In each of three matched pairs of communities, one community was designated as the intervention site and the other as the control. After an extended baseline period, the intervention began and included a high-intensity mass media campaign and extensive community involvement. Goals of the intervention were to improve health behaviors; lower cholesterol, blood pressure, and cigarette smoking, and increase physical activity; and reduce cardiovascular disease morbidity and mortality by 15%. Results of the campaign intervention were modest, finding improvements in message exposure, activities, and coronary heart disease risk factors usually within chance levels, and "no evidence of any cumulative effect on the estimated risk of dying from coronary heart disease" (Luepker et al., 1994, p. 1391).

These studies are only illustrative of a variety of targeted campaigns, including the antismoking campaigns and seat belt campaigns. In short, since the 1970s, although there are no overarching grand theories of how the media influence audiences, we have learned a variety of lessons, such as when mass media are helpful and successful in health campaigns, how such intended planned campaigns relate to larger issues of media portrayals of social behavior, and how news coverage of health issues can influence audience and policymakers' views of health issues.

SOME KEY LESSONS LEARNED

Although the results of these community-wide public health campaigns showed that the mass media had stronger effects for certain types of messages to certain audiences under certain conditions, the experience gleaned from these studies helped to focus attention on some important conditions for maximizing the use of mass media in the development of targeted health communication campaigns. Three important insights for conducting health communication campaigns become evident in examining the results of previous large-scale campaigns. First, synergistic strength is gained from use of a planned integrated strategy for matching intervention messages to audiences via multiple channels involving more than mass media. Second, campaign outcomes are likely to be more successful when there is careful identification and matching of target population to the recommended behaviors, messages and media channels for delivery. Third, campaigns need to recognize and respond to the social and political contexts within which most health behavior is embedded. Targeted communication cannot be expected single-handedly to generate effects.

Social Marketing Approach

There is synergistic strength gained from use of an integrated strategy for matching intervention messages to audiences via multiple channels. Public health campaigns today are more likely to use an integrated strategy for planning, development, and delivery of the intervention by employing a social marketing approach. Indeed, social marketing is the current buzzword in developing targeted advertising strategy.

Social marketing is "the adaptation of commercial marketing technologies to programs designed to influence the voluntary behavior of target audiences to improve their personal welfare and that of the society of which they are a part" (Andreasen, 1994, p. 110). It involves the use of marketing techniques (including the four "P's" of product, price, promotion, and place) to influence individual behavior.

The process of managing social marketing involves several steps. These include:

1. An assessment of the environment in which the campaign will occur.
2. The identification of the target-adopter population and characteristics to be used to segment the audience into groups with common characteristics.
3. The design of campaign objectives and strategies.
4. A careful consideration of the "marketing mix" or "4P's." This consideration of the marketing mix requires an understanding of what behavior (or product) the campaign is attempting to influence (e.g., regular condom use); the physical, social and psychological costs (or price) related to complying with the campaign recommendations (e.g., will my partner think I sleep around or that I think he sleeps around if I ask him to wear a condom); the packaging and presentation (or promotion) of the product/behavior to compensate for costs to the individual to comply (e.g., example with condoms); and finally, the availability (or place/distribution) of the recommended response (e.g., availability of condoms in vending machines in college dormitories).
5. The management of the social marketing process involves planning, organization, implementation, control and evaluation of the social marketing program. In short, social marketing used the traditional advertising strategies to "sell" a health message. Overall, social marketing has been widely used in health communication campaigns in both the United States and abroad, where it has been used to promote family planning, infant health, and condom use to prevent HIV transmission (Rogers, 1996), and it is the approach of one of the largest government-sponsored social interventions ever enacted in the United States, the National Youth Anti-Drug Media Campaign.

Importance of Segmentation and Targeting: Stages of Change Models

A second important insight for maximizing campaign effectiveness is careful identification of and matching the message to the target population in terms of that audience's health beliefs, behaviors, and media use. Although the notion that individuals respond differently to messages (e.g., McGuire, 1976) or adopt behaviors at different rates (e.g., Rogers, 1962, 1983) is not new, a useful model of stage conceptualization for application to health communication was developed by Prochaska and DiClemente, beginning in the early 1980s. The Transtheoretical Model or stages of change model (SOC) posits five stages through which individuals progress towards behavior change (Prochaska & DiClemente, 1983, 1985; Prochaska, DiClemente, & Norcross, 1992). The model allows communicators to identify the stage where the target audience members can be placed along a continuum from ignorance or indifference (i.e., no action) to commitment to a behavior (i.e., consistent action). Research documenting the model has involved behavior change in the areas of smoking cessation (Prochaska & DiClemente, 1983), substance use (DiClemente & Hughes, 1990), weight control (O'Connell & Velicer, 1988; Prochaska, Norcross, Fowler, Follick, & Abrams, 1992), and sun screen use (Rossi, 1989), among others.

The SOC model interfaces neatly with the social marketing approach discussed earlier in that it benefits from up-front research that takes into account the perspective of the target groups, and it presents a systematic strategy for careful behavior-based segmentation of the target and provides a means for matching intervention and messages to enhance adoption of change. Because the model allows for a wide range of change processes within each stage of change, it is linked to various social psychological theories of persuasion and attitude and behavior change, such as social cognitive theory and others.

Importance of the Environmental Context:
Edutainment and Media Advocacy

Finally, we've realized the need to account for the complexity of social, political, and economic contexts within which most health behavior is embedded; that is, the third consideration for implementing successful health communication campaigns results from the knowledge gained from the large community-wide public health campaigns of the 1970s. Any persuasive health campaign is embedded in a larger set of social and political notions about healthy behavior—whether it is social acceptance or rejection of smoking or seat-belt use. Both larger societal news of health behaviors and media portrayals of social behaviors are contexts within which intentional mass media health campaigns operate.

There is a tendency by public health professionals to look to the media as a way of directly changing behavior. The underlying assumption is that people practice risky behaviors because they lack accurate information to fully understand the consequences of their actions. Public health campaigns attempt to inform populations about these health matters. But the mass media present a constant stream of health-related messages from other sources, through news, advertising, talk shows and entertainment programming. It is against this backdrop that individuals process health promotion messages. Television is a particularly popular source for health information and, like other media, conveys this information through characters in the media who can be seen as role models of behaviors relevant to health, through a specific perspective about the nature of health and illness, and through advertising of health-related products and lifestyles that are not necessarily all that healthy. Both intended and targeted media health messages need to be coupled with advocacy for healthy behavior messages throughout media.

Two approaches to using mass media for health promotion that target attempts to influence media coverage of health issues are media advocacy and the notion of entertainment–education or "edutainment." Media advocacy makes strategic use of mass media to advance a social or public policy initiative (Smoking Control, 1988; Wallack, Dorfman, Jernigan, & Themba, 1993). In order to reframe public debate to increase public support for more effective policy approaches to public health problems, media advocacy uses a range of strategies to gain increased media coverage. Although media coverage of health issues in the news, entertainment, and public service will tend to increase awareness and knowledge of health issues, the essence of media advocacy is to involve the public in the policy generating process (Wallack, 1990). We've recently seen media advocacy in the area of tobacco use reframe the problem of youth and smoking from one of individual commitment to quit smoking to one of eliminating access of cigarettes to youth through the removal of vending machines and tighter rules on cigarette sales to minors.

The use of entertainment education attempts to capitalize on the advantages of entertainment program to capture wide audience attention to influence them. It seeks to take advantage of the appeal of popular media to show individuals how they can live healthier and happier lives (Singhal & Rogers, 1999). When television characters seek psychiatric help, discuss safe sex practices, or get health checkups, such as mammograms, these characters are sending powerful health messages that are influential. Singhal and Rogers (1999) offered a comprehensive look at a variety of entertainment education programs worldwide, across different media (e.g., television, radio, etc.), and also addressed issues concerning effects found and research methodologies. They concluded that using entertainment fare to educate about health is a flexible, adaptable, and versatile media strategy that holds promise for influencing short-term health behavior when used properly (Singhal & Rogers, 1999).

The recent announcement and controversy over the White House attempts to encourage the broadcast networks use of antidrug messages in their programs illustrates the growing popularity of this intervention strategy—but also the potential political problems of having federal agencies attempt to influence programmers.

In short, there are now theoretical models of how to shape media messages to produce individual level effects like increasing awareness of healthy practices and attitude and behavioral changes. Indeed, there are several theoretical formulations of persuasion that are discussed in this volume.

Also, we are more aware of the media health messages conveyed in the news, and through the embedded portrayals of health practices in daytime soap operas and the various portrayals of illness on prime-time programs as well as that of physicians and health care institutes. Every day the media send messages about alcohol, drugs, food, nutrition, sex, and sexuality, as well as the efficacy of our health institutions to help us when we are sick. Studies often show that portrayals in the media are often in serious conflict with realistic guidelines for health, nutrition, and medicine, and that people who spend more time with media, particularly TV, may have beliefs about health that conflict with good practices. Thus there is a growing interest in media advocacy and the use of entertainment for health education.

CONCLUSION

Let us try to summarize the study of the mass media's role in health campaigns and communicating health messages. The relative success of major demonstration projects in the 1970s and later showed that media, when used appropriately, could enable behavior outcomes. We now believe media messages are part of any intervention strategy. But we have no grand theoretical formulation of how media affect attitudes or behavioral change. The social marketing approach to designing messages is in many ways atheoretical, campaign specific, and leads to non-cumulative findings about the process of persuasion even when it works.

The shifts toward concern for "prevention" as a means of addressing societal health issues has opened the door for health promotion and health education as means for addressing health issues. This in turn has led to increased importance of communication (in mass media and small media and interpersonal formats). Thus there is now a larger role for entertainment as education and advocacy in news coverages of issues. Developing health campaigns involves more than well-constructed public service announcements or pamphlets.

Finally, the continued availability of federal funding for health-related projects and, most recently, the shift to availability of funds for "paid-for media" will ensure research activity in this area. We should expect more research on the development of media health campaigns and the role of media in health education. It is hard to find a major health education initiative today that would not both monitor and use mass media for influencing the public health. Finally there has been a reintegration of communication study with other social sciences, like social psychology, sociology, anthropology, and so on. Efforts are more integrated across disciplines now (as anyone sitting on a grant review panel can attest), and more often, communication experts are being added to research teams to assess the quality of the communication component of interventions and campaigns.

REFERENCES

Andreasen, A. R. (1994). Social marketing: Its definition and domain. *Journal of Public Policy & Marketing, 13,* 108-114.

Chaffee, S. H. & Hockheimer, J. L. (1985). The beginnings of political communication research in the United States: Origins of the "limited effects" model. In E. M. Rogers, & F. Balle (Eds.), *The media revolution in America and Western Europe* (pp. 60-95). Norwood, NJ: Ablex.

Delia, J. B. (1987). Communication research: A history. In C. Berger & S. Chaffee (Eds.), *Handbook of communication science* (pp. 20-98). Newbury Park, CA: Sage.

Dennis, E. E., & Wartella, E. A. (1996). *American communication research: The remembered history.* Mahwah, NJ: Lawrence Erlbaum Associates.

DiClemente, C. C. & Hughes, S. O. (1990). Stages of change profiles in treatment. *Journal of Substance Abuse, 2,* 217-235.

Farquhar, J. W., Fortmann, S. P., Flora, J. A., Taylor, B., Haskell, W. L., Williams, P. T., Maccoby, N., & Wood, P. D. (1990). Effects of community wide education on cardiovascular disease risk factors: The Stanford five-city project. *Journal of the American Medical Association, 264,* 359-365.

Hovland, C., Lumsdaine, A., & Sheffield, S. (1949). *Experiments in mass communication* (Vol. 3). Princeton, NJ: Princeton University Press.

Katz, E. (1987). Communications research since Lazarsfeld. *Public Opinion Quarterly, 51,* 25-45.

Katz, E., & Lazarsfeld, P. F. (1955). *Personal influence: The part played by people in the flow of mass communications.* Glencoe, IL: Free Press.

Klapper, J. T. (1960). *The effects of mass communication.* Glencoe, IL: Free Press.

Lashley, K. S., & Watson, J. B. (1922). *A psychological study of motion pictures in relation to venereal disease campaigns.* Washington: U.S. Interdepartmental Social Hygiene Board.

Lasswell, H. D. (1948). The structure and function of communication in society. In L. Bryson (Ed.), *Communication of ideas* (pp. 37-51). New York: Harper & Row.

Lazarsfeld, P. F., Berelson, B. R., & Gudet, H. (1948). *The people's choice.* New York: Columbia University Press.

Lippmann, W. (1922). *Public opinion.* New York: Harcourt Brace.

Luepker, R. V., Murray, D. M., Jacobs, D. R., Jr., Mittelmark, M. B., Bracht, N., & Carlaw, R. (1994). Community education for cardiovascular disease prevention: Risk factor changes in the Minnesota Heart Health Program. *American Journal of Public Health, 84,* 1383-1393.

Maccoby, N., & Solomon, D. S. (1981). Heart disease prevention: Community studies. In R.E. Rice & W.J. Paisley (Eds.), *Public communication campaigns* (pp. 105-126). Beverly Hills, CA: Sage.

McGuire, W. J. (1976). Some internal psychological factors influencing consumer choice. *Journal of Consumer Research, 2,* 302-319.

McGuire, W. (1985). Attitude and attitude change. In G. Lindzey & E. Aronson (Eds.), *Handbook of social psychology* (2nd ed., Vol. 2, pp. 233-346). Reading, MA: Addison-Wesley.

McGuire, W. J. (1996). The Yale communication and attitude change program of the 1950s. In E. Dennis & E. A. Wartella (Eds.), *American communication research: The remembered history* (pp. 39-60). Mahwah, NJ: Lawrence Erlbaum Associates

O'Connell, D. O., & Velicer, W. F. (1988). A decisional balance measure of the stages of change model for weight loss. *International Journal of the Addictions, 23,* 729-740.

Peterson, R. E., & Thurstone, E. L. (1933). *Motion pictures and the social attitudes of children.* New York: Macmillan.

Prochaska, J. O., & DiClemente, C. C. (1983). Stages and processes of self-change in smoking: Toward an integrative model of change. *Journal of Consulting and Clinical Psychology, 51,* 390-395.

Prochaska, J. O., & DiClemente, C. C. (1985). Common processes of change in smoking, weight control and psychological distress. In. S. Shiffman & T.A. Willis (Eds.), *Coping and substance abuse* (pp. 345-363). New York: Academic Press.

Prochaska, J. O., DiClemente, C. C., & Norcross, J. (1992). In search of how people change: Application to addictive behaviors. *American Psychologist, 47,* 1102-1114.

Prochaska, J. O., Norcross, J. C., Fowler, J. L., Follick, M. J., & Abrams, D. B. (1992). Attendance and outcome in a work site weight control program: Processes and stages of change as process and predictor variables. *Addictive Behaviors, 17,* 35-45.

Rogers, E. M. (1962). *Diffusion of Innovations.* New York: Free Press.

Rogers, E. (1982). The empirical and critical schools of communication research. In. M. Burgoon (Ed.), *Communication yearbook* (pp. 125-144). New Brunswick, NJ: Transaction Books.

Rogers, E. M. (1983). *Diffusion of Innovations* (3rd ed.). New York: Free Press.

Rogers, E. M. (1994). *A history of communication study: A biographical approach.* New York: Free Press.

Rogers, E. M. (1996). The field of health communication today. *American Behavioral Scientist, 38,* 208-214.

Rossi, J. S. (1989). Exploring behavioral approaches to UV risk reduction. In A. Moshell & L. W. Blankenbaker (Eds.), *Sunlight, ultraviolet radiation, and the skin* (pp. 91-93). Bethesda, MD: National Institutes of Health.

Selnow, G. F., & Crano, W. D. (1987). *Planning, implementing, and evaluating targeted communication programs: A manual for business communicators*. New York: Quantum Books.

Singhal, A. & Rogers, E. M. (1999). *Entertainment-education: A communication strategy for social change*. Mahwah, NJ: Lawrence Erlbaum Associates.

Smoking control media advocacy guidelines. (1988). Washington, DC: Advocacy Institute for the National Cancer Institute, National Institutes of Health.

Sproule, J. M. (1983). The Institute for Propaganda Analysis: Public education in argumentation, 1937--1942. In D. Zarefsky, M. O. Sillars, & J. Rhodes (Eds.), *Argument in transition* (pp. 57-85). Annandale, VA: Speech Communication Association.

Star, S., & Hughes, H. (1950). A report on an educational campaign: The Cincinnati plan for the United Nations. *American Journal of Sociology, 55*, 389-400.

Wallack, L. (1990). Improving health promotion: Media advocacy and social marketing approaches. In C. Atkin & L Wallack (Eds.), *Mass communication and public health* (pp. 147-163). Newbury Park, CA: Sage.

Wallack, L., Dorfman, L., Jernigan, D., & Themba, M. (1993). *Media advocacy and public health*. Newbury Park, CA: Sage.

Wicker, A. W. (1969). Attitudes vs. actions: The relationship of verbal and overt behavioral responses to attitude objects. *Journal of Social Issues, 25*, 41-78.

3

Promising Strategies for Media Health Campaigns

Charles Atkin
Michigan State University

Devising effective mass communication drug prevention strategies poses a difficult challenge to campaign design specialists and media professionals. This chapter reviews conventional strategies from the general health campaign literature and offers some promising innovative approaches that may achieve greater success in addressing the drug problem. The recently initiated national drug campaign blueprint is well grounded in theory and sophisticated in basic design. The Office of National Drug Control Policy (ONDCP) and the Partnership for a Drug-Free America (PDFA) approaches are consistent with many principles in this chapter, and certain tactics are cited as examples of effective strategy. Nevertheless, anti-drug campaign designers can profit by considering additional strategic factors and by fine-tuning the current strategies.

APPROACHING CAMPAIGN DESIGN

Disciplined campaign designers must undertake tedious homework before progressing to the fun phase of message creation. The starting point in health campaign design is a conceptual analysis of the situation comprising several forms of assessment. The first step is to analyze the behavioral aspects of the health problem, to determine which actions should be performed by which segments of the population. In particular, the designer needs to specify focal segments of the population whose health behavior is to be changed. For each segment, one can trace backward from the ultimate focal behaviors to identify the proximate and distal determinants of action, and then create models of the pathways of influence. In most cases, the model will differ for each health topic, and it varies according to focal behaviors sought and population segments targeted.

The next phase is to assess the model from a communication perspective, specifying target audiences and target behaviors that can be directly influenced by campaign messages. The communication campaign can then be designed to impact on most promising pathways. This requires a comprehensive plan for combining the myriad strategic components subject to manipulation by the campaigner.

In formulating the plan, the campaign strategist is faced with basic decisions about allocating resources among the prospective pathways, focal behaviors, types of messages, channels, and dissemination options. Should the campaign seek to change fundamental behaviors, or chip away at more readily altered peripheral actions? Should the most resistant or receptive segments be the focus of campaign efforts? What proportion of the resources should be devoted to direct influence on the focal segment versus indirect pathways via stimulating interpersonal influencers and leveraging or combating environmental determinants? Which influencers should be targeted? What is the optimum combination of awareness messages, instructional messages, and persuasive messages? How many messages should the attack the competition (the unhealthy behavior) versus promote the healthy alternative? Is it more effective to disseminate the messages via expensive TV channels or primarily utilize mini-media? (See Selnow, chap. 12, this volume.) Should the campaign messages be scheduled in concentrated bursts or spread out over a lengthy period of time?

In media-based campaigns, development of the strategy entails sensitive application of mass communication theories and best practices principles. The strategic guidelines presented in this chapter draw on models, processes, generalizations, and recommendations in the voluminous research literature on media health campaigns, particularly theoretical perspectives and reviews by Ajzen and Fishbein (1980), Atkin (1981, 1994, 2001), Atkin and Wallack (1990), Backer and Rogers (1993), Backer, Rogers, and Sopory (1992), Bandura (1986), Becker (1974), Boster and Mongeau (1984), Bracht (2001), Burgoon and Miller (1985), Cappella et al. (2001), DeJong and Winsten (1990, 1999), Donohew, Sypher, and Bukoski (1991), Dozier, Grunig and Grunig (2001), Hale and Dillard (1995), Janz and Becker (1984), Maibach and Parrott (1995), McGuire, (1989, 1994), Petty, Baker, and Gleicher (1991), Prochaska and DiClemente (1983), Rogers (1983), Rosenstock (1990), Singhal and

Rogers (1999), Slater (1999), Stephenson and Witte (2001), Wallack and DeJong (1995), and Wartella and Middlestadt (1991).

The applicability of the general principles depends on the specific context (especially types of audiences to be influenced and type of product being promoted), so effective campaign design usually requires extensive formative evaluation inputs and message pretests. Surveys, focus groups, and lab testing provide useful information to guide campaign development and to provide feedback on effective and ineffective components (Atkin & Freimuth, 1989).

KNOWING YOUR LIMITS

Health campaigns that are directly targeted to the focal segment of the population tend to have a modest degree of impact, and the effects on fundamental values and behavior patterns are very limited. But impact is highly variable, depending on the palatability of the advocated behavior and the receptivity of target audience (see Wartella and Stout, chap. 1, this volume). Recent meta analysis studies of comprehensive community-based campaigns shows that the media contribute to a 5 -10% change in behavior (Snyder, 2001). Although a small increase in market share is considered successful in commercial advertising campaigns, it is often disappointing to health campaigners and their sponsors (see Derzon & Lipsey, chap. 10).

The limited potency of the media leads to several implications and recommendations for campaign designers. First, set realistic expectations of success, especially in the short run. Be prepared for a long haul, because many campaigns will take years to achieve and maintain significant impact. Second, employ some of the promising ideas presented throughout this chapter, and take care to avoid wasting resources on ineffective strategies. Give more emphasis to relatively attainable impacts, by aiming at more receptive segments of the audience and by creating or promoting more palatable positive products. Augment the relatively small set of packaged campaign stimuli with message multipliers, by stimulating information-seeking and sensitization and by generating public relations publicity. Use a greater variety of persuasive incentives to motivate the audience, and include more educational material to help them perform the behaviors. Finally, meager direct effects may be overcome by shifting campaign resources to indirect pathways of facilitating and controlling the behavior of the focal segment via interpersonal, organizational, and societal influences. Most of these strategies involve a broader diversity of approaches than conventionally employed in health campaigns.

AVOIDING CAMPAIGN PITFALLS

The campaign designer must adeptly steer through minefield of audience resistance barriers at each stage of response, from exposure to processing to learning to yielding to behavioral implementation. Perhaps the most elemental problem is reaching the audience and attaining attention to the messages. Other key barriers include misperception of susceptibility to negative outcomes, deflection of persuasive appeals, denial of applicability to self, rejection of unpalatable recommendations, and inertia.

Owing to the wide variety of pitfalls, audience members are lost at each stage of message response. The messages may be regarded as offensive, disturbing, boring, stale, preachy, confusing, irritating, misleading, irrelevant, uninformative, useless, unbelievable, or unmotivating. Moreover, insufficient quantitative dissemination may render some of the campaign messages   invisible. The guidelines throughout this chapter should be helpful in avoiding the problematic barriers to effectiveness, and formative evaluation data help identify weaknesses. This section focuses on one significant problem area, where messages that do attract attention may end up producing counterproductive boomerang effects.

Beware of Boomerangs

Designers need to be vigilant of unintended side effects that run counter to the campaign objectives or to that undermine other health practices. Hippocrates' motto, "First do no harm," is applicable to media campaigns because imprecisely-targeted messages reach a variety of audiences, and because there is limited control over how receivers interpret media content. The problem is more acute for negative messages that depict problem behaviors and attempt to threaten individuals. The boomerang concept permeates design considerations, especially the selection and presentation of target responses, incentives, evidence, and messengers. In making strategy decisions, campaigners should be mindful of the following types of boomerang effects.

Inadvertent social norming may occur when alarming prevalence statistics or portrayals of misbehavers or victims (which serve to impress sponsors and to motivate influencers) may serve to normalize the unhealthy behavior. Reformed celebrities delivering warnings may be perceived as unhealthy role models (and healthy celebrities may get into subsequent trouble).

Portraying the proscribed behavior as undesirable may promote the competition as audience becomes curious, learns it is fun, or regards it as challenging; in particular, it may be risky to portray risky behavior because it may be appealing to risk-takers in the audience (see Donohew, Palmgreen, Lorch, Zimmerman, & Harrington, chap. 7, this volume).

Campaigners are constantly wrestling with the question of whether the forbidden fruit appeal might sell the fruit. If adolescents are told that they're too young to perform a behavior or simply warned not to do it, there's always the chance that psychological reactance may lead to the opposite response (Burgoon, Alvaro, Grandpre, & Voloudakis, in press).

Highly threatening fear appeals may backfire without a strong efficacy component, and the use of exaggerated claims may undermine source credibility for other messages in the campaign. Frequent emphasis on a negative incentive may produce desensitization, as the audience becomes accustomed to this harmful outcome. On the other hand, an underwhelming threat may also be counterproductive if the harmful outcome is less severe than expected, yielding a negative violation of expectations (see Siegel & Burgoon, chap. 8, this volume).

Finally, there are larger issues involving counterproductive problem shifting within the health domain. For example, if adolescents are successfully scared away from marijuana, they may drink more alcohol because it is seen as relatively less harmful. If teenage drinkers adopt the heavily-promoted designated driver practice, it may disinhibit drunkenness among their nondriving companions. If teenage drivers are convinced that safety belts will protect them, they may drive faster and suffer high-speed crashes. More fundamentally, the conventional campaign focus on individual behavior change puts the onus of responsibility on the "victim" while deflecting attention from social and structural determinants of the health problem (Wallack & Dorfman, 2001).

Concerns about counterproductive effects should not automatically doom a particular strategy. An approach that produces boomerang may still be advantageous if it yields a "net gain" whereby a larger proportion of the focal segment is influenced in the desired direction. Rough message pretesting is the best method to guard against counterproductive features that may produce negative net results. In general, careful formative evaluation inputs can help avoid the range of undesired responses that might occur.

EXERCISING SELF-DISCIPLINE

In designing and implementing successful health campaigns, the disciplined approach requires that the campaign team perform a thorough situational analysis, develop a pragmatic strategic plan, and execute the creation and placement of messages in accordance with principles of effective media campaign practices. It usually is advantageous to rely on research inputs at each phase in the production process.

This approach is seldom fully practiced because many organizations that sponsor health campaigns (and campaign designers) succumb to various irresistible temptations: they are occasionally contemptuous (regarding the focal segment as misbehavers who are ignorant and misguided), righteous (admonishing unhealthy people about their incorrect behavior), extremist (rigidly advocating unpalatable ideals of healthy behavior), politically correct (staying within tightly prescribed boundaries of propriety to avoid offending overly sensitive authorities and interest groups), colleague-oriented (seeking to impress professional peers and overly-reliant on normative practices for the genre), or self-indulgent (attempting sophisticated executions where creativity and style overwhelm substantive content considerations). Thus, campaigns tend to overemphasize creative self-expression, clever sloganeering, artistic production values, celebrity spokespersons, exciting visual channels, and powerful fear appeals threatening severe harm. This approach can occasionally produce creatively brilliant messages that win awards and generate positive reactions from the audience, but the overall campaign does not necessarily contribute to changes in health behavior.

It should be kept in mind that public service campaigns differ from other media forms such as news and entertainment because the messages are purposively focused on achieving bottom-line impact on behavior. In many respects, campaigns in the health and prosocial domains are similar to commercial advertising campaigns. It is useful to adapt concepts from the social marketing perspective, which emphasizes an audience-centered consumer orientation and calculated attempts to package the social product and utilize the optimum combination of components to attain pragmatic goals. Because it is more difficult to sell healthy practices than commercial goods, there is even a greater need for health campaigners to exercise pragmatic self-discipline.

Health specialists are not always conscious of the fact that they differ substantially from their audiences in knowledge, values, priorities, and level of involvement, so they lack the perspective of the "average" person. Research data from samples of the target audiences can help overcome the gulf between sender and receiver.

Moreover, diligent efforts are needed to improve the working relationship between campaign designers and evaluation researchers versus the media professionals who implement message creation and dissemination. A major role of the strategist in the collaborative process is to develop a framework for setting specifications and providing feedback as messages are prepared, channels are selected, and campaign stimuli are placed.

DIVERSIFYING APPROACHES TO CAMPAIGNS

Over the past few decades, a relatively limited array of strategies typically has been utilized in media-based health campaigns. The field may be well advised to diversify the approaches to campaign design beyond conventional practices. Like most health campaigns, ONDCP relies on a narrow set of approaches, which may be improved by considering a broader set of communication tactics that are coordinated in a more conceptually sophisticated manner.

In creating a media campaign strategy, there are many dimensions to consider, each with multiple options. For example, designers can choose among a variety of direct and indirect pathways to take, about 50 basic persuasive appeals to be created, perhaps 25 to 30 different channels to be utilized, 5 to10 types of target behaviors to be advocated, 10-15 types of target audiences to be influenced, 10 to15 kinds of source messengers to deliver the content, 5 to10 types of instructional skills to be taught, and an array of stylistic executions to be produced.

A basic theme of this chapter is that disciplined diversification can yield greater success in health campaigns. Rather than putting too many eggs in one basket (or frying pan in the case of drug public service announcements (PSAs), it is advisable to use a large variety of messages. Even excellent messages can wear out with heavy repetition, especially if the message features highly distinctive stylistic devices (e.g., clever slogan, humorous portrayal). Most messages can achieve near-maximum impact after a relatively small number of exposures; presentation of additional variations will achieve greater incremental impact because the degree of effectiveness of alternative versions tends to be roughly equivalent. There are a large number of potentially influential persuasive appeals, so scattershot incentives can strike multiple responsive chords across segments with diverse predispositions.

Similarly, there are a variety of focal segments of the population that the campaign might seek to influence, both directly and indirectly via messages targeted to audiences of influencers and policymakers. The next section suggests factors to consider in deciding which focal segments should be identified and given varying degrees of emphasis in allocating campaign resources.

PRIORITIZING FOCAL AUDIENCE SEGMENTS

A typical health campaign might subdivide the population on a dozen dimensions (e.g., age, sex, ethnicity, stage of change, susceptibility, self-efficacy, values, personality characteristics, and social context), each with multiple levels. Combining these dimensions, there are thousands of potential subgroups that might be defined for targeting purposes.

Because audience receptivity is often a more central determinant of campaign effectiveness than the potency of the campaign stimuli, there will be differential success depending on which segment is targeted. For example, one form of segmentation might be based on the stage of readiness for change in health practices. To achieve the maximum degree of communication impact, campaign designers often attempt to pick off the easy targets. In the case of drug campaigns, two basic predispositional categories of young people are most readily influenced by media messages.

Reinforcing the Healthy Core

Just as political campaigners try to protect their base constituency, health campaigners need to maintain the healthy practices of the "choir" by devoting a portion of resources to reinforcing messages. The ONDCP campaign seeks to give support to youth that have resisted drug usage in order to maintain the "loyal franchise." This segment merits moderate priority, because these nonusers are very favorably predisposed to the anti-drug messages but they are only slightly likely to use drugs in the absence of campaign reinforcement (see Fishbein et al., chap. 5, this volume).

Targeting "At-Risk" Pre-Users. Another key segment is younger adolescents who haven't yet tried drugs but whose background characteristics suggest a probability that they might use drugs in the near future. Compared to the core, this segment of the population is higher priority because of the greater risk of drug use combined with momentary receptivity. However, it is difficult to produce longer-term abstinence effects because situational forces and opportunities may change rapidly and because campaign messages might inadvertently accelerate temptation. Health campaigners face a more challenging advance-marketing task than commercial advertisers, who can readily induce youthful anticipation of forbidden fun when preselling beer, cigarettes, cosmetics, and motorcycles.

Ignoring the Hard Core. On the other hand, the hard-core users are not readily influenced by campaigns. For many unhealthy practices, those performing risky behavior are highly resistant during early phases (especially during the teenage years). Although this segment is in greatest need of change, it may be fruitless to invest heavy resources to induce immediate discontinuation. As they mature or experience negative consequences, some of these individuals may progress to a readiness stage where they are receptive to cessation messages at some later time. In the meantime, focusing campaign messages on adolescent casual users may have a greater chance of success, based on the effectiveness of 1980s anticocaine efforts (although much of the impact was confined to adult casual users).

Beyond this set of examples, campaigners also need to consider other demographic, social, and psychological-based subgroups (e.g., higher versus lower income, high versus low sensation-seekers). Influencing these varied population segments requires a complex mix of narrowly customized messages and broadly applicable multitargeted messages that use diverse appeals and optimally ambiguous recommended actions.

Addressing the Competition

Prevention campaign messages often focus on the harmful consequences of the unhealthy *practice* rather than promoting a positive alternative to compete with it. This is especially the case for substances (alcohol, tobacco, and other drugs), where the positive product lacks inherently appealing features. Although threats can be effective if handled skillfully, the heavy reliance on negatively attacking the competition tends to restrict the strategic arsenal to a narrow array of options.

The overly negative approach can be lightened by implementing two forms of diversification. First, the nature of attacks might be shifted from the conventional emphasis on severity of harm to a refutational discounting of supposed advantages of the unhealthy practice. Messages can acknowledge that the competition has certain attractive aspects, and then argue that each seeming positive consequence is unlikely to be experienced, not so positive after all, or relatively unimportant. The classic persuasion literature on one-sided versus two-sided messages indicates that it is more effective to raise and refute the opposing side if the audience is sophisticated and knowledgeable about the topic, predisposed against the position being advanced, perceives a manipulative intent, and is already aware of the pro-arguments. For example, a message might employ the straw man refutation technique by citing and disproving the inflated claim that "everybody uses drugs."

Second, the predominant anticompetition tenor of campaign messages can be diversified by shifting the emphasis from negative incentives associated with an unhealthy practice to mirror-image positive incentives associated with the healthy practice, which is one of the strategies described in the next section.

DIVERSIFYING INCENTIVE APPEALS

Unlike superficial awareness messages or simple exhortations, persuasive messages add a motivational element in the form of positive or negative reasons to perform the desired behavior. In selecting incentives, the key criteria are the salience of the promised or threatened consequences, the malleability of beliefs about the likelihood of experiencing these outcomes, and potential persuasiveness of the arguments that can be advanced. Incentive appeals should build on the existing needs and values that are identified in formative evaluation, rather than seeking to change fundamental orientations. It usually is more effective to emphasize mild but likely consequences than remote or improbable consequences that are higher in valuation.

Thus, threats of death, illness, injury, or other serious physical harm should play a limited role in health campaigns. Alarming fear appeals can be quite influential if handled adeptly (see next section on fine-tuning of fear), but other incentives should be given greater emphasis. The campaign design team should brainstorm softer reasons why the audience should perform the healthy practice. This diversified approach encompasses messages featuring threats of a less severe nature, negative incentives beyond the physical health domain, and positive incentives.

Minor Health Threats. While serious harm is a major motivator, the severity x susceptibility formula can also be maximized by featuring non-severe outcomes that have a higher probability of occurrence. In the case of drug campaigns, the negative incentives might be loss of stamina, weight gain, or physiological addiction. Not only are these outcomes far more frequent, but elevated levels of susceptibility may be perceived because observed or experienced conditions may be misattributed to drugs rather than other origins.

Other Negative Incentives. Beyond the realm of physical health, there are dozens of potential motivational appeals along the social, psychological, economic, or legal dimensions that may be used in drug prevention. In the social incentive category, drug campaigns can present negative appeals about looking uncool, alienating friends, incurring peer disapproval, losing trust of parents, or having a detrimental influence on others such as younger siblings. The constellation of psychological, cognitive, moral and aspirational incentives might include reduced ability to concentrate, low grades, feeling lazy and unmotivated, losing control, making bad decisions, and anxiety about getting caught or experiencing harm, guilt, and loss of self-respect. Among the economic incentives are diminished job prospects, fines, cumulative cost of purchasing drugs, and inability to spend on other needs and desires. Messages can also highlight penalties for violating laws and policies, such as incarceration, loss of driver's license, or suspension from school.

Positive Incentives. For each of the negative consequences of performing the proscribed practice, there is usually a mirror-image positive outcome that can be promised for performing the healthy alternative (e.g., avoiding drugs or enjoying a drug-free lifestyle). In the physical health dimension, messages can offer prospects ranging from a longer life-span to enhanced athletic performance. Positive social incentives include being cool, gaining approval and respect, forming deeper friendships, building trust with parents, and being a good role model. On the psychological dimension, messages might promise such outcomes as gaining control over one's life, positive self-image, attaining one's goals, feeling secure, or acting intelligently. Exaggerated rewards may work well as motivators, even though the likelihood is rare; just as negative strategies frequently use long-shot prospects of severe harm, positive approaches could promise lottery-type payoffs that are more believable to positivists.

Multiple Incentives. There are dozens of persuasive appeals that are potentially effective, and the degree of potency is fairly equivalent in many cases. Thus, campaigns can usually achieve greater impact by employing a variety of different appeals rather than concentrating on a handful of persuasive incentives. In prioritizing among incentives, the designer should consider the absolute potency and the relative contribution vis-à-vis other concurrent appeals and influence that has already been achieved in the past. Preproduction research can test basic concepts to determine the absolute effectiveness of each one and to examine optimum combinations, and pretesting research can compare the relative influence of executions of various appeals.

FINE-TUNING FEAR APPEALS

A pervasive strategy in health campaigns is to motivate behavior change by threatening the audience with harmful consequences from initiating or continuing an unhealthy practice. Fear appeals can be risky because there may be boomerang effects or null effects due to defensive responses by the audience members who attempt to control their fear rather than control the danger (Witte, 1994). The three crucial defensive mechanisms are selective avoidance of the message itself (due to unpleasant or alarming depictions), selective perception of the information (particularly the perceived likelihood of negative outcomes), and denial of applicability to self.

Despite these problems, the research indicates that well-designed fear appeals are quite effective in changing behavior (Witte & Allen, 2000). Several types of message content increase the odds of a functional response. First, provision of efficacy information is crucial; if the fear-arousing message (or companion messages in the campaign) presents credible and understandable ways for the individual to effectively address the threat, then constructive responses are more likely. Depending on the prior beliefs and abilities of the message recipient, there may be a need for self-efficacy instructional material (demonstrating how to perform behaviors and boosting the confidence that the individual can do so successfully) or response efficacy material (convincing the individual that the recommended behavior will reduce the danger).

Second, messages need to overcome people's natural tendency to be unrealistically optimistic about odds of avoiding negative events. This can be achieved by emphasizing susceptibility evidence and personal applicability, and by featuring negative outcomes that are less severe but more probable. To avoid the perception of empty threats, It is also advantageous to coordinate claims with reality forces that can't be readily dismissed.

Third, fear appeals are inherently compelling and thus have great potential to attract attention and impel greater involvement during processing. However, care must be taken to avoid overly disturbing depictions or noncredible content that might turn off the audience at early stages of message response.

Fear appeals tend to be more effective if the audience can be motivated to engage in central processing of the content, especially a substantive appraisal of the risk (Petty & Cacioppo, 1986). One technique for elevating elaboration likelihood is taking advantage of people's accuracy in estimating risk to others by prompting self-relevance introspection with questions (e.g., will the negative outcomes happen to others... aren't you also vulnerable?). Another approach involves stimulating recipients to think about an array of health-related outcomes varying in severity (e.g., imminent death, slightly premature mortality, serious illness, mild symptoms) and to determine for themselves which ones are personally applicable. As indicated in the section on incentives, the campaign can expand the menu of threats to include non-ealth negative consequences (social, psychological, legal, moral, and economic).

To avoid the defensive resistance problem, some fear appeals should be aimed at audiences who are in a position to influence the focal segment. Indirect strategies for targeting influencers are discussed later in this chapter.

ACCENTUATING THE POSITIVE

As in political campaigns that feature mudslinging, audiences receiving negative messages about health practices often are turned off. To achieve greater diversification, the facile prescription is "don't always say don't." Because campaign messages that attack the unhealthy behavior with warnings and threats are overused, there is a need to give careful attention to implementing the positive approach.

In campaign messages that promote a positive product directly to a focal segment, there is a continuum of prospective target responses that can be explicitly recommended for adoption. These actions can vary in the acceptability to the audience, based on a cost-benefit ratio. The key component to be minimized is the cost factors, such as effort and sacrifice required to perform the behavior, social disapproval, monetary expense, and psychological challenges. This barrier can be overcome with smaller or softer products that demand lower investment and generate fewer drawbacks.

The recommended behavior options also must be judged from the societal perspective in terms of political, legal, moral, and economic considerations. For example, "moderate drinking" or "safe sex" may be more palatable (and pragmatically functional) than abstinence to teenagers, but explicit advocacy of these behaviors is troublesome because of alcohol laws, religious values, and parental objections. Instituting a "safe ride" program or "free condom" distribution for high school students incurs substantial economic costs as well.

The various target audiences that the campaign seeks to influence may also call for different types of products to be promoted. Thus, the campaign can create a "product line" of various behaviors featuring audience-appropriate forms of packaging. In creating this menu, the designer should take into account receptivity versus resistance of the audience and the potency of the incentives associated with each product. With resistant audiences, it may be fruitless to advocate a sizable degree of change that is beyond the recipients' latitude of acceptability; for many health behaviors, the initial product representation should reflect the incremental "foot in the door" strategy rather than the "door in the face" strategy (Stiff, 1994).

The array of products promoted to the focal audience can be packaged in a manner to make the recommended actions more appealing. In the case of substance prevention campaigns, the healthy product typically involves nonuse of the unhealthy product: alcohol, tobacco, and other drugs.

This is a major challenge in substance-abuse campaigns where the positive product is essentially "nothing," so creative packaging is needed to sell nonuse. One option is the "drug-free lifestyle", and another is "abstinence"; however, this type of terminology has not been overwhelmingly effective in the alcohol, tobacco, and sexual domains. Some messages might instead promote modest-cost products such as prebehaviors (e.g., sign pledge card, state intentions publicly, wear red ribbon) or limited forms of abstaining (e.g., drug-free week, delay until later). A different approach is to promote concrete alternative products to displace the unhealthy substance (e.g., choosing soft drinks instead of alcohol at a party, playing sports instead of doing drugs after school).

It is crucial that antidrug campaigners develop more attractive labels and images for the product line, especially because the competition features a drug line with appealing names such as "ecstasy" and "crystal meth."

STRATEGIC AMBIGUITY

The conventional rule of thumb in message construction is to be clear and straightforward, a proven technique for facilitating comprehension in educational and persuasive applications. In general, there is greater learning of material conveyed with simplified vocabulary, short sentences, sparse copy, graphic depictions and a single major point per message. In certain situations, however, it may be advantageous to communicate basic content components with ambiguous visual and verbal message executions that produce differential interpretations among audience segments. During message processing, ambiguity should reduce counterarguing and reactance, and increase introspection and elaboration (thus minimizing the boomerang effect and maximizing audience involvement).

This approach is typically implemented by featuring vaguely-worded behavioral recommendations or by presenting suggestive portrayals, arguments, and evidence. The ambiguity allows the individual receivers to draw their own implications based on predispositions; the strategic aspect involves manipulating the message content in a manner that plays off the perceptual tendencies of various subgroups.

Multi-Targeted Messages. Strategically ambiguous executions are especially applicable to spot messages on TV, where targeting tends to be imprecise. If there are multiple segments that will attend the message, it can be both efficient and effective to influence several simultaneously with obliquely-targeted or multitargeted messages.

The strategic ambiguity approach is adapted from the crafty communication practices of corporate executives and political candidates. It has been used quite shrewdly by the alcohol companies in their "private service" campaigns dealing with risky drinking, which use ambiguous slogans such as "know when to say when" or "think when you drink" to simultaneously attain multiple objectives:

1. Combat the drunk driving or alcohol poisoning problems among extreme drinkers (without significantly undermining consumption levels by regular heavy drinkers who perceive the drinking limitations in a liberal manner).
2. Favorably impress opinion leaders and the general public who perceive that the companies are exhibiting social responsibility by ostensibly targeting heavy drinkers with moderate-drinking messages.
3. Promote product usage by portraying consumption in what viewers perceive to be a noncommercial context (Atkin, Wallack, & DeJong, 1992).

Likewise, politicians excel at waffling on controversial issues and in projecting images and "glittering generality" concepts that are appealing to diverse constituencies. In the 2000 presidential primaries, candidate John McCain successfully convinced voters all along the ideological spectrum that he would "reform the political system"; liberals, moderates, and conservatives drew quite different interpretations that the nature of this reform would be consistent with their divergent priorities.

This approach can be illustrated with a recent drug PSA airing in California, showing people concocting methamphetamine from 30 volatile chemicals in the kitchen; the fear appeal portrays the house exploding in dramatic manner. The ostensible audience is persons with in-home meth labs, and the implicit conclusion is to shut it down before it blows up. The message is likely to produce a minimal effect because people in this segment will deny that it will happen to them, or they will try to be more careful.

Nevertheless, the ambiguity of the recommended response enables several other audiences to be influenced: Neighbors who suspect that a home lab is operating nearby might notify the authorities, prospective meth-makers might think twice before starting a lab in their kitchen; and teenage users might become convinced that the explosive concoction is too risky to use. Moreover, upscale adults might conclude that meth poses a serious societal problem, feel that the government is doing a good job by scaring the lab operators, and support investing more tax dollars for police crackdowns.

One design advantage of ambiguity is that these messages do not require high-precision media targeting, thus reducing the need to tailor messages to small segments. Even when the message is primarily aimed at a single audience segment, there are advantages of ambiguity and vagueness because the self-generated interpretation may be more persuasive than the concept that is concretely operationalized in a message. In the next three subsections, this simpler form of strategic ambiguity is applied to the presentation of recommendations, consequences, and evidence in health messages.

Recommended Response. An explicitly-specified ideal behavior often falls outside the focal audience's latitude of acceptance, and explicit advocacy tends be highly admonishing with words such as *don't* and *never* (Sherif & Hovland, 1961). The alternative is to present vaguely-worded softened recommendations (e.g., indefinite time frames, limited situational applications) or to specify nothing and let recipients construct their own implication. Implicit conclusions tend to be more effective if the audience is knowledgeable about the topic, predisposed against the position being advanced, or perceives a manipulative intent (Hovland, Janis, & Kelley, 1953).

For adolescent audiences, the ambiguous recommendation demands less psychological sacrifice and triggers less reactance than with idealized exhortation, and plays to youth's self-concept as independent thinkers who reach their own conclusions.

This approach is also promising with adult audiences. For example, one drug campaign message to parents says, "Be a good role model—if you use drugs, your children are more likely to use them too. Your child is very aware of your habits." This message doesn't exhort parents to stop using drugs, it does not suggest that they carefully disguise their drug use, and it doesn't tell these users how to rationalize their habit in discussions with children; the appropriate response is left open-ended.

Portrayal of Consequences. Certainly there are advantages of presenting explicit and graphic depictions of harmful outcomes that can vividly demonstrate severity or intensify fearful emotions. Nevertheless, ambiguous portrayals may be functional in overcoming defensive reactions and unleashing creatively imaginative interpretations.

Messages can be vague in specifying exactly what is the harmful consequence, by using subtle symbolic representations of harm or depicting someone experiencing distress of an uncertain nature; this allows the audience to imagine their own harmful outcome as they would while watching a nonexplicit horror film (e.g., "Heroin can end your life. Even while you're still in it."). For high-threat messages that seek to emphasize severity of harm, it may be advantageous to cite ambiguous consequences that are not readily observable (e.g., fried brain cells or silent disapproval by peers), and thus are not readily refutable by those in a counterarguing mode. Messages might also cite concrete consequences of ambiguous origin (e.g., bad grades in school or loss of friends), for which the audience member can make the attribution that the outcomes are due to the risky behavior rather than other sources.

Presentation of Evidence. It often is important to support persuasive incentives with convincing evidence, particularly to augment the credibility of susceptibility claims. For fear appeals where there is a low level of actual vulnerability, the likelihood of harm can be buttressed by depicting rare but vivid cases rather than underwhelming statistical figures; this tactic may also heighten relevance and comprehensibility. In implementing social norming appeals where the actual norm isn't highly impressive (e.g., only 56% of adolescents have never tried pot, which hardly makes abstinence normative), it may be ineffective to cite the exact statistic. Instead, the message can present weasel-words such as "most" or "majority" (which might be interpreted as 60% or 80%), cite raw figures such as "millions," or refer to the "increasing number" (which has the added feature of momentum).

MATCHING THE MESSENGERS

The *messenger* is the model appearing in the message who delivers information, demonstrates behavior, or provides a testimonial. As in many types of campaigns, the health messenger is helpful in attracting attention, personalizing abstract concepts by modeling actions and consequences, bolstering belief formation due to source credibility, and facilitating retention due to memorability. The leading categories of health campaign messengers are expert specialists such as doctors, famous figures such as celebrities and trade characters, individuals with health-related experiences such as victims and survivors, ordinary real persons, and government officials such as the President or Surgeon General.

Although health campaigners conventionally favor certain types of messengers, none is necessarily superior to others in all situations. In selecting the appropriate messenger, the crucial factor is which component of influence model needs a boost. For example, celebrities help draw attention to a dull topic, experts enhance response efficacy, ordinary people heighten self-efficacy, victims convey the severity of harmful outcomes, and victims who share similar characteristics of the audience should augment susceptibility claims.

INCORPORATING INSTRUCTIONAL MATERIAL

Beyond the emphasis on glamorous persuasive devices, there is also a practical need to present mundane educational content that simply facilitates audience learning. This type of material serves to "show and tell" the audience how to perform complex behavior, to feel personally efficacious, to resist peer pressure, and to avoid being corrupted by unhealthy messages in the media environment. Although schools often try to teach peer resistance and media literacy skills, campaign messages can serve a valuable supplementary function in arming the audience to cope with environmental influences. Given the potentially detrimental health effects of commercial advertising, entertainment media portrayals, and certain web sites, it may be wise to devote a modest proportion of campaign messages to inoculating viewers and listeners against these influences that might undermine the campaign.

Stimulating Information-Seeking

Campaign messages that have the broadest reach can deliver only a superficial amount of informational and persuasive content, which is seldom customized to the individual recipient. The conventional mass media are inherently a somewhat crude tool for health campaigns because of targeting imprecision and depth limitations that restrict the presentation of multiple appeals, elaborate evidence, and detailed instruction. To overcome these shortcomings, campaigners should stimulate the audience to seek out additional material from specialized sources.

A key role of awareness messages is to arouse interest or concern, and to motivate further exploration of the subject. In particular, messages should include elements designed to prompt active seeking from elaborated information sources such as web sites, hot-line operators, books, counselors, parents, and opinion leaders. Campaigners need to refine triggering strategies to motivate or facilitate search activity (e.g., health websites should feature related links, and topical material should be positioned adeptly on search engines for self-initiated searching).

Facilitating information-seeking not only extends the exposure to the campaign material, but the content and style of the specialty messages will be more on target for individual needs and tastes, and the capacity of these channels enables more extensive information to be accessed.

Triggering Sensitization

The everyday environment experienced by the focal segment of the population has a rich array of existing influences that can complement the health campaign messages, but many of these stimuli are simply not salient enough to be recognized or processed. In the mass media, there are numerous news stories, advertisements, entertainment portrayals, and other public service campaigns that present content consistent with campaign goals. Similarly, individuals may not be conscious of certain social norms, interpersonal influences, behavioral models, or societal conditions that might contribute to performance of the target behavior. A small proportion of campaign messages can serve a triggering function for priming the audience to cue into the procampaign stimuli.

For example, the media-cuing messages in a drug campaign might help recipients take notice of daily news reports of prosecution of drug offenders, feature stories about celebrities whose careers are impaired by drug abuse, sports telecasts exhibiting athletes who pursue a drug-free lifestyle, or AIDS prevention messages with antineedle themes. The campaign messages can also raise consciousness of behaviors and consequences that are absent in environment: that there are no advertisements for illicit drugs, that drug-using entertainment characters seldom attain rewards, and that no government or business leaders advocate drug use.

Channeling Concepts

Conceptually, channel selection is dictated by the usage patterns of the target receivers and the nature of the message. Pragmatically, the limited resources of the campaigner also play a role. It is usually more feasible to stage a pseudo event that generates news coverage than to acquire time or space in the ideal media vehicle, it is more feasible to achieve a minor product placement in an entertainment program than to capture the whole plotline, and it is more feasible to place a PSA on a low-rated mature adult radio station than a hot teen station (see Selnow, chap. 12, this volume). In these circumstances, campaign designers should adapt the message to the channel that can be accessed and the audience that can be reached. Although the practical "take what you can get" philosophy often yields a less than optimal strategy, the trade-off is that it actually can be implemented.

In disseminating messages, designers most commonly rely on television, radio, newspapers, and printed materials, especially broadcast spots, press releases, and pamphlets. This narrow array of preferred choices has not consistently produced impressive results, and it may be worth exploring a more diverse variety of channels, modes, and vehicles.

Mini-media. Rather than confining strategies to the major mass communication channels, campaigns can broaden the approach to include secondary media such as billboards, posters, flyers, banners, comic books, table tents, theater slides, bookmarks, buttons, shirts, and bumper stickers. Although lacking the glamour of a TV spot or the depth of a booklet, these forms of communication can serve valuable functions in a campaign at a fairly low cost.

Enhanced Public Relations. Health campaigners have traditionally underutilized public relations techniques for generating news and feature story coverage in the mass media. With recent trends making health topics increasingly central among journalistic priorities for newspapers, news magazines, and television newscasts, along with the long-standing interest in specialty magazines and cable channels and in daytime TV talk shows, campaigns should take greater advantage of these opportunities for message dissemination.

Public relations in the health domain should move beyond the passive distribution of press releases to aggressively place guests on talk shows, regularly feed feature writers with compelling story ideas, and creatively stage pseudo-events to attract journalist attention (including the dramatization of health-related statistics using "creative epidemiology" techniques). The source of the campaign messages is especially important, as public relations efforts tend to attain greater media acceptance when sponsored by high-profile and widely respected organizations that feature distinctive or compelling messengers (e.g., celebrity spokespersons, government officials, and charismatic experts who have gained prominence, along with victims and survivors who provide a human interest angle).

In achieving impact on the audience, there are several advantages of public relations messages over prepackaged stimuli such as PSAs, pamphlets, and Web pages. First, there is likely to be greater audience reach at a lower cost. In particular, placements in the mainstream media can attract attention from influencers and policymakers, which is useful for indirect and media advocacy strategies. On the other hand, there may be limitations on the frequency of disseminating certain ideas that are considered to be "old news" by the gatekeepers, and it may be difficult to reach key focal segments (youth, disadvantaged, uninformed) unless diligent efforts are made to place the messages in alternative channels.

Second, messages appearing in the news media (and some entertainment settings) tend to have greater credibility than messages such as PSAs that are packaged in an advertising format; this should facilitate belief-formation regarding health consequences and acceptance of recommended behaviors. Third, health issues gaining visibility in the mainstream news media can benefit from the agenda-setting effect, whereby problems and solutions are perceived as more urgent and significant. This is particularly important in media advocacy strategies targeted to opinion leaders and policymakers in society.

One drawback of public relations is the lack of control over the form of information presentation, as media professions apply their journalistic or creative priorities in translating the message. Although skilled public relations practitioners can carefully package and frame key concepts in a manner that is relatively bulletproof, the campaign material appearing in media outlets may not be exactly what the designer seeks.

Entertainment-Education. The practice of embedding health-related material in entertainment programming (or creating entertainment programming as a vehicle for health education) has become widespread in developing countries (Singhal & Rogers, 1999). Because the interesting and enjoyable style of presentation attracts large audiences and conveys information in a relevant and credible manner, this approach has proved to be quite successful in promoting health in Africa, Asia, and South America. Entertainment-education has been used sparingly in the United States, with narrow applications in efforts to promote the designated driver, safety belts, safe sex, and drug abstinence, along with child-oriented topics such as alcohol, occupational roles, and conflict resolution. Despite reticence on the part of the domestic entertainment industry (and recent controversy in the case of drug-related themes in TV shows), this practice has considerable promise for U.S. health campaigns.

Interactive Media Stimuli. There are now thousands of Web sites and CD-ROM disks offering a wide array of health materials, and many campaigns are utilizing this channel. In addition to the provision of prepackaged pages and streaming video, the interactive capacity of these technologies offers a promising advance over standard media messages. Screening questionnaires can assess each individual's capabilities, readiness stage, stylistic tastes, knowledge levels, and current beliefs, and then direct them to narrowly-targeted customized messages that are precisely designed to address their needs and predispositions. Not only does this approach increase the likelihood of learning and persuasion, but it decreases the possibility of boomerang effects. Furthermore, entertaining interactive formats such as games are particularly well suited for youthful focal segments.

Multi-audience Media. While certain media channels allow precise targeting, others such as broadcast news and public service spots, newspapers, general-interest magazines, and billboards reach broader audiences. Messages in the general-audience media should be carefully designed to include components that will simultaneously influence several distinct audiences, as discussed in the strategic ambiguity section. This approach typically encompasses a combination of fundamental themes, broadly appealing incentives, and multilevel implications in order to hit two or more birds with one stone. For example, a feature story might include elements that will alarm and motivate influencers, warn preusers, and increase fear among those practicing unhealthy behaviors.

Influencing the Influencers

It often is valuable for campaigners to supplement the direct approach (educating and persuading the focal segment) by influencing other target audiences who can exert interpersonal influence or help reform environmental conditions that shape behaviors of the segment to be changed. Mass media campaigns have considerable potential for producing effects on institutions and groups at the national and community level, as well as motivating personal influencers in close contact with the focal individuals. These audiences are more likely to be receptive to media messages, and their indirectly-stimulated control activities are more likely to be effective than campaign messages directly targeted to the focal segment. This subsection focuses on interpersonal influencers; the next subsection examines higher-order organizations. Through the two-step flow, the media messages first affect these influentials, who subsequently intervene to facilitate or compel individual behavioral practices (see Wartella & Stout, chap. 2, this volume).

For adolescent segments of the population, there are various peer and authority figures in positions to personally educate, persuade, or control the focal individuals: parents, siblings, friends, coworkers, bosses, teachers, club leaders, coaches, medical personnel, police officers, and store clerks. These influencers offer added types of persuasive potency that the media lack because they can provide positive and negative reinforcement, exercise control (by making rules, monitoring behavior, and enforcing consequences), shape opportunities, facilitate behavior with reminders at opportune moments, and serve as role models. Furthermore, influencers can customize their messages to the unique needs and values of the individual.

An important role of the campaign is to stimulate interpersonal influence attempts by inspiring, prompting, and empowering influencers, especially those who are hesitant to wield their authority. The influencers are likely to be responsive to negative appeals that arouse concern about harmful consequences to those they are trying to help behave appropriately. Thus, messages should be designed to motivate facilitators and enforcers to take action.

In the case of drug prevention, parents can play a major role by initiating dialog with their children and teenagers about drugs (and more basic issues of right and wrong), by clearly establishing expectations and aggressively enforcing rules, by using praise to boost self-esteem, by teaching resistance to peer pressure, by participating in joint recreational activities, by regulating or coviewing corruptive media content, and by making efforts to provide an experiential taste of harmful health consequences (e.g., touring a section of town plagued by drug problems or visiting a rehab center).

Persuasive appeals may be needed to influence parents regarding the vulnerability of their own family members (e.g., "the problem doesn't just apply to other children…your children are at risk), the degree of risk (e.g., "harm is more severe than in the past due to stronger forms of marijuana and dangerous new inhalants"), and parental efficacy (e.g., "you are a stronger influence than you realize… you can make a difference").

Educational materials are also needed to inform parents about which actions to take and how to successfully implement the guidelines. In particular, campaigners need to educate parents who are former drug users on how to avoid hypocrisy by directly confronting it through the use of talking points (e.g., "we all make mistakes… don't repeat them," "if we know then what is known now," "it is a lot stronger drug now").

Just as educational messages produce greater resistance to negative influences, other messages can enhance receptivity to enforcement and interpersonal persuasion. By softening up the focal segment so its members will respond constructively to indirect prohealth influences, the campaign can heighten the likelihood that individuals will accept attempts by others to control their behavioral decisions. One message theme is to put a positive spin on the motives of these interpersonal sources, so the focal segment perceives the influencers to be acting out of altruism, concern, or responsibility to fulfill their authority role.

Altering the Environment

Individuals' decisions about health practices are strongly shaped by the constraints and opportunities in their societal environment, including monetary expenses, laws, entertainment role models, commercial messages, social forces, and community services (e.g., price of drugs, penalties for possession, drug abuse depictions in movies, prohibition of advertising for marijuana, peer approval of drug use, drug interdiction efforts, and access to rehab or recreational facilities). Through the interventions of government, business, educational, medical, media, religious, and community organizations, many of these influential factors can be engineered to increase the likelihood of healthy choices or to discourage unhealthy practices. In particular, media messages tend to be more effective when supplemented with direct service delivery components.

Eliminate the Negative. There are numerous types of mass media messages that undermine the effects of health campaigns, particularly advertisements (e.g., commercials for beer or proprietary medicines) and entertainment (e.g., dramas or songs that glamorize unhealthy practices). Aggressive campaigners may attempt to reduce these corruptive influences by prodding regulators to restrict content or encouraging social responsibility on the part of corporations and media organizations that produce the messages. Similarly, restrictions on marketing and sales policies for products such as alcohol and tobacco can reduce access to unhealthy products.

Policy Initiatives. A promising campaign thrust involves carefully-targeted efforts designed to influence policymakers who can change the environment that impinges on a health practice. Depending on the health domain, these leaders can legislate propriety by passing laws or raising taxes, they can promote responsibility by exercising moral leadership, and they can facilitate appropriate behavior by creating opportunities for the focal segment.

More fundamental long-range approaches might seek to restructure basic socioeconomic conditions, because these underlying factors are key predictors of health status. Health campaigners can cooperate with organizations that are attempting to institute basic changes in society by reducing poverty, improving schools, eliminating racism, assisting dysfunctional families, broadening access to the health care system, and enhancing employment opportunities.

Media Advocacy. Over the past decade, advocates of reform have refined techniques that combine community organizing and media publicity to advance healthy public policies (Wallack, Dorfman, Jernigan, & Themba, 1993). A portion of campaign messages are designed to influence public opinion, government policymakers, and organization leaders in order to change the environmental conditions affecting public health that shape behaviors of individuals. This approach crosses over into the political sphere by seeking to raise the volume of voices for social change, to increase the sense of urgency, and to acquire greater legitimacy for advocated policies.

The media advocacy strategy relies heavily on agenda setting of health issues. By generating publicity in the news media, the elevated media agenda can shape the public agenda and the policy agenda pertaining to new initiatives, rules, and laws. An important element is changing the public's beliefs about the effectiveness of policies and interventions that are advanced, which leads to supportive public opinion (and direct pressure) that can help convince institutional leaders to formulate and implement societal constraints and opportunities. The ultimate target audience may be government officials, employers, business execs, health care system administrators, religious leaders, media professionals, school administrators, or heads of civic organizations; they are reached directly by the news and editorial content and indirectly via inputs from the aroused public.

Media advocacy also can play a role in the debate between proponents of treatment versus prevention, and more specifically the relative priority of school-based programs versus paid media campaigns. Summative evaluation data demonstrating campaign effectiveness can be strategically publicized to secure support for greater investment of resources in subsequent media-based campaigns. Furthermore, evidence of campaign success in addressing health problems may impress the general public and community opinion leaders who are in a position to provide localized support services to complement media messages.

Maximizing Quantitative Potency

The elusive ideal in campaign design is the magic bullet, where the right message appeal is sent through the right channel to the right target audience with impressive effects. Wallack (1989) referred to this unlikely scenario as the "media fantasy." In reality, the media function more like a shotgun than a rifle, spraying tiny pellets across broad audiences. In certain respects, this scattershot approach may actually be functional for hitting the moving targets and reaching the evasive quarry; besides, it is difficult to aim precisely with the modest budget for ammunition. The primary implication, however, is that many messages must be disseminated to achieve meaningful impact. Although not sufficient to ensure success without high quality content, substantial quantity is almost invariably a necessary condition for effective campaigns.

Quantitative Factors. A great volume of stimuli is needed to attain adequate reach and frequency of exposure. Moreover, maximum saturation conveys significance of the problem, which is an essential facilitator of agenda setting and heightened salience. Prominent placement of messages in conspicuous positions within media vehicles serves to enhance both exposure levels and perceived significance. To provide a common thread unifying the varied messages, the campaign should feature continuity devices (e.g., logo, slogan, jingle, messenger), which increase memorability and enable the audience to cumulatively integrate material across multiple exposure impressions. Another quantitative consideration involves the scheduling of a fixed number of presentations; depending on the situation, campaign messages may be most effectively concentrated over a short duration, dispersed thinly over a lengthy period, or distributed in intermittent bursts of "flighting" or "pulsing."

Unfortunately, the limited resources available for most public service campaigns greatly restrict the quantity of messages disseminated. Unlike commercial advertisers who can place numerous messages in the media and rely on high-repetition soft-sell strategies based on principles of mere exposure or other peripheral paths of influence, campaign designers need to achieve the most "bang for the buck" by making each message provocative, involving, and engaging to attract attention and facilitate processing.

To maximize quantity, campaigners need to diligently pursue monetary resources from government, industry, or association sources to fund paid placements and leveraged media slots, to aggressively lobby for free public service time or space, to skillfully employ public relations techniques for generating entertainment and journalistic coverage, and to utilize the low-cost Internet channel of communication. Moreover, pseudo-quantity can be boosted by sensitizing audiences to appropriate content already available in the media and by stimulating information-seeking from specialty sources.

The Perpetual Campaign. Although campaigns ostensibly have a beginning and end, the realities of health promotion and prevention often require exceptional persistence over long periods. Campaigners can seldom let up because focal segments of the population are in constant need of influence. There are always newcomers moving into the "at risk" stage, backsliders who are reverting to prior misbehavior, evolvers who are gradually adopting the recommended practice at a slow pace, waverers who need regular doses reinforcement to stay the course, and latecomers who are finally seeing the light after years of unhealthy habits.

CONCLUSION

Relatively few media campaign messages score exactly on target, although some come close; the perfect message requires greater customization than can be normally attained through mass communication. Nevertheless, campaigners keep using the media because the extremely large audiences can be reached efficiently; even if only a few percent are influenced, the small impact may translate to millions of individuals practicing healthier behaviors.

The odds of success can be improved if more effective strategies are employed in future health campaigns. This chapter has advocated greater diversification of pathways, products, incentives, and channels beyond the approaches conventionally used in health campaigns. This requires the disciplined formulation of strategies based on careful analysis of the situation, sensitive application of communication theory, and regular collection of formative evaluation information.

In particular, the formulation of a comprehensive strategic plan is needed to effectively integrate the optimum combinations of campaign components that will directly and indirectly influence behaviors. The ideas outlined in this chapter offer some promising approaches for designers to consider in developing media-based campaigns to prevent drug abuse and other health problems.

REFERENCES

Ajzen, I., & Fishbein, M. (1980). *Understanding attitudes and predicting social behavior.* Englewood Cliffs, NJ: Prentice-Hall.

Atkin, C. (1981). Mass media information campaign effectiveness. In R. Rice & W. Paisley (Eds.), *Public communication campaigns* (pp. 265-280). Beverly Hills, CA: Sage.

Atkin, C. (1994). Designing persuasive health messages. In L. Sechrest, T. E. Backer, E. M. Rogers, T. F. Campbell, & M. L. Grady (Eds.), *Effective dissemination of clinical health information* (AHCPR Publication No. 95-0015, pp. 99-110). Rockville, MD: Public Health Service, Agency for Health Care Policy and Research.)

Atkin, C. (2001). Theory and principles of a media health campaign. In R. Rice & C. Atkin (Eds.), *Public communication campaigns: Theory, practice and effects* (pp. 49-68). Thousand Oaks, CA: Sage.

Atkin, C., & Freimuth, V. (1989). Formative evaluation research in campaign design. In R. Rice & C. Atkin (Eds.), *Public communication campaigns* (pp. 131-150). Newbury Park, CA: Sage.

Atkin, C., & Wallack, L. (1990). *Mass communication and public health: Complexities and conflicts.* Newbury Park, CA: Sage.

Atkin, C., Wallack L., & DeJong, W. (1992). *The influence of responsible drinking TV spots and automobile commercials on young drivers.* Washington, DC: AAA Foundation for Traffic Safety.

Backer, T., & Rogers, E. (1993). *Organizational aspects of health communication campaigns: What works?* Newbury Park, CA: Sage.

Backer, T., Rogers, E., & Sopony, P. (1992). *Designing health communication campaigns: What works?* Newbury Park, CA: Sage.

Bandura, A. (1986). *Social foundations of thought and action: A social cognitive theory.* Englewood Cliffs, NJ: Prentice-Hall.

Becker, M. H. (1974). The health belief model and personal health behavior. *Health Education Monographs, 2,* 324-508.

Boster, F., & Mongeau, P. (1984). Fear arousing persuasive messages. In R. Bostrom (Ed.), *Communication Yearbook* (Vol. 8, pp. 330-375). Beverly Hills, CA: Sage.

Bracht, N. (2001). Community partnership strategies in health campaigns. In R. Rice & C. Atkin (Eds.), *Public communication campaigns: Theory, practice and effects* (pp. 323-342). Thousand Oaks, CA; Sage.

Burgoon, M., Alvaro, E. M., Grandpre, J., & Voloudakis, M. (in press). Revisiting the theory of psychological reactance: Communicating threats to attitudinal freedom. In J. Dillard & M. Pfau (Eds.), *Handbook of persuasion.* Beverly Hills, CA: Sage.

Burgoon, M., & Miller, G. (1985). An expectancy interpretation of language and persuasion. In H. Giles & R. St Clair (Eds.), *Recent advances in language, communication, and social psychology* (pp. 199-229). London: Lawrence Erlbaum Associates.

Cappella, J., Fishbein, M., Hornik, R., Ahern, R. K., & Sayeed, S. (2001). Using theory to select messages in antidrug media campaigns: reasoned action and media priming. In R. Rice & C. Atkin (Eds.), *Public communication campaigns: Theory, practice and effects* (pp. 214-230). Thousand Oaks, CA: Sage.

DeJong, W., & Winsten, J. (1990). The use of mass media in substance abuse prevention. *Health Affairs, 2,* 30-46.

DeJong, W., & Winsten, J. A. (1999). The use of designated drivers by US college students: A national study. *Journal of American College Health, 47,* 151-156.

Donohew, L., Sypher, H., & Bukoski, W. (1991). *Persuasive communication and drug abuse prevention.* Hillsdale, NJ: Lawrence Erlbaum Associates.

Dozier, D., Grunig, L., & Grunig, J. (2001). Public relations as communication campaign. In R. Rice & C. Atkin (Eds.), *Public communication campaigns: theory, practice and effects* (pp. 231-248). Thousand Oaks, CA: Sage.

Hale, J. L., & Dillard, J. P. (1995). Fear appeals in health promotion: Too much, too little or just right? In E. Maibach & R. Parrott (Eds.), *Designing health messages: Approaches from communication theory and public health practice* (pp. 65-80). Newbury Park, CA: Sage.

Hovland, C. I., Janis, I. L., & Kelley, H. H. (1953). *Communication and persuasion.* New Haven, CT: Yale University Press.

Janz, N. K., & Becker, M. H. (1984). The health belief model: A decade later. *Health Education Quarterly, 11,* 1-47.

Maibach, E. & Parrott, R. (1995). *Designing health messages: Approaches from communication theory and public health practice.* Thousand Oaks, CA: Sage.

McGuire, W. (1989). Theoretical foundations of campaigns. In R. Rice & C. Atkin (Eds.), *Public communication campaigns* (pp. 43-66). Newbury Park, CA: Sage.

McGuire, W. (1994). Using mass media communication to enhance public health. In L. Sechrest, T. E. Backer, E. M. Rogers, T. F. Campbell, & M. L. Grady (Eds.), *Effective dissemination of clinical health information* (AHCPR Publication No. 95-0015, pp. 125-151). Rockville, MD: Public Health Service, Agency for Health Care Policy and Research.

Petty, R., Baker, S., & Gleicher, F. (1991). Attitudes and drug abuse prevention: Implications of the Elaboration Likelihood Model of persuasion. In L. Donohew, H. Sypher, & W. Bukoski (Eds.), *Persuasive communication and drug abuse prevention* (pp. 71-90). Hillsdale, NJ: Lawrence Erlbaum Associates.

Petty, R. E., & Cacioppo, J. T. (1986). *Communication and persuasion: Central and peripheral routes to attitude change.* New York: Springer-Verlag.

Prochaska, J., & DiClemente, C. (1983). Stages and processes of self change of smoking: Toward an integrative model. *Journal of Consulting and Clinical Psychology, 51,* 390-395.

Rogers, R. (1983). Cognitive and physiological processes in fear appeals and attitude change: A revised theory of protection motivation. In J. Cacioppo & R. E. Petty (Eds.), *Social psychophysiology* (pp. 153-176). New York: Guilford Press.

Rosenstock, I. (1990). The health belief model: Explaining health behavior through expectancies. In K. Glanz, F. M. Lewis, & B. K. Rimer (Eds.), *Health behavior and health education: Theory, research and practice* (pp. 39-62). San Francisco, CA: Josey-Bass.

Sherif, M., & Hovland, C. I. (1961). *Social judgment theory.* New Haven, CT: Yale University Press.

Singhal, A. & Rogers, E. (1999). *Entertainment-education: a communication strategy for social change.* Mahwah, NJ: Lawrence Erlbaum Associates.

Slater, M. (1999). Integrating application of media effects, persuasion, and behavior change theories to communication campaigns: A stages-of-change framework. *Health Communication, 11,* 335-354.

Snyder, L. (2001). How effective are mediated health campaigns? In R. Rice & C. Atkin (Eds.), *Public communication campaigns (pp. 181-192).* Thousand Oaks, CA: Sage.

Stephenson, M., & Witte, K. (2001). Creating fear in a risky world. Generating effective health risk messages. In R. Rice & C. Atkin (Eds.), *Public communication campaigns: Theory, practice and effects* (pp 88-104). Thousand Oaks, CA: Sage.

Stiff, J. (1994). *Persuasive communication.* New York: Guilford Press.

Wallack, L. (1989). Mass communication and health promotion: A critical perspective. In R. Rice & C. Atkin (Eds.), *Public communication campaigns* (pp. 353-368). Newbury Park, CA: Sage.

Wallack, L., & DeJong, W. (1995). Mass media and public health: Moving the focus from the individual to the environment. In S. E. Martin & C. P. Mail (Eds.) *Effects of the mass media on the use and abuse of alcohol* (pp. 253-268). NIAAA Research Monograph No. 28. Bethesda, MD: NIAAA.

Wallack, L. & Dorfman, L. (2001). Putting policy into health communication: The role of media advocacy. In R. Rice & C. Atkin (Eds.), *Public communication campaigns: theory, practice and effects* (pp. 389-402). Newbury Park, CA: Sage.

Wallack, L., Dorfman, L., Jernigan, D., & Themba, M. (1993). *Media advocacy and public health.*Newbury Park, CA: Sage.

Wartella, E. & Middlestadt, S. (1991). Mass communication and persuasion: The evolution of direct effects, limited effects, information processing, and affect and arousal models. In L. Donohew, H. Sypher, & W. Bukoski (Eds.), *Persuasive communication and drug abuse prevention* (pp. 53-69). Hillsdale, NJ: Lawrence Erlbaum Associates.

Witte, K. (1994). Fear control and danger control: an empirical test of the extended parallel process model. *Communication Monographs, 61*, 113-134.

Witte, K. & Allen, M. (2000). A meta-analysis of fear appeals: Implications for effective public health campaigns. *Health Education and Behavior, 27*, 591-615.

II

CONTEMPORARY
THEORIES AND RESEARCH

4

Using Interactive Media Tools to Test Substance Abuse Prevention Messages

Michael Burgoon, Eusebio M. Alvaro, Katherine Broneck,
Claude Miller, Joseph R. Grandpre, John R. Hall,
and Cynthia A. Frank

University of Arizona

Social awareness of public health issues has reached an unprecedented level, given the serious and aversive consequences of disease, disability, and even death that are potentially preventable. High-risk behaviors (e.g., tobacco use, risky sexual behavior, and illegal drug use) have contributed to pandemic prevalence of infectious diseases including HIV/AIDS, increasing rates of cancer and cardiovascular disease, and a plethora of economic and health problems associated with drug abuse. Because attitudinal and behavioral modifications are required to manage such potentially preventable maladies, unprecedented efforts have been mounted to develop communication campaigns aimed at disease prevention and control and substance abuse abatement. As is usually the case with only such campaign development, policymakers and researchers have turned to tried-and-true communication channels such as print products and general broad-based radio and television spots to "educate" and "inform" the general public of the aversive consequences of specific health-related behaviors.

Over time, the amount of money spent on health campaigns has increased geometrically. Concomitantly, there has been a monumental increase in the information available to the body politic about a number of health issues, preventable diseases, and dangerous behaviors. However, there is increasing evidence that the correlation between the amount of information available and the *acceptance* of advocated behavioral/attitudinal change is disappointingly low. One can point to a number of campaigns conducted at great expense over long periods of time that have resulted in little or no change in outcome measures of import.

It is possible that traditional print and broadcast media may not be the optimal channels for either reaching or impacting relevant target groups such as youth, adolescents, and specific minority groups. It is becoming increasingly apparent that these target groups are not particularly amenable to change as a result of the passive reception of messages exhorting them to alter behaviors. Finding ways to tailor prevention messages to specific audience segments is difficult, if not impossible, with a reliance on such traditional media sources.

Increasingly, there is recognition that new communication technologies, including those allowing for interactivity, require research attention. In a society where the target groups of interest are increasingly computer literate and prefer the web to the newspaper or the television, it appears appropriate to conduct theoretically-driven research taking advantage of all the richness and flexibility of new communication technology. The addition of computer-based interventions is mandated as a next step, given the relative lack of success in the unidirectional message campaigns used in past (traditional) public health campaigns.

INTERACTIVE MEDIA

As previously suggested, new communication technologies incorporate the interactivity of the microcomputer with traditional media and other new information technologies to form an innovative information delivery system simultaneously using multiple communication channels (i.e., audio, video, text, still imagery and interactive games). The term *interactive technology* refers to computer-based media that enable users to access information and services of interest, control how the information is presented, and respond to the information and messages in the same context in which they were delivered (Street & Rimal, 1997).

In a number of applied research venues, the advantages of using such sophisticated communication systems cannot be ignored. Interactive multimedia computer programs can be designed to deliver information to very discrete target populations (e.g., adolescents, minorities) while demanding the continual participation of the end user. Traditional media and information technologies (i.e., printed materials, slides, and videotape presentations) generally cater to relatively broadly defined target populations while promoting passive learning by demanding very little active participation by the end user. Active participation on the part of the end user has been found to promote better comprehension and receptivity of information (McGrane, Toth, & Alley, 1990). Moreover, pation also challenges end users to make decisions, reso and practice new behaviors. Interactive media can be easily programmeu to link messages (using hypertext) with related data banks, and thereby provide more detailed explanations of subject areas end users find particularly interesting or difficult to understand. In addition, interactive multimedia computer programs have been found to increase end users' self-awareness, thereby making attitudes more salient and accessible than does traditional media (Metheson & Zanna, 1988).

User Advantages. Long before the advent of computer-based interactive technology, communication researchers found that when an individual is highly involved with a task (Brynes & Kiger, 1990; Cacioppo & Petty, 1981; Crano, 1983; Schilling, El-Bassel, & Gilbert, 1992), has hands-on experience with it (Toth, 1987), is empowered by it (Bates, 1979; Jones, 1987), and perceives the task as having important personal consequences (Crano, 1995, 1997), the probability that the individual will manifest knowledge-consistent behavior is significantly increased. New media, unlike traditional mass media, challenge users to make decisions, resolve problems, and practice new behaviors. These actions, in turn, increase feelings of self-efficacy and confidence, and reduce uncertainty about behavior change (Kalichman, Hunter, & Kelly, 1992). In addition, new media can be easily programmed to provide positive feedback to the user, acting as a "qualified observer," and in this sense fulfill a fundamental role in what educators consider to be the ideal learning environment (Pollack & Breault, 1987). Further, end users can be made responsible for teaching other users how to use the interactive system, providing many opportunities for "postbehavior consolidating," which also has been found to be an important variable in learning and implementing new behaviors (McGrane et al., 1990).

Research Advantages. There are several added advantages of using interactive computer systems for those conducting social influence research in health, organizational, and educational contexts. For example, interactive media programs can be designed to track each individual user's approach to the materials offered; measure the time each user spends perusing each message; monitor each user's total time spent on specific tasks; record each user's choice of additional information links; and provide detailed data summaries of the user's interaction with the program at the end of each experiment. Such computer-mediated measures have been shown to provide significantly more objective evaluation of users' behavior and performance during exposure to information than traditional coding or self-report measures (Pollack & Breault, 1987). In addition, interactive modules can be designed to control each participant's access to experimental messages by programming participant assignment to experimental conditions, while simultaneously collecting comprehensive data on variables of interest.

MULTIMEDIA/INTERACTIVITY IN HEALTH PROMOTION AND DISEASE PREVENTION

The majority of health promotion and disease prevention messages use brochures, television and radio spots, billboards, and magazine ads to promote better, healthier lifestyles. Moreover, many of the traditional forms of health messages are usually unidirectional, one-to-many presentations. Message recipients cannot interact with or ask questions as the information is being presented. Consequently, health care researchers have started using interactive technologies such as the Internet, computerized compact disc programs (CD-ROMs), and video games to distribute interactive health prevention messages.

Health promotion and disease prevention messages delivered via interactive multimedia often fall into one or a blend of four mediated presentational categories: problem solving, informational, networking, and personalized messages. A fifth category of research-oriented applications includes projects that largely use interactive multimedia as a research tool. Such applications often draw on the preceding four message categories for content. Each of these applications is discussed in detail before moving on to an overview of two applied research projects designed to test the relative efficacy of drug prevention messages by using interactive multimedia technology.

Problem Solving. Problem-solving programs are self-management and decisional in nature. They provide a computerized environment where users are faced with various health related problematic situations. Users are asked to make decisions based on what they would do given these situations. Forerunners in self-management health prevention programs are the Health Hero video game series (Lieberman, 1995; Lieberman & Brown, 1995) and the Body Awareness Resource Network (BARN) (Bosworth, 1994; Bosworth, Gustafson, & Hawkins, 1994; Hawkins, Gustafson, Chewning, Bosworth, & Day, 1987).

The Health Hero video game series consists of four video games targeting children and addressing health issues such as smoking, asthma, and safety. Knowledge about each given topic is presented through animated sequences explaining and demonstrating healthy behaviors. Players manipulate their game characters through a computerized environment where they make health decisions based on the information presented earlier in the game.

Video games regarding health goals allow people to make health decisions and in turn receive immediate, cumulative feedback on their performance. Lieberman (1997) argued that by being motivated to win the game, the people playing the game will learn the skills and information necessary to win, thereby internalizing information about the health prevention message that was being presented. Field tests as well as controlled laboratory studies have demonstrated that after playing the Health Hero video games, children are more apt to retain health information for more than 1 month (Lieberman, 1995), have more self-esteem, self-efficacy, and self confidence about the health related topics (Lieberman, 1995), and express interest in learning more about the health topics (Lieberman & Brown, 1995).

The BARN project also incorporates video games and quizzes to provide information on a variety of health topics (Bosworth et al., 1994). The simulations and computerized games allow users of the program to explore the health risks involved when poor decisions are made (Bosworth, 1994). Evaluations of the BARN have found that after completing the program, health behaviors changed positively and risk-taking activities decreased among the users (Bosworth et al., 1994; Hawkins et al., 1987). It was found that students who interacted with the BARN program kept seeking more information about different health topics as time progressed, just as did those who used the Health Hero video game series. The desire to achieve more knowledge, as well as the often-cited issue of lack of understanding printed material, can lead to the use as well as the need for informational programs.

Informational. Informational programs allow users to be educated more thoroughly about a given health subject. Printed health prevention materials often are found to be problematic for certain populations because of low reading levels (Kinzie, Schorling, & Siegel, 1993), knowledge gaps, and translation problems due to language barriers or word choice (Hawkins et al., 1987). Therefore interactive CD-ROMs, which blend text, dialogues, and digitized informational videos, are being used to help educate these populations. Informational programs have been tested across a wide variety of topics and populations. The research efforts include evaluations for contraceptive decisions (Chewning et al., 1999), diabetes (Brennan, 1993), asthma (Huss et al., 1992), rheumatoid arthritis (Wetstone, Sheehan, Votaw, Peterson, & Rothfield, 1985), and multiple health topics (Hawkins et al., 1987; see also Krishna, Balas, Spencer, Griffin, & Boren). These studies demonstrate that informational multimedia programs can increase knowledge and recall of the health topic and interventions and lead to positive changes in both behavioral intentions and comprehension of the health information being presented.

Networks. Once health promotion and disease prevention information is presented, there is a chance that users will want to seek more information about the relevant health topic or ask questions about what they have just seen. Therefore, establishing networking programs that enable interaction with other sources of information is important. Computer networks and the Internet have been used along with health programs to facilitate such extended interaction. The Comprehensive Health Enhancement Support System (CHESS), Stanford Health-Net, and Internet-based web sites help to link people to others who can answer questions anonymously, divulge information, and share stories.

CHESS is a program that has informational modules, expert sections, discussion groups, personal stories, and instant library sections for users to use (Gustafson, Hawkins, Boberg, Pingree, Serlin, Graziano, & Chan, 1999). An earlier program, the Stanford Health-Net, also used a health information library, electronic mail, electronic bulletin board, and referral listings (Robinson, 1989). Results from studies of both systems demonstrate that networking allows for increases in emotional and social support, self-efficacy, and understanding of the health-related materials among the users (Gustafson, et al., 1993) and an overall positive impact on community health behaviors (Robinson, 1989).

Studies addressing the use of the Internet as an interactive context for health prevention messages provide mixed results. Although the Internet can be used as a tool by which to network and change health behavior through health promotion and disease prevention messages (Cassell, Jackson, & Cheuvront, 1998), the quality of health information on the Internet varies greatly. Thus, optimal use of the Internet for networking, information retrieval, and persuasion may not be achieved until approaches and procedures to enhance credibility of web-based information can be delineated (Eng, Gustafson, Henderson, Jimison, & Patrick, 1998; Gustafson, Robinson, Ansley, Adler, & Brennan, 1999; Starr, 1997).

Personalized. Computer surveys and basic word processing programs are also being used to create personalized messages to users. Computer-tailored messages are created for the individual user. Messages are precreated on word processing programs and merged into a newsletter template depending on how users answer health related questions. Studies on personalized health prevention messages have covered varied foci from nutrition education (Brug, Campbell, & Van Assema, 1999) to smoking prevention and cessation (Dijkstra, De Vries, & Roijackers, 1999; Strecher, 1999; Strecher et al., 1994). Results indicate that tailoring health promotion and disease prevention messages to the user does lead to desired attitudinal change (Brug et al., 1999), cessation (for a review, see Strecher, 1999), and prevention behaviors (Skinner, Strecher, Hospers, 1994).

Research Applications. Interactive videos have been used to research health prevention messages, attitude, and general knowledge of the viewers. Levenson and Signer (1986) found that the interactive video allowed for more knowledge, retention of information presented, and information on how to best construct health prevention messages. However, the Internet as well as CD-ROM programs can also be used to test survey research messages. The Internet has been used in studies such as the Drug Information Assessment and Decisions for Schools (DIADS) to conduct surveys about drug prevention (Bosworth, 1994). Ongoing studies on drug prevention and sun safety among adolescents and adults have used CD-ROMs created from Toolbook and Director to assess television commercial effectiveness in persuading students to engage in health promotion behaviors (Alvaro, Grandpre, Burgoon, Miller, & Hall, 2000; Grandpre, Alvaro, Burgoon, Miller, & Hall, in press). Through computerized interactivity, information gathered on health prevention messages can be manipulated for better persuasive effects. Findings from these on-going studies have already facilitated the design and implementation of better health prevention messages.

To better understand how interactive technology can be used in producing and conducting theoretically driven research, the following discussion focuses on two specific health-related research projects conducted in the past 3 years. The first project examined the impact of multimedia messages on adolescent's attitudes and behavioral intentions toward tobacco use. The second project focused on adolescent's reactions to antidrug advertisements concerning marijuana and inhalants.

MULTIMEDIA EXPERIMENTATION PART I: TOBACCO PREVENTION

The first study to be reviewed used psychological reactance theory (Brehm, 1966; Brehm & Brehm, 1981) as a basis to examine the relative impact of explicit, implicit, controlling, and noncontrolling language on tobacco-related knowledge, attitudes, and behaviors in adolescents. This study (funded by the Arizona Disease Control Research Commission: ADCRC Contract 9904, Michael Burgoon, principal investigator) examined theoretically based approaches to designing more effective tobacco prevention messages. More specifically, a major goal of the project was to identify message design characteristics that avoid message failure and the potential for boomerang effects in reactant populations.

The research team (see Alvaro et al., 2000; Grandpre et al, in press) sought to better understand the nature of effective tobacco prevention messages by investigating how adolescents react to messages that either directly and explicitly outline a desired course of action and curtail free choice (explicit messages) or simply present facts while encouraging freedom of choice (implicit messages) on the part of the message receiver. The study involved public school children at the 4th, 7th and 10th grade levels in a metropolitan city located in the southwestern United States.

Design and Procedure

This study employed a 3 (grade: 4, 7, 10) x 2 (message type: implicit or explicit) x 3 (message position: prosmoking, antismoking, or antismoking with restoration) factorial design. The ToolBook® computer program was used to randomly assign students to one of the six experimental conditions, thus ensuring equal distribution among message conditions. In all, 924 students from a wide range of socioeconomic and ethnic backgrounds, drawn from 22 different elementary, middle, and high schools, took part in the study.

At the beginning of the data collection phase of the study, six PII 300-MHz multimedia personal computers were installed in a secure and quiet place at each school (e.g., the school library). On arrival, participants were seated at a computer and supplied with headphones to listen to the audio portion of the message (produced using SoundForge®), which constituted the central experimental manipulation. Participants were then instructed on how to begin the session—ostensibly presented as a web site developed for research purposes. The experimenters decided to present the experimental session as a web site in order to provide participants with a feeling of familiarity and anonymity. The latter issue was quite important in that many of the items imbedded in the electronic questionnaire were of a sensitive nature. It also was the researchers' belief that study participants would be more comfortable interacting with the software in a relatively familiar online environment—one that many adolescents feel confident in navigating.

Experimental sessions began with an informed assent statement which asked participants to indicate assent to participate by entering an assigned identification number. This assent statement was followed by a user-friendly questionnaire designed in, and administered by, ToolBook®

software (based on screen-captured images of web pages designed using FrontPage® and viewed through Netscape®), which consisted of preliminary demographic data on the participant. All data were deposited in an individual log that captured all subsequent data generated in the session.

Once participants answered the demographic questions, the Tool-Book® program randomly assigned them to one of the six message conditions. The assigned condition was noted in each participant's log file and a Director® projector program initiated playback of the assigned message. Each of the different messages was of 2 min duration and used exactly the same core visual elements and background sound (produced using PhotoPaint®, SoundForge®, and Premiere®). The two restoration messages included an additional 30-sec tag sequence.

Following the experimental message, participants responded to various outcome and mediating variables (by using radio buttons and/or check boxes) administered by the ToolBook® program and subsequently recorded in a participant's log file. The last part of the questionnaire included a screen that contained checkboxes allowing the participants to select all of the topics on which they would like to receive further information. Finally, on completion of the questionnaire, the participants were presented with a text-based debriefing that described the project as well as their role in it. The entire session lasted an average of 15 to 25 min for each respondent, with time largely depending on the participant's reading ability.

MESSAGE PRODUCTION

Creation and presentation of each of the six experimental messages necessitated the use of a number of software programs including MS Word®, MS FrontPage®, Corel PhotoPaint®, Adobe Premiere®, Sonic Foundry SoundForge®, Macromedia Director®, and Asymetrix Tool-Book®. Interactive multimedia computer programs were used to merge photographic stills, music, full-motion video, audio voice-over, and text, to give each of the six messages a common appearance modeled after extant broadcast-quality prosmoking and tobacco prevention messages.

A customized ToolBook® master program was developed to allow the manipulation of specific message characteristics across all six messages while maintaining consistently high production values. Each message maintained a uniform presentation of visual elements, (e.g., video, stills, and text) and audio style (e.g., use of narration and music), as well as overall affective tone. It was important to control the coherence and consistency of all six experimental messages in that, in a real-world context, the medium and channels used by tobacco companies and tobacco prevention advocates vary greatly. More specifically, tobacco prevention messages are able to take advantage of all available media, whereas pro-smoking messages are restricted to print media—even though latent pro-smoking messages can be found in movies and other media. Use of the ToolBook® programming was vital not only for the staging of the multimedia production, but also because it allowed the researchers to administer the experimental messages and collect all data in the same medium at the same time.

A narrative device fashioned after the television program *Mystery Science Theater 3000* was used to provide a general theme and context for the experimental messages. The core of each message involves a teen brother and sister couple providing a running critical commentary on programming that they are watching on the family television set. The commentary is the primary vehicle by which the experimental manipulations are delivered and, as such, it is spun in one of four directions: prosmoking and explicit message, prosmoking and implicit message, tobacco prevention and explicit message, and tobacco prevention and implicit message. For the restoration messages, 30-sec endings were tagged onto both the core tobacco prevention messages.

To enhance intrinsic motivation, a complex (and identical) three-part visual message design was used to structure the core content in all six conditions. The first sequence is comprised of clips of sporting events, including Winston Cup drag racing and baseball games showing players using smokeless tobacco. The second sequence focuses on a series of movie clips taken from classic and contemporary films. The clips show cool and glamorous characters smoking cigarettes. The final sequence involved a montage of tobacco print ads that were scanned from magazines, set to music, and edited in a rapid series of shots designed to mimic a music video style.

The two tobacco prevention "restoration" messages were identical in every way to the two other two anti-smoking messages except for a 30-sec audiovisual clip tagged onto the end. The end clip is designed to restore a participant's threatened freedom of choice by explicitly stating that any decision to be made in regard to tobacco use is solely up to the viewer.

SUMMARY

The primary research finding arising from this study (for a detailed presentation of the results see Alvaro et al., 2000, and Grandpre et al, in press;) is that explicit messages—especially those that use threatening and controlling language to spell out a desired course of action—elicit cognitive processing that results in higher levels of psychological reactance, and consequent message rejection. Study participants exposed to explicit messages felt controlled and manipulated—*regardless of the position being advocated*. Explicit messages were rated more negatively and sources of these messages were perceived as less trustworthy. Another significant finding was that implicit messages that leave conclusions up to message receivers resulted in more negative attitudes toward tobacco use than explicit messages—again *regardless of the position being advocated!*

The strong need for autonomy and self-expression that is part and parcel of adolescence makes it apparent that persuasive messages targeting this group should be complex and information rich, and should be designed to emphasize choice rather than control. Of special note is the fact that tobacco prevention campaigns that deliver explicit messages using controlling language actually can elicit more *positive* attitudes toward tobacco use, particularly among high risk groups (see Alvaro et al., 2000; Grandpre et al., in press). The need for future research is self-evident.

MULTIMEDIA EXPERIMENTATION PART II: DRUG PREVENTION MESSAGES

Following up on the successful use of multimedia technology in the aforementioned tobacco prevention study, a second, and more complex, experimental investigation targeting adolescent drug use was designed to include an additional interactive component. This second study, funded by the National Institute on Drug Abuse (grant DA12578 to William Crano and Michael Burgoon), is designed to investigate mass mediated drug prevention public service announcements (PSAs) targeting children and adolescents at different stages of development and of different ethnic backgrounds. One goal of the study was to assess the relative effectiveness of drug prevention PSAs—specifically those addressing marijuana and inhalant use—in regard to changing adolescents' attitudes, knowledge, beliefs, and intentions to use marijuana or inhalants. Another goal of this research effort was to assess the relative impact of various message features on adolescent responses to drug prevention PSAs.

Design and Procedures

The experiment was a 2 (topic: marijuana, inhalants) x 3 (tag line: explicit tag, implicit tag, no tag) x 2 (discussion group source: adult, peer) x 2 (discussion group message: explicit, implicit) factorial design.

Much as in the previously reported study, ToolBook® software was used to develop the master program. The course of the experiment was set following a participant's expressed assent—indicated via the entry of an anonymous user identification number. On responding to a number of demographic questions, participants were randomly assigned to one of 24 experimental conditions whereupon they were presented with a drug prevention message.

As in the tobacco prevention study, after viewing a drug prevention message, participants responded via mouse click to a number of items designed to assess a number of variables of theoretical interest: perceived control, source and message evaluation, message elaboration, behavioral intentions to use or avoid drug use, and information seeking. On completion of the principal criterion measures, participants were exposed to an interactive module designed to encourage further involvement with the experimental treatments. After completing the interactive module, participants were debriefed via computer before being thanked and excused.

EXPERIMENTAL MESSAGES

The messages created specifically for this study differ substantially from those used in the prior tobacco prevention study. The messages differed in content, form, and in the manner in which they were generated by the computer programs. This study used 24 unique messages; however, they were generated by combining the same core audiovisual components in various ways.

The messages all followed the same basic pattern. There were two components common to all messages: marijuana-prevention and inhalant-prevention PSAs developed by the Partnership for a Drug-Free America (PDFA), as well as a "focus group" that was ostensibly viewing and commenting on the drug-prevention PSAs. Messages began with a screen informing experiment participants that they would be viewing excerpts of a focus group commenting on a series of three drug-prevention PSAs. Next, a drug-prevention PSA from the PDFA campaign was presented in its entirety and was followed by a 15 to 20-sec video segment featuring a focus group apparently discussing that particular PSA. This focus group was composed either of adults or peers, and the discussion was scripted so as to use either explicit or implicit language in forwarding a drug prevention position. In some instances, the PSA was followed by a tag line also using either implicit or explicit language (i.e., "Don't do drugs" or "Drugs...you decide"). The entire sequence of a PSA followed by a "focus group" discussion of that PSA was repeated three times with different ads and discussion content—the type of language used (explicit or implicit) was consistent across all three "focus group" discussion segments.

Participants in the 12 marijuana message conditions saw the same 3 marijuana--prevention PSAs, and participants in the 12 inhalant prevention message conditions saw the same 3 inhalant-prevention PSAs. However, the composition of the "focus groups" (i.e., adults/peers) and the type of language used in the "focus group" discussion segments (i.e., explicit or implicit language) varied as a function of treatment condition.

After viewing the drug prevention message and responding to a number of items assessing a host of variables of interest, participants were presented with an interactive module. The interactive module was segmented into three parts: a segment that first asked participants to rank the 3 PSAs they had just watched; a segment that provided false-feedback; and a final segment that allowed participants the option of reranking the PSAs. In the initial segment, three still pictures from the respective PSAs were presented in the order the PSAs were originally viewed, and participants were asked to judge the PSAs they felt to be "best," "okay," and "worst." They did this by using the computer mouse to drag and drop first, second, and third-place ribbons on the respective photos.

A screen then reproduced the pictures of the PSAs in their newly ranked order and informed participants that some of the PSAs were designed by adults and some by their peers. The feedback was "false" in that, unbeknownst to the participant, the computer program had generated one of two random conditions where they were informed that either: (a) their first and second place picks were designed by adults, and their third by peers; or (b) their first and second place picks were designed by peers, and their third by adults. Participants were then given a choice to either rerank the PSAs or proceed without making any changes to their initial rankings. If they chose to rerank the PSAs, the third segment presented them with the opportunity to do so by asking them once again to use the mouse to drag and drop the appropriate ribbons to indicate the new rankings.

SUMMARY

Complete results are not yet available for this study; although data collection has been completed, analysis is ongoing. Preliminary results indicate that, regardless of the type of antidrug commercial (marijuana or inhalant) or grade level, adolescents are significantly more accepting of *implicit* antidrug messages that emphasize some freedom of choice than of explicit messages that tell them what to do. Students perceived implicit messages as less controlling and commanding and as allowing for more decisional freedom than explicit messages. These results provide complete support for the hypotheses of this study, derived from the reactance theory framework (Brehm, 1966; Brehm & Brehm, 1981). The students in this study experienced significantly more reactance when they perceived their decisional freedom as being impinged on by being told to stay away from drugs. This was clearly demonstrated when the students were asked about their intent to use marijuana in the future. Students who viewed explicit messages were significantly more likely to express intent to try marijuana in the future than students who viewed the implicit messages, regardless of whether the source was an adult or a peer. Viewing messages that the students perceived as controlling and commanding led to a perceived loss of decisional freedom and increased psychological reactance. To restore this perceived loss of freedom, students expressed more intent to try marijuana in the future.

When asked specifically about whether the group (peers or adults) commenting on the commercial was trying to control their thoughts, behaviors, or decisions about drugs, students perceived the adults in the explicit language condition as trying to exert the most control. However, students perceived the adults in the implicit language condition as the least controlling, even less so than the two peer conditions. This is an important finding because students in the implicit condition were more accepting of the antidrug message presented by adults than those presented by their own peers.

A possible explanation for this unintended yet interesting finding may be found in Language Expectancy Theory (Burgoon & Miller, 1985; see also Siegel & Burgoon, chap. 8, this volume). This theory states that people hold expectations of how specific others will act and react in a particular situation. The acceptance of a particular message often hinges on how one expects the source of the message to act. For instance, one would expect to be told to stop smoking or lose weight when presenting to a physician, but not when visiting an auto-mechanic. If one's expectations of another's behavior are violated in a positive way, one should be more accepting of the message presented. On the other hand, a negative violation will result in the nonacceptance of the message. In the case of this study, it appears that students expected the adult group to use more explicit language and simply tell them what to do. However, the use of more implicit, noncontrolling language in the adult/implicit condition resulted in a positive violation of the students' expectations and greater acceptance of the message (see also Burgoon, 1975, 1990, 1995; Burgoon, Birk, & Hall, 1991; Burgoon, Dillard, & Doran, 1983; Burgoon & Miller, 1985, 1990).

In addition to these positive findings, feedback from participants, school officials, and community leaders has been quite positive. The experiment was perceived as engaging, and participants required very little extrinsic motivation to take part in the study. The participating students also had minimal difficulty in comprehending and responding to the various on-screen questionnaire items. Moreover, participants were excited and intrigued by the technology used in the study.

DISCUSSION AND CONCLUSION

Multimedia interventions such as those just described are largely designed to be efficacy trials, where experimenters have fairly extensive control over the delivery of the interventions, and the primary goal is to assess the relative impact of theoretically relevant features of the source of message, or message modality. However, it should be noted that the school officials in both the studies mentioned saw the projects as fulfilling a health education need for their students. Although they understood the scientific merit of the research, their interest was primarily in the potential benefits that students gained by being exposed to innovative health promotion and prevention messages. The latter focus may be quite valid in that an encouraging outcome of both studies is that the use of interactive multimedia may have resulted in facilitating participants' intrinsic motivation to attend to drug prevention messages. Throughout the studies, students and school officials alike were intrigued by the technology being used. It was readily apparent that study participants were quite motivated to attend to the multimedia messages and that a high level of interest was maintained for the duration of the study. Thus, although the researchers' main goal was to test the relative efficacy of drug prevention messages, one somewhat unintended effect of the studies may have been increasing attention to, and involvement with, drug prevention information in general.

A second, and related, observation is that school officials also saw participation in the described studies as an opportunity for students to become familiar with social science research. To this end, the experimenters have been concerned with providing adequate and timely feedback to all study participants. For example, in the initial tobacco study, the researchers delivered poststudy multimedia presentations to audiences composed of students, teachers, and/or administrators. The presentations were specifically tailored to each group but they all addressed the overall design of the projects, the study results for particular schools as well as overall study results, and how the information will be used in the future. These presentations were responded to with substantial enthusiasm and often led to insightful questions from students about various health issues as well as about scientific research processes in general. Students were especially impressed with the fact that their contributions to these exciting studies would potentially have an impact in the design of future tobacco prevention efforts. Similar extended "debriefings" currently are underway for those schools participating in the more recent drug prevention project.

Although the use of interactive technology in research efforts is certainly one of the more exciting new aspects of social science research, one caveat should be noted. Using technology to enhance a research project can and will take considerable time and effort on the part of the researcher. Developing the messages and questionnaires, programming the components to work in unison, and insuring the smooth retrieval of data is no small undertaking. Once the program is constructed it should be pilot tested to guarantee that respondents can and will be able to interact with it in a satisfactory manner. Both the studies reported here involved extensive pilot testing with members of the populations of interest. In addition, given the fact that serious technological problems may arise in the field, a highly competent and trained staff is essential during data collection. Therefore, one should consider time and monetary constraints as well as one's own computer prowess before attempting to apply technology to any research endeavor. Lastly, it is important to note that although the technology examined in this chapter may greatly enhance the ability of the researcher to collect and analyze important and interesting data, it can also constrain the researcher's ability to examine theoretically important phenomena—pragmatic considerations may determine message design.

Future Directions

Given the encouraging results from the research projects discussed here, there are several avenues to consider regarding the future of using interactive technology in social science research. First, the emergence of more sophisticated interactive technology has paved the way for an in-depth examination of the similarities of, and differences between, several interaction modalities. This new technology not only provides a new and exciting technique to collect data in the laboratory and field, but also permits the incorporation of different communication modalities into the design of any study.

In addition, interactive technology allows for the manipulation of proximity and synchronicity in that subjects can be separated by time and space, but still interact via computers. Projects using the Internet as a medium by which health promotion and disease prevention interventions may be disseminated will doubtlessly draw increasing interest over the coming years. Such projects could also be extended to investigate the relative merits of communication modality in disseminating health information. Does the independence associated with seeking out a web-site from home, or a location of one's choosing, further enhance the benefits of using interactive multimedia technology?

Of special significance is the fact that interactive multimedia technology permits construction of targeted messages that are responsive to the characteristics of specific participants or populations. One can design a study so that, depending on answers to certain diagnostic questions, a participant receives a message from someone of his or her own ethnic group, gender, age level, education level, and socioeconomic level, or from someone completely different. The reading level of the questionnaire can also be immediately adjusted on the basis of the education level of the participant, or in reaction to the time it takes the participant to answer each question.

This technology also affords participants the opportunity to create their own prevention messages through the selection and combination of extant message components. The subject, in creating these messages, could manipulate several message components such as source, explicitness of the message, visual cues and graphics, rate and tone, and length of message, as well as the inclusion of text and background music. Data could be collected indicating exactly which components participants perceive to be important in delineating effective prevention messages. Moreover, interactive multimedia technology allows participants the freedom to design messages from scratch rather than simply commenting on one of several preproduced messages. In this way, as well being a tool by which to answer important research questions, multimedia interventions become truly interactive and provide the target audience with a clear and distinct voice in the development of prevention campaign messages.

ACKNOWLEDGMENTS

The research discussed in this chapter was funded by the Arizona Disease Control Research Commission (contract 9904 to Michael Burgoon, principal investigator) and by the National Institute on Drug Abuse (grant DA12578, William Crano and Michael Burgoon, principal investigator). All conclusions and interpretations are those of the authors and do not necessarily reflect those of the funding agencies.

Please address any correspondence to the first author at: Health Communication Research Office, Arizona Cancer Center, 1522 East Drachman St., P.O. Box 210475, Tucson, AZ 85721-0475. (520) 626-5453 or (520) 626-6695 (Fax), or e-mail mburgoon@u.arizona.edu

REFERENCES

Alvaro, E. M., Grandpre, J. R., Burgoon, M., Miller, C. H., & Hall, J. R. (May, 2000). *Adolescent reactance and anti-smoking campaigns II*. Paper presented at the International Communication Association annual conference, Acapulco, Mexico.

Bates, J. A. (1979). Extrinsic reward and intrinsic motivation: A review with implications for the classroom. *Review of Educational Research, 19*, 557-576.

Bosworth, K. (1994). Computer games and simulations as tools to reach and engage adolescents in health promotion activities. *Computers in Human Services, 11*, 109-119.

Bosworth, K., Gustafson, D. H., and Hawkins, R. P. (1994). The BARN system: Use and impact of adolescent health promotion via computer. *Computers in Human Behavior, 10*, 467-482.

Brehm, J. W. (1966). *A theory of psychological reactance*. New York: Academic Press.

Brehm, S. S., & Brehm, J. W. (1981). *Psychological reactance: A theory of freedom and control*. San Diego, CA: Academic Press.

Brennan, P. F. (1993). Differential use of computer network services. In C. Safran (Ed). *Proceedings of the seventeenth annual symposium on computer applications in medical care, Oct 30-Nov 3, Washington, DC*. (pp. 27-31). New York: McGraw-Hill.

Brug, J., Campbell, M., & Van Assema, P. (1999). The application and impact of computer-generated personalized nutrition education: A review of the literature. *Patient education and counseling, 36*, 145-156.

Brynes, D. A., & Kiger, G. (1990). The effect of a prejudice-reduction simulation on attitude change. *Journal of Applied Social Psychology, 20*, 341-356.

Burgoon, M. (1975). Toward a message-centered theory of persuasion: Empirical investigations of language intensity III. The effects of source creditability and language intensity on attitude change and person perception. *Human Communication Research, 1,* 251-256.

Burgoon, M. (1990). The effects of message variables on opinion and attitude change. In J. Bradac (Ed.), *Messages in communication sciences: Contemporary approaches to the study of effects* (pp. 129-164). Newbury Park, CA: Sage.

Burgoon, M. (1995). Language expectancy theory: Elaboration, explication and extension. In C. Berger & M. Burgoon (Eds.), *Communication and social influence processes* (pp. 29-52), East Lansing: Michigan State University Press.

Burgoon, M., Birk, T. S., & Hall, J. R. (1991). Compliance and satisfaction with physician-patient communication: An expectancy theory interpretation of gender differences. *Human Communication Research, 18,* 177-208.

Burgoon, M., Dillard, J. P., & Doran, N. (1983). Friendly or unfriendly persuasion: The effects of violations of expectations by males and females. *Human Communication Research, 10,* 283-294.

Burgoon, M., & Miller, G. R. (1985). An expectancy interpretation of language and persuasion. In H. Giles & R. St. Clair (Ed.), *The social and psychological contexts of language* (pp. 199-229). London: Lawrence Erlbaum Associates.

Burgoon, M. & Miller, G. R. (1990). Social psychological concepts and language: Social influence. In H. Giles & P. Robinson (Eds.), *Handbook of social psychology and language* (pp. 51-72). London: John Wiley and Sons.

Cacioppo, J. T., & Petty, R. E. (1981). Effects of tent of thought on the pleasantness ratings of P-O-X- triads: Evidence for three judgmental tendencies in evaluating social situations. *Journal of Personality and Social Psychology, 40,*1000-1009.

Cassell, M. M., Jackson, C., & Cheuvront, B. (1998). Health communication on the Internet: An effective channel for health behavior change? *Journal of Health Communication, 3,* 71-79.

Chewning, B., Mosena, P., Wilson, D., Erdman, H., Potthoff, S., Murphy, A., & Kuhnen, K. K. (1999). Evaluation of a computerized contraceptive decision aid for adolescent patients. *Patient Education and Counseling, 38,* 227-239.

Crano, W. D. (1983). Assumed consensus of attitudes: the effect of vested interest. *Personality and Social Psychology Bulletin, 9,* 597-608.

Crano, W. D. (1995). Attitude strength and vested interest. In R. E. Petty & J. A. Krosnick (Eds.), *Attitude strength: Antecedents and consequences. The Ohio State University series in attitudes and persuasion* (Vol. 4, pp. 131-171). Hillsdale, NJ: Lawrence Erlbaum Associates.

Crano, W. D. (1997). Vested interest, symbolic politics, and attitude-behavior consistency. *Journal of Personality and Social Psychology, 72,* 485-491.

Dijkstra, A., De Vries, H., & Roijackers, J. (1999). Targeting smokers with low readiness to change with tailored and nontailored self-help materials. *Preventive Medicine, 28,* 203-211.

Eng, T. R., Gustfason, D. H., Henderson, J., Jimison, H., & Patrick, K. (1998). Introduction to evaluation of interactive health communication applications. *American Journal of Preventive Medicine, 16,* 10-15.

Grandpre, J., Alvaro, E. M., Burgoon, M., Miller, C., & Hall, J.R. (in press). Adolescent reactance and anti-smoking campaigns: A theoretical approach. *Health Communication.*

Gustafson, D. H., Hawkins, R., Boberg, E., Pingree, S., Serlin, R. E., Graziano, F., & Chan, C. L. (1999). Impact of a patient-centered, computer-based health information/support system. *American Journal of Preventive Medicine, 16,* 1-9.

Gustafson, D. H., Robinson, T. N., Ansley, D., Adler, L., & Brennan, P. F. (1999). Consumers and evaluation of interactive health communication applications. *American Journal of Preventive Medicine, 16,* 23-29.

Gustafson, D. H., Wise, M., McTavish, F., Taylor, J. O., Wolberg, W., Stewart, J., Smalley, R. V., & Bosworth, K. (1993). Development and pilot evaluation of a computer-based support system for women with breast cancer. *Journal of Psychosocial Oncology 11,* 69-93.

Hawkins, R. P., Gustafson, D. H., Chewning, B., Bosworth, K., & Day, P. M. (1987). Reaching hard-to-reach populations: Interactive computer programs as public information campaigns for adolescents. *Journal of Communication, 37,* 8-28.

Huss, K., Huss, R. W., Squire, E. N., Carpenter, G. B., Smith, L. J., & Salata, K. Computer education for asthmatics: What effects? (1992). *Journal of Nursing Care Quality, 6,* 57-66.

Jones, M. K. (1987). Interactive videodisc and the self-directed learner. *Optimal Information Systems,* January-February, 62-64.

Kalichman, S. C., Hunter, T. L., & Kelly, J. A. (1992). Perceptions of AIDS susceptibility among minority and non-minority women at risk for HIV infection. *Journal of Consulting and Clinical Psychology, 60,* 725-732.

Kinzie, M. B., Schorling, J. B., & Siegel, M. (1993). Prenatal alcohol education for low-income women with interactive multimedia. *Patient Education and Counseling, 21,* 51-60.

Krishna, S., Bala, E. A., Spencer, D. C., Griffin, J. Z., & Boren, S. A. (1997). Clinical trials of interactive computerized patient education: Implications for family practice. *Journal of Family Practice, 45,* 25-33.

Levenson, P. M. & Signer, B. (1986). A comparison of noninteractive and interactive video instruction about smokeless tobacco. *Journal of Educational Technology Systems, 14,* 193-202.

Lieberman, D. A. (1995). *Three studies of an asthma education video game.* Report to the National Institute of Allergy and Infectious Diseases, National Institutes of Health, Bethesda, MD.

Lieberman, D. A. (1997). Interactive video games for health promotion: Effects on knowledge, self-efficacy, social support, and health. In R. L. Street, W. R. Gold, & T. Manning (Eds.), *Health promotion and interactive technology: Theoretical applications and future directions* (pp. 103-120). New Jersey: Lawrence Erlbaum Associates.

Lieberman, D. A., & Brown, S. J. (1995). Designing interactive video games for children's health education. In K. Morgan, R. M. Satava, H. B. Sieburg, R.

Matthews, & J. P. Christensen (Eds.), *Interactive technology and the new paradigm for healthcare* (pp. 201-210). Amsterdam: IOS Press.

McGrane, W. L., Toth, F. J., & Alley, E. B. (1990). The use of interactive media for HIV/AIDS prevention in the military community. *Military Medicine, 155*, 235-240.

Metheson, K., & Zanna, M. P. (1988). The impact of computer-mediated communication on self-awareness. *Computers in Human Behavior, 4*, 221-233.

Pollack, R. A., & Breault, G. (1987). Improving teacher effectiveness through the use of interactive microcomputer bideodisc instruction. *Education and Computing, 3*, 213-215.

Robinson, T. N. (1989). Community health behavior change through computer network health promotion: Preliminary findings from Stanford Health-Net. *Computer Methods and Programs in Biomedicine, 30*, 137-144.

Schilling, R. F., El-Bassel, N., & Gilbert, L. (1992). Drug use and AIDS risks in a soup kitchen population. *Social Work, 37*, 353-358.

Skinner, C., Strecher, B., & Hospers, H. (1994). Physicians' recommendations for mammography: do tailored messages make a difference? *American Journal of Public Health, 84*, 43-49.

Starr, P. (1997). Smart technology, stunted policy: Developing health information networks. *Health Affairs, 16*, 91-105.

Strecher, V. J. (1999). Computer-tailored smoking cessation materials: A review and discussion. *Patient Education and Counseling, 36*, 107-117.

Strecher, V. J., Kreuter, M., Boer, D. D., Kobrin, S., Hospers, H. J., & Skinner, C. S. (1994). The effects of computer-tailored smoking cessation messages in family practice settings. *Journal of Family Practice, 39*, 262-270.

Street, R. L., & Rimal, R. N. (1997). Health promotion and interactive technology: A conceptual foundation. In R. L. Street, W. R. Gold, & T. Manning (Eds.), *Health promotion and interactive technology: Theoretical applications and future directions* (pp. 103-120). Mahwah, NJ: Lawrence Erlbaum Associates.

Tinsley, B. J. (1992). Multiple influences on the acquisition and socialization of children's health attitudes and behavior. An integrative review. *Child Development, 63*, 1043-1069.

Toth, F. J. (1987). The video generation. *Navy Medicine, 18*, 200-215.

Wetstone, S. L., Sheehan, T. J., Votaw, R. G., Peterson, M. G., & Rothfield, N. (1985). Evaluation of a computer based education lesson for patients with rheumatoid arthritis. *Journal of Rheumatology, 12*, 907-912.

5

The Role of Theory in Developing Effective Antidrug Public Service Announcements

Martin Fishbein, Joseph Cappella, Robert Hornik

University of Pennsylvania

Sarah Sayeed

City University of New York

Marco Yzer and R. Kirkland Ahern

University of Pennsylvania

During the past decade there has been a growing recognition of the usefulness of theory in the development of behavior change interventions (see e.g., National Institutes of Health [NIH], 1997). Theories of behavioral prediction and behavior change are useful because they provide a framework to help identify the determinants of any given behavior, an essential first step in the development of successful interventions to change that behavior. Clearly, the more one knows about the factors underlying a decision to perform or not perform a given behavior, the greater is the probability that one can design an intervention that will successfully influence that decision. The purpose of this chapter is to show the relevance of behavioral theory for developing messages to prevent and reduce illicit drug use. It is important to recognize, however, that although behavioral theories can identify the critical beliefs underlying a given behavior, they do not tell us how to change those beliefs.

THEORIES OF BEHAVIORAL PREDICTION

Although many theories have been applied to health-related behavioral prevention research—for example, the Theory of Planned Behavior (e.g., Ajzen, 1985, 1991; Ajzen & Madden, 1986), the Theory of Self-Regulation and Self-Control (e.g., Kanfer, 1970), the Theory of Subjective Culture and Interpersonal Relations (e.g., Triandis, 1972), the Transtheoretical Model of Behavior Change (Prochaska & DiClemente, 1983, 1986, 1992; Prochaska, DiClemente & Norcross, 1992; Prochaska, Redding, Harlow, Rossi, & Velicer, 1994), the Information/Motivation/Behavioral-Skills Model (Fisher & Fisher, 1992), the Health Belief Model (Becker, 1974, 1988; Rosenstock, 1974; Rosenstock, Strecher & Becker, 1994), Social Cognitive Theory (Bandura, 1977, 1986, 1991, 1994), the Theory of Reasoned Action (Ajzen & Fishbein, 1980; Fishbein & Ajzen, 1975; Fishbein, Middlestadt & Hitchcock, 1991)—there is growing consensus that there is only a limited number of variables that need to be considered in predicting and understanding any given behavior (see, e.g., Fishbein, 2000; Fishbein et. al., 2001). For example, consider the three theories that have most strongly influenced prevention research.

The Health Belief Model (HBM). According to the Health Belief Model, the likelihood that someone will adopt (or continue to engage in) a health protective behavior is primarily a function of two factors. First, the person must feel personally threatened by some disease (e.g., lung cancer). That is, he or she must feel personally susceptible to (or at risk for) a condition that is perceived to have serious negative consequences. Second, the person must believe that the benefits of taking the preventive action (e.g., stopping smoking) outweigh the perceived barriers to (and/or costs of) taking that action. Note that the costs and benefits of performing one behavior (e.g., trying marijuana) may be very different from those associated with performing another behavior (e.g., using marijuana regularly). For example, although one might believe that using marijuana regularly could "damage my brain," this belief might not occur with respect to trying marijuana.

Social Cognitive Theory (SCT). Social cognitive theory also identifies two factors as primary determinants underlying the initiation and persistence of an adaptive behavior. First, the person must have self-efficacy with respect to the behavior. That is, the person must believe that he or she can (i.e., has the capability to) perform the behavior in question in the face of various circumstances or barriers that make it difficult to perform that behavior. Second, one must have some incentive to perform the behavior. More specifically, the expected positive outcomes of performing the behavior must outweigh the expected negative outcomes. Social cognitive theory has focused on three types of perceived (or expected) outcomes: physical outcomes (e.g., performing the behavior will make me healthy), social outcomes (e.g., performing the behavior will please my parents), and self-standards (e.g., performing the behavior will make me feel proud).

The Theory of Reasoned Action (TRA). According to the Theory of Reasoned Action, performance or nonperformance of a given behavior is primarily determined by the strength of a person's intention to perform (or to not perform) that behavior, where intention is defined as the subjective likelihood that one will perform (or try to perform) the behavior in question. The intention to perform a given behavior is, in turn, viewed as a function of two basic factors: the person's attitude toward performing the behavior (i.e., one's overall positive or negative feeling about personally performing the behavior) and/or the person's subjective norm concerning the behavior (i.e., the person's perception that his or her important others think that he or she should, or should not, perform the behavior in question.

The Theory of Reasoned Action also considers the determinants of attitudes and subjective norms. Attitudes are viewed as a function of behavioral beliefs (i.e., beliefs that performing the behavior will lead to certain outcomes) and their evaluative aspects (i.e., the evaluation of those outcomes); subjective norms are viewed as a function of normative beliefs (i.e., beliefs that a specific individual or group thinks one should or should not perform the behavior in question) and motivations to comply (i.e., the degree to which, in general, one wants, or does not want, to do what the referent thinks one should do). Generally speaking, the more one believes that performing the behavior will lead to positive outcomes and/or will prevent negative outcomes, the more favorable will be one's attitude toward performing the behavior. Similarly, the more one believes that specific referents (i.e., individuals or groups) think that one should (or should not) perform the behavior and the more one is motivated to comply with those referents, the stronger will be the perceived pressure (i.e., the subjective norm) to perform (or to not perform) that behavior.

Based on these three theories, we can identify four factors that may influence an individual's intentions and behaviors:

1. The individual's perception that he/she is personally susceptible to acquiring a given disease or illness.
2. The individual's attitude toward performing the behavior, which is based on one's beliefs about the positive and negative consequences of performing that behavior.
3. Perceived norms, which include the perception that those with whom the individual interacts most closely support the individual's attempt to change, and that others in the community also are changing.

4. Self-efficacy, which involves the individual's perception that he or she can perform the behavior under a variety of difficult or challenging circumstances.

Although there is considerable empirical evidence to support the role of attitude (or outcome expectancies), perceived norms, and self-efficacy as determinants of intention and behavior (Holden, 1991; Kraus, 1995; Shephard, Hartwick, & Warshaw, 1988; Strecher, McEvoy, Becker, & Rosenstock, 1986; van den Putte, 1991), this is not always the case for perceived susceptibility (or perceived risk – see, e.g., Fishbein et al., 1996; Gerrard, Gibbons & Bushman, 1996). Indeed, as shown later, it appears that perceived risk may best be viewed as having an indirect effect on intention. Based on these and other considerations, Fishbein (2000) recently proposed an integrative model of behavioral prediction (See Figure 5.1).

AN INTEGRATED THEORETICAL MODEL

Looking at Figure 5.1, it can be seen that any given behavior is most likely to occur if one has a strong intention to perform the behavior, if one has the necessary skills and abilities required to perform the behavior, and if there are no environmental constraints preventing behavioral performance. Indeed, if one has made a strong commitment (or formed a strong intention) to perform a given behavior, and if one has the necessary skills and abilities to perform the behavior, and if there are no environmental constraints to prevent the performance of that behavior, the probability is close to 1 that the behavior will be performed (Fishbein, 2000; Fishbein et al., 2001).

One immediate implication of this model is that very different types of interventions will be necessary if one has formed an intention but is unable to act on it, versus if one has little or no intention to perform the behavior in question. In some populations or cultures, the behavifor may not be performed because people have not yet formed intentions to perform the behavior, whereas in others, the problem may be a lack of skills and/or the presence of environmental constraints. In still other cultures, more than one of these factors may be relevant. Clearly, if people have formed the desired intention but are not acting on it, a successful intervention will be directed either at skills building or at removing (or helping people to overcome) environmental constraints.

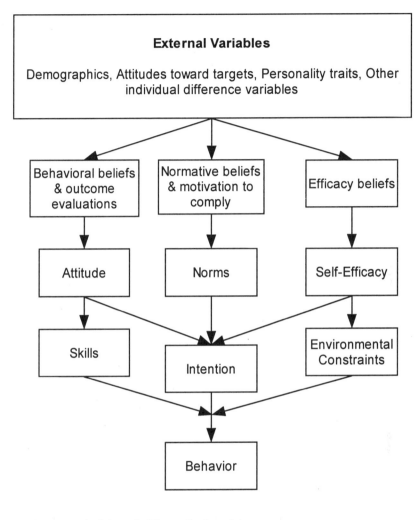

FIGURE 5.1 An integrated theoretical model.

On the other hand, if strong intentions to perform the behavior in question have not been formed, the model suggests that we consider three primary determinants of intention: the attitude toward performing the behavior, perceived norms concerning performance of the behavior, and one's self-efficacy with respect to performing the behavior. It is important to recognize that the relative importance of these three psychosocial variables as determinants of intention will depend on both the behavior and the population being considered. Thus, for example, one behavior may be primarily determined by attitudinal considerations, whereas another may be primarily influenced by feelings of self-efficacy. Similarly, a behavior that is attitudinally driven in one population or culture may be normatively driven in another. Thus, before developing interventions to change intentions, it is important first to determine the degree to which that intention is under attitudinal, normative, or self-efficacy control in the population in question. Once again, it should be clear that very different interventions are needed for attitudinally controlled behaviors than for behaviors that are under normative influence or are strongly related to feelings of self-efficacy. Clearly, one size does not fit all, and interventions that are successful at changing a given behavior in one culture or population may be a complete failure in another.

The model in Figure 5.1 also recognizes that attitudes, perceived norms, and self-efficacy are all, themselves, functions of underlying beliefs – about the outcomes of performing the behavior in question, about the normative proscriptions and/or behaviors of specific referents, and about specific barriers to behavioral performance. Thus, for example, as described earlier, the more one believes that performing the behavior in question will lead to "good" outcomes and prevent "bad" outcomes, the more favorable should be one's attitude toward performing the behavior. Similarly, the more one believes that specific others think one should (or should not) perform the behavior in question, and the more one is motivated to comply with those specific others, the more social pressure one will feel (or the stronger the subjective norm) with respect to performing (or not performing) the behavior. Finally, the more one perceives that one can (i.e., has the necessary skills and abilities to) perform the behavior, even in the face of specific barriers or obstacles, the stronger will be one's self-efficacy with respect to performing the behavior.

It is at this level that the substantive uniqueness of each behavior comes into play. For example, the barriers to trying and/or the outcomes (or consequences) of trying marijuana may be very different from those associated with using marijuana occasionally or regularly. Yet it is these specific beliefs that must be addressed in an intervention if one wishes to change intentions and behavior. And although an investigator can sit in his or her office and develop measures of attitudes, perceived norms, and self-efficacy, he or she cannot tell you what a given population (or a given person) believes about performing a given behavior. Thus one must go to members of that population to identify salient outcome, normative, and efficacy beliefs. To put this somewhat differently, one must understand the behavior from the perspective of the population one is considering.

Finally, the figure also shows the role played by more traditional demographic, personality, attitudinal, and other individual difference variables (e.g., perceived risk or sensation seeking). According to the model, these types of variables play primarily an indirect role in influencing behavior. That is, for example, although men and women may hold different beliefs about performing some behaviors, they may hold very similar beliefs with respect to others. Similarly, rich and poor, old and young, those from developing and developed countries, those who do and do not perceive they are at risk for a given illness, those with favorable and unfavorable attitudes toward law enforcement, and those who have or who have not used drugs may hold different attitudinal, normative, or self-efficacy beliefs with respect to one behavior but may hold similar beliefs with respect to another. Thus, there is no necessary relation between these "external" or "background" variables and any given behavior. Nevertheless, external variables such as cultural and personality differences and differences in a wide range of values should be reflected in the underlying belief structure.

It is probably worth noting that theoretical models such as the one presented in Figure 5.1 have often been described as "Western" or "U.S." models that do not apply to other cultures or countries. However, as we have tried to show, when properly applied these types of models recognize, and are sensitive to, cultural and population differences. For example, as described earlier, the relative importance of each of the variables in the model is expected to vary as a function of both the behavior and the population being investigated. Moreover, these types of models require one to identify the behavioral, normative, and self-efficacy beliefs that are salient in a given population. Thus, when properly applied, these types of models are both population and behavior specific.

APPLYING THE MODEL

The first step in using this or any other behavioral prediction or behavior change model is identifying the behavior we wish to understand and/or change. Unfortunately, this is not nearly as simple or straightforward as is often assumed. First, it is important to distinguish between behaviors, behavioral categories, and goals. One of the lessons we have learned is that the most effective interventions are those directed at changing specific behaviors (e.g., walk for 20 min three times a week), rather than behavioral categories (e.g., exercise) or goals (e.g., lose weight) (see Fishbein, 1995, 2000). In the drug domain, we often have considered goals (e.g., getting into a treatment program) or behavioral categories (e.g., using drugs) rather than specific behaviors (e.g., snorting cocaine at a party with my friends).

Note that the definition of a behavior involves several elements: the action (snorting), the target (cocaine), and the context (at a party with my friends). Clearly, a change in any one of the elements changes the behavior under consideration. Thus, for example, snorting cocaine is a different behavior than injecting cocaine (a change in action), and both of these are different behaviors than is snorting a popper (a change in target). Similarly, snorting cocaine at a party with my friends is a different behavior than snorting cocaine at home when I'm alone. Moreover, it is important to include the element of time, and time itself can be viewed in two ways. For example, smoking marijuana once or twice a year is a different behavior than smoking marijuana once or twice a week, and smoking marijuana in a given 2-week time period (e.g., during spring break) is a different behavior than smoking marijuana in a different 2-week time period (e.g., during final exams) or in a 2-month time period.

As a simple illustration of the importance of considering time, Table 5.1 presents some data from a mall-based touch-screen computer survey of 600 adolescents conducted by Opinion One, a marketing survey research firm. Table 5.1 shows the percent of these adolescents who engaged in prior marijuana use, but distinguishes between "ever use" and "use in the past 12 months" as well as in frequency of use in the past 12 months. Here it can be seen that if we had simply asked our respondents if they had ever used marijuana, almost 41% would have said "Yes." In contrast, by asking about use in the past 12 months, we find that only 25% of the adolescents say "Yes." And if we ask if they have smoked marijuana six or more times in the past 12 months, we find that only 14% say "Yes."

Not only do these data suggest that ever using marijuana in the past 12 months is a different behavior than using marijuana six or more times in the past 12 months, they also point out the fact that we probably are

TABLE 5.1
Opinion One Survey: Percent of Adolescents
Engaging in Prior Marijuana Use

Engagement	Frequency	Percent
Never	352	58.7
Yes, not in past year	100	16.7
1-5 timmes in past year	66	11.1
>5 times in past year	82	13.7

dealing with very different populations when we consider those who have or have not used marijuana in the past 12 months. Similarly, we may be dealing with different populations when we consider those who used majuana five times or less and those who used it six times or more.This can perhaps best be seen by looking at the adolescents' intentions to use marijuana in the next 12 months. For illustrative purposes, Table 5.2 shows the percent of ever and never users who (a) intend to use marijuana "even once or twice, in the next 12 months" and (b) intend to use marijuana "nearly every month for the next 12 months," with intentions being measured on a four point *definitely will not, probably will not, probably will*, and *definitely will* scale. Those responding *probably* or *definitely will* are here considered "intenders." Note that only 3% of never-users intend to use marijuana *even once or twice* and only 1% intend to use marijuana *nearly every month*. In marked contrast, 44% of ever-users say they will use marijuana *once or twice* and 25.5% say they will use it *nearly every month*. Similarly, although 80% of never-users say they *definitely will not* use marijuana even once or twice, 93% say they definitely will not use it *nearly every month*. The corresponding numbers are 31% and 50% for ever-users.

One immediate implication of these findings is not only that using marijuana once or twice is a different behavior than using marijuana nearly every month, but, more important, that very different campaigns (or interventions) are necessary for "ever" and "never" users. For the never-users, the problem is not one of changing intentions, but of making sure that existing intentions do not change and that they are acted on. The same is true for some of the ever-users, but for other ever-users, it would be important to change intentions to use marijuana—particularly intentions to use marijuana even once or twice in the next 12 months.

To further illustrate these differences in behavior and populations, Table 5.3 shows the differences in the psychosocial determinants of these intentions. To reduce the questionnaire burden, although all ever-

TABLE 5.2
Percent of Never and Ever-Users Who Intend to Use Marijuana
"Even Once or Twice in the Next 12 Months" [T] or Intend to Use
Marijuana "Nearly Every Month for the Next 12 Months" [R]

Intention	Never-Users, All		Ever Users, All	
	T	R	T	R
Percent with positive intentions	3.2	1.1	43.7	25.5
Percent who definitely say NO	80.1	93.1	31.2	49.8

users were asked only about use *nearly every month*, non-users were randomly assigned to answer questions about either *use even once or twice* or *use nearly every month*. Attitudes are measured on a 7-point (-3 to +3) scale; subjective norms (-2 to +2) and self-efficacy (1 to 5) were measured on 5-point scales. It is important to note, however, that although attitudes and norms were assessed with respect to the two specific behaviors (i.e., using marijuana *once or twice* or *nearly every month*), self-efficacy was assessed more generally with respect to *saying NO* to marijuana. Thus, there is no reason to expect differences in self-efficacy between the two groups of never-users.

The data in Table 5.3 seem to imply that although never-users see little difference between using marijuana even once or twice and using marijuana nearly every month, the behavior of using marijuana nearly every month is seen quite differently by never-users and ever-users. More specifically, as expected, never-users do not differ in their perceived ability to *say no* to marijuana, irrespective of whether they answered other questions about "trial" or "regular" use. More important, never-users appear to have equally negative attitudes and subjective norms with respect to these two behaviors. In marked contrast, compared to never-users, ever-users are significantly less negative to monthly use, feel significantly less social pressure to not use marijuana on a regular basis, and are significantly less certain they could say no to marijuana under a variety of circumstances. However, before concluding that "trial" use and "regular" use are similar behaviors for never-users, it is important to look at some of the beliefs underlying these attitudes and subjective norms.

Although respondents were asked different sets of questions about the consequences of "trial" and "regular" use, there were eight outcomes that were common to both sets. Table 5.4 shows the mean belief strength of never-users with respect to these eight outcomes for both "trial" and "regular" use. There, for example, it can be seen that never-users believe

TABLE 5.3
Attitudes, Norms, and Self-Efficacy as a Function
of Behavior and Population

Population	Behavior	Attitude	Norms	Efficacy
Never-users	Once or twice	-2.30[a]	-1.71[a]	4.31[a]
Never-users	Nearly every mo.	-2.50[a]	-1.76[a]	4.37[a]
Ever-users	Nearly every mo.	-0.96[b]	-1.29[a]	4.08[b]

Note: Column values with different superscripts are significantly different (*p* < .05).

TABLE 5.4

Never-Users' Beliefs About Using Marijuana "Even
Once or Twice" and "Almost Every Month"

Belief	Once or Twice	Every Month	t
Be like coolest kids	-1.27	-1.24	0.48
Trouble with law	0.57	1.09	3.19**
Use stronger drugs	-0.46	0.29	4.78**
Decreased judgment	0.41	0.82	2.82**
Damage my brain	1.09	1.30	2.22*
Upset my parents	1.40	1.60	2.05*
Against my morals	0.63	0.93	1.98*
Have good time	-0.70	-0.66	0.67

$*p < .05, **p < .01.$

that using marijuana once or twice is significantly less likely to lead to the use of stronger drugs ($M = -.46$) than is using marijuana nearly every month ($M = +.29$). Similarly, never-users are significantly more likely to believe that "regular" use will decrease their judgment ($M = +.82$) and get them in trouble with the law ($M = +1.09$) than will "trial" use ($M = +.41$ and $+.57$, respectively). Thus, although never users have equally strong negative attitudes toward "trial" and "regular" use of marijuana, they do see some real differences between these two behaviors. It is interesting to note, however, that in contrast to substantial differences in behavioral beliefs, never-users have very similar normative beliefs about these two behaviors. That is, never users believe that their friends and parents are equally disapproving of trial and regular use.[1]

Perhaps not surprisingly, just as never-users believe that there are different consequences associated with "trial" and "regular" use, ever-users and never-users hold significantly different beliefs about the consequences of using marijuana "almost every month." For example, Figure 5.2 shows that never users, those who have ever used but not in the past 12 months, those who have used one to five times in the past 12 months, and those who have used six or more times in the past 12 months differ systematically vis-à-vis their belief that regular use of marijuana would be

---

[1] Recall that self-efficacy questions did not ask the adolescents if they could avoid "regular" or "trial" use; instead, all respondents were asked to indicate how certain they were that they could say no to marijuana under different circumstances. Thus, one would not expect the never users to differ on this variable.

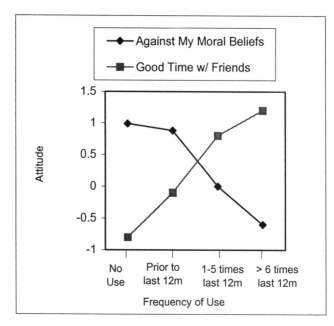

FIGURE 5.2 Beliefs about using marijuana nearly every month as a function of prior use: Acting against moral beliefs and having a good time with friends.

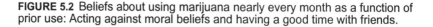

"acting against my moral principles." More specifically, it can be seen that the more marijuana one has smoked in the past 12 months, the less likely is one to believe that marijuana smoking would be morally reprehensible. Similarly, it can be seen that the four "use groups" also differ significantly with respect to their beliefs that regularly smoking marijuana (i.e., almost every month) would lead to "having a good time with my friends." Although never-users do not believe that "regular" marijuana use would lead to this outcome, those who have smoked marijuana six or more times in the past 12 months think it is likely that smoking marijuana almost every month will lead to *good times with friends*. Similar patterns were found with respect to many of the other positive and negative outcome beliefs. These findings should make it clear that very different interventions will be necessary for different populations (e.g., ever-users and never-users), as well as for "trial" and "regular" use. Unfortunately, although the choice of a behavior is under the control of the interventionist, he or she may not always know about the size or number of different subpopulations comprising a given target population.

For example, consider a school-based program where the principal of the school is anxious to have an antidrug program but is reluctant to allow students to be asked questions about their own illicit drug use behaviors. Here one cannot develop separate interventions for ever-users and never-users, let alone for those who use occasionally or those who use regularly. One can try to identify those factors that are most likely to influence a given behavior in the population as a whole—but which behavior should one consider? Although many different factors can influence this decision, the Office of National Drug Control Policy (ONDCP) has targeted "trial" use for never-users and "regular" use for occasional users as the two behaviors they would most like to prevent. However, as we saw earlier, over 95% of the never-users in our sample reported that they did not intend to use marijuana even once or twice during the next 12 months. Clearly, for this population, we need to understand the factors that maintain these intentions and that enable the adolescents to act on them. Because we currently do not have data to explore this issue (i.e., longitudinal data linking intentions at Time 1 to behavior at Time 2 are not yet available), and because over 40% of our sample had indicated that they had previously used marijuana, we decided, as an initial step, to focus on young adolescents' intentions *to use marijuana nearly every month for the next 12 months.*

TESTING THE INTEGRATED MODEL

The data we present come from a school-based, posttest only, randomized trial evaluating the effectiveness of two sets of antidrug public service announcements (PSAs). Two hundred and forty-two (242) students with a mean age of 14.6 years were randomly assigned to one of three conditions. In all three of these conditions, participants first viewed a public broadcasting program on how to make a documentary. The PSAs were distributed throughout the program in two of these conditions. After viewing the programs, the students filled out a lengthy questionnaire that assessed all of the psychosocial variables described in the integrated model as well as a number of demographic, personality, and other individual difference variables. The effects of these interventions will be reported in the future. Because the main purpose of this chapter is to illustrate how theory can be used to develop effective messages, we consider the data from the sample as a whole. It is worth noting, however, that the findings presented next for the total sample were very similar to findings we obtained when we considered only those in the control condition.

The first thing we considered was the distribution of intentions. It can be seen in Table 5.5 that only 15 of the 242 adolescents (6.2%) indicated a positive intention to use marijuana almost every month for the next 12 months, whereas 204 (84.3%) said they definitely would not perform this behavior. Clearly, although most members of this population do not need an intervention to reduce their intentions to use marijuana "regularly," there is some variation in intentions. Although such a skewed distribution may severely constrain correlations, let us explore the extent to which the integrated model described earlier can help us predict and understand these adolescents' intentions to use marijuana almost every month.

Figure 5.3 shows how the model fit the data. Taken together, attitudes, norms, and self-efficacy accounted for 41% of the variance in intentions ($R = .64$). Although all three of the psychosocial predictors significantly influenced intentions, attitudes were most important (beta = .32), followed by norms (beta = .27) and self-efficacy (beta = -.17).[2] Equally important, the behavioral beliefs we considered significantly predicted attitude ($r = .61$, $p < .001$) and the normative beliefs significantly predicted the normative pressure the adolescents were experiencing ($r = .71$, $p < .001$). Thus, it pays to try to identify the specific behavioral, normative, and self-efficacy beliefs that discriminate between those who do and do not intend to use marijuana almost every month for the next 12 months.

TABLE 5.5
School Based Sample: Pattern of Intentions
to Use Marijuana Almost Every Month for
the Next 12 Months

Response	Frequency	Percent
Definitely would not	204	84.3
Probably would not	23	9.5
Probably would	6	2.5
Definitely would	9	3.7

---

[2] It is important to recognize that while attitudes and norms were assessed with respect to the behavior in question (i.e., using marijuana almost every month for the next 12 months), self-efficacy was assessed more generally with respect to "saying no" to using marijuana. Thus, the relative importance of self-efficacy as a determinant of intentions to use marijuana "regularly" may be underestimated.

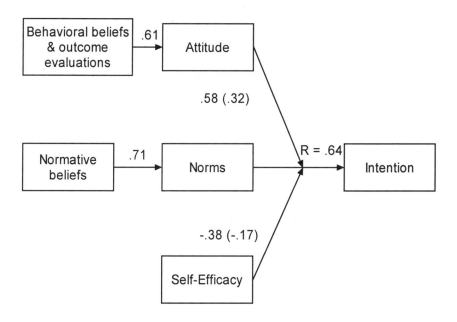

FIGURE 5.3 An integrative model: Findings from an adolescent sample (n = 242). Note: All correlations (and regression weights) significant at $p < .01$.

The Role of "External" Variables

First, however, let us consider whether "other variables" can help to explain the adolescents' intentions to use marijuana almost every month. In addition to assessing demographic variables such as gender, ethnicity, and age, we assessed a number of individual difference variables. More specifically, the adolescents were asked if turning down drugs would make them feel left out, or if it would make their friends think they weren't cool. They also were asked whether their friends would respect them and/ or accept them and their decision if they turned down drugs. These four items did not form a single scale; rather, analyses suggested two measures: (a) the belief that "saying no" leads to positive consequences and (b) the belief that "saying no" leads to negative consequences. Respondents were also asked, "How often do you spend your free time in the afternoons hanging out with friends without adult supervision?" *Time spent with friends* was indicated on a 5-place *Never* (1) to *Always or Almost Always* (5) scale. They were also asked to indicate how many times, in the last 7 days, they got together with friends who "get in trouble a lot," "fight a lot," "take things that don't belong to them," and who "smoke cigarettes or chew tobacco." These four items did have internal consistency (alpha = .80), and thus were summed to create a single *Time with risky friends* measure. *Sensation seeking* was also assessed with four internally consistent items (alpha = .78): I would like to explore strange places; I like to do frightening things; I like new and exciting experiences, even if I have to break the rules; and I prefer friends who are exciting and unpredictable. Finally, being under parental supervision was measured by two items reflecting the adolescents' beliefs that their parents knew of their whereabouts.

Table 5.6 shows the correlation between each of these "external variables" and the adolescents' intentions to use marijuana almost every month for the next 12 months. It also shows the correlation between each of the external variables and the three major psychosocial determinants of that intention (i.e., attitudes, norms, and self-efficacy). Consistent with the findings of others, most of the external variables are significantly related to the intention to use marijuana regularly. For example, the more one is a sensation seeker and the more one spends time with "risky" friends, the more likely he or she is to intend to use marijuana regularly. In contrast, the more adolescents perceive that they are under parental supervision, the less likely they are to form an intention to use marijuana regularly. Note, however, that each variable that is significantly related to intention also is related to at least one of the underlying psychosocial determinants. Consistent with this result, regression analyses indicated that none of these external variables contribute to the prediction of intention over and above the contribution of attitudes, norms, and self-efficacy.

TABLE 5.6

Correlations of "External Variables" with Adolescents' Intentions,
Attitude, Norms, and Self-efficacy On Using Marijuana
Almost Every Month for the Next 12 Months

External Variable	Correlations with :			
	Intention	Attitude	Norms	Self-efficacy
Saying No - Negative	.07	.17	.08	-.24***
Saying No - Positive	-.12	-.11	-.15*	.32***
Time with friends	.13*	.16*	.15*	.02
Time with risky friends	.34***	.50***	.33***	-.20**
Sensation seeking	.20**	.39***	.23***	-.09
Parental supervision	-.27***	-.29***	-.17**	.32

Note: *p < .05, **p < .01, ***p < .001.

Given that the variance in intention to use marijuana regularly appears to be primarily determined by attitudes, norms, and self-efficacy, let us now consider the beliefs that underlie these variables.

Identifying Target Beliefs

Because attitude was the most important determinant of intention, we will consider behavioral beliefs. Because we assessed a large number of behavioral beliefs (or outcome expectancies), it seemed parsimonious to determine whether these beliefs could be viewed as representing a smaller set of underlying dimensions. We thus clustered the beliefs into four conceptual groupings: physical and mental costs; social costs; self-esteem costs; and positive outcomes. It should be noted that the three cost groupings are based on the three classes of outcome expectancies identified by Bandura (1986). Rather than distributing positive outcomes among the costs however, we viewed them as a separate dimension. To test the unidimensionality of these four conceptual groupings we examined each of them for its internal consistency. In Table 5.7 it can be seen that, consistent with our conceptual analysis, all four scales were internally consistent with alphas ranging from .74 to .91.

Before considering whether these scales discriminated between intenders and nonintenders, it is important to demonstrate that these scales can predict the attitude toward using marijuana almost every month. That is, we saw earlier that the weighted sum of all the beliefs correlated .61 with attitude. If the four scales represent true underlying belief dimensions, the attitude should be predicted almost as well from the four scale scores as from the full set of underlying beliefs. Consistent with this expectation, the sum of the four scales (weighted by the evaluations of the outcomes–that is, costs were weighted -1 and positive outcomes were weighted +1) correlated .64 with attitude.[3]

Table 5.7 also shows the correlation of each of the four belief scales with the intention to use marijuana almost every month. In addition, the table presents the mean scale score for intenders and nonintenders. It can be seen that all four types of beliefs are significantly correlated with intentions, and that all four discriminate between intenders and nonintenders. Note that although nonintenders believe that smoking marijuana almost every month will lead to all three types of costs and no positive

---

[3] Consistent with this result, the weighted sum of the four scale scores correlated strongly ($r = .97$) with the sum of the beliefs x evaluations, based on all of the underlying beliefs.

TABLE 5.7
Internal Consistency of Behavioral Belief Scales,
Correlations with Intentions, and Mean Scale Scores
of Intenders (INT) and Non-intenders (N-INT)

Scale	Alpha	r	N-INT	INT
Physical & mental costs	0.91	-.30	.92	.12
Social costs	0.91	-.37	.78	-.43
Positive outcomes	0.74	.39	-.65	.37
Self-esteem costs	0.91	-.34	.91	-.05

Note: All correlations, and the differences between intenders and
non-intenders, significant at $p < .01$.

outcomes, those who intend to smoke marijuana almost every month do
not believe that there are social costs, do believe that there are positive
outcomes, and are relatively uncertain about the costs to their self-
esteem as well as about physical and mental costs. These findings suggest that all four dimensions are legitimate targets for an intervention. But
which specific beliefs should an intervention address? Although it is clear
that we want to change beliefs that are highly correlated with the intention
we wish to change, Hornik and Woolf (1999) pointed out that we must
also consider whether it is in fact possible to change the belief. That is,
can one support the belief with a plausible argument based on strong evidence? Unfortunately, although empirical evidence can be used to identify beliefs that are highly correlated with intention, deciding whether a
particular belief can or cannot be changed is largely a subjective judgment. Nevertheless, it is reasonable to assume that beliefs based on
direct experience will be more difficult to change than beliefs based on
inference or on information provided by some outside source (see Fishbein, von Haeften, & Appleyard, in press).

Tables 5.8-5.11 show the correlations between each of the four belief
dimensions or scales, (and the items comprising each scale) with the
intention to use marijuana almost every month. In addition, the tables
show the mean scale and individual item scores for both intenders and
nonintenders. Starting with beliefs about positive outcomes, it can be
seen in Table 5.8 that five of the eight individual beliefs comprising this
scale did discriminate between intenders and nonintenders. Note that the
two items with the strongest correlations (and with the biggest mean differences) relate to having a good time, either in general or with one's
friends. That is, consistent with the data from our initial survey (see Figure
5.2), although intenders believe that smoking marijuana "regularly" will
lead to these outcomes, nonintenders do not. According to Hornik and

TABLE 5.8

Correlations between Positive Outcome Scale (alpha = .74)
and Each Scale Item with Intention to Use Mariuana Almost
Every Month, and the Mean Scale and Item Scores for
Intenders (INT) and Non-intenders (N-INT)

Scale/Item	r-intention	N-INT	INT
POSITIVE OUTCOMES	.39	-.65	.37
Be like coolest kids	.27	-1.45	-.13
Fit in with group I like	.28	-1.06	.20
Have a good time	.40	-.62	1.13
Have good time w/ friends	.44	-.67	1.27
Get away from problems	.18	-.87	- .47*
Become more creative	.26	-.86	.27
Be like other teens	.15	-.30	.20*
Feel dreamy or mellow	-.06	.68	.47*

Note: * indicates a nonsignificant difference between means.

Woolf (1999), the question that one needs to ask is whether it will be possible to develop messages that will convince the intenders that their regularly smoking marijuana will not lead to "good times." Unfortunately, because this belief is most likely based on the adolescents' direct experience, this may be a rather difficult thing to do.

Looking at the beliefs with the next highest correlations, we can see that although nonintenders do not believe that regular marijuana use will help them fit in with a group they like or allow them to be like the coolest kids, intenders appear to be relatively uncertain about these two consequences (although they tend to believe that regular smoking will help them fit in with a group they like but will not make them be like the coolest kids). Here again, because the adolescents are the ones defining the group they like, it would probably be difficult to change their beliefs about whether regular use of marijuana would help them fit in with that group. And although it may be possible to develop messages to strengthen the intenders' belief that regular use of marijuana will not make them "one of the coolest kids," it is important to note that for at least some adolescents, "being like one of the coolest kids" is not seen as a good thing, but is actually evaluated negatively. Thus a message directed at this belief may be convincing at least some intenders that regular use will prevent "bad things" from happening—that is, they don't want to be seen as "one of the coolest kids" and smoking marijuana will help them avoid this label. If this is in fact the case, decreasing their belief that smoking marijuana makes them "one of the coolest kids" may actually strengthen rather than weaken their attitudes and intentions concerning regular use.

Looking again at Table 5.8, it appears that there is probably only one positive outcome belief that discriminates between intenders and nonintenders that may be relatively easy to change, namely the belief that regular use makes one more creative. Clearly one could try to persuade intenders that although they think that regular use of marijuana increases their creativity, the "facts" are that they actually lose creativity. But this seems more like a message about the physical and mental costs of regular marijuana use than a message about positive consequences of using marijuana. So let us look more closely at the adolescents' beliefs about the physical and mental costs of regular use of marijuana.

In Table 5.9 we see that nonintenders believe regular marijuana use will make them lose ambition and motivation, make them become forgetful, make it difficult for them to express their thoughts, and make them anxious and/or depressed. In contrast, those intending to use marijuana nearly every month are essentially uncertain or tend to disbelieve that these negative outcomes will occur. It would appear that, like the belief about "creativity", most of these beliefs are amenable to change.

TABLE 5.9

Correlations between the Physical and Mental Costs Scale (alpha = .91) and Each Scale Item with Intention to Use Marijuana Almost Every Month and Mean Scale and Individual Item Scores for Intenders (INT) and Non-intenders (N-INT)

Scale/Item	r-intention	N-INT	INT
PHYSICAL/MENTAL COSTS	-.30	.92	.12
Lose ambition	-.26	.75	-.20
Become anxious	-.15	.48	-.33
Lose athletic skills	-.26	.96	-.13
Start avoiding problems	-.13	.53	.00*
Damage my brain	-.07	1.35	1.33*
Become depressed	-.29	.77	-.03
Decrease judgmen	-.27	.99	-.01
Difficulty expressing thoughts	-.26	.79	-.33
Become forgetful	-.21	.97	.13
Damage my lungs	-.18	1.45	.80
Lose motivation	-.25	1.01	.00
Feel tired	-.13	1.00	.60*

Note: * indicates a nonsignificant difference between means.

Although space does not allow for a complete discussion of each belief dimension, Tables 5.10 and 5.11 present the relevant data concerning social costs and costs to one's self-esteem. Note that with respect to both dimensions, most of the individual beliefs comprising the dimension are highly correlated with intention and discriminate between intenders and nonintenders. It appears, however, that it would be more difficult to change beliefs about social costs (because they are more likely to be based on direct observation) than about costs to one's self-esteem. Thus, in general, it appears that the messages with the greatest potential of being effective will be those directed at changing beliefs about mental costs (including the loss of creativity) and loss of self-esteem.

Turning to normative beliefs, Table 5.12 shows that although all six normative beliefs discriminate between intenders and nonintenders, the most important referents to adolescents are their girl/boyfriend and other close friends. Just as we argue that it will be hard to change adolescents' beliefs about the social costs of regular marijuana use, we argue that it will also be difficult to change their perceptions about the normative proscriptions of these referents. Intenders are already aware that their parents, grandparents, and teachers would disapprove of their regular use of marijuana. Thus, attempts to change normative beliefs will probably not produce large changes in regular use intentions.

TABLE 5.10

Correlations Between the Social Costs Scale (alpha = .91)
and Each Scale Item with Intention to Use Marijuana
Almost Every Month and Mean Scale and Individual
Item Scores for Intenders (INT) and Non-intenders (N-INT)

Scale/Item	r-intention	N-INT	INT
SOCIAL COSTS SCALE	-.37	.78	-.43
Lose friends	-.31	.42	-1.00
Feel lonely	-.24	.42	-.47
Be a loser	-.36	.58	-1.20
Lose boy/girlfriend	-.35	.75	-.67
Lose friends' respect	-.33	.74	-.80
Look stupid	-.26	.91	-.33
Destroy relationships	-.31	.96	-.27
Upset parents	-.10	1.46	1.27

Note: * indicates a nonsignificant difference between means.

TABLE 5.11

Correlations Between the Costs to Self-Esteem Scale
(alpha = .91) and Each Scale Item with Intention to Use
Marijuana Almost Every Month and Mean Scale and Individual
Item Scores for Intenders (INT) and Non-intenders (N-INT)

Scale/Item	r-intention	N-INT	INT
SELF-ESTEEM COSTS	-.34	.91	-.05
Not able to find job	-.33	.75	-.80
In trouble with law	-.21	.97	.13
Mess us my life	-.36	1.20	-.07
Spend to much money	-.07	1.35	1.33*
Be a bad role model	-.23	1.04	.27
Against my morals	-.35	1.09	-.27
Won't be a good person	-.23	.44	- .27*
Do worse in school	-.25	1.09	.13
Start using stronger drugs	-.28	.28	-.93

Note: * indicates no significant difference between means.

Finally Table 5.13 shows that although nonintenders are quite certain they could say "no" to marijuana under all circumstances, intenders are, at best, only slightly certain. It is interesting to note that although all adolescents seem to agree that it is "easiest" to say no to marijuana when it is

TABLE 5.12

Correlations between the Normative Belief Scale
(alpha = .79) and Each Scale Item with Intention to Use
Marijuana Almost Every Month and Mean Scale and Individual
Individual Item Scores for Intenders (INT) and Non-intenders (N-INT)

Scale/Item	r-intention	N-INT	INT
NORMATIVE BELIEFS	.58	-1.53	-.32
Friends	.47	-1.37	.39
Parents/caregivers	.39	-1.88	-1.23
Girlfriend/Boyfriend	.56	-1.43	.77
Grandparents	.39	-1.87	-.92
Teachers	.39	-1.84	-1.15
People your age	.31	-.76	.23

Note: All mean differences statistically significant ($p < .05$).

TABLE 5.13

Correlations between the Efficacy Beliefs Scale
(alpha = .91) and Each Scale Item with Intention to Use
Marijuana Almost Every Month and Mean Scale and Individual
Item Scores for Intenders (INT) and Non-intenders (N-INT)

Scale/Item	r-intention	N-INT	INT
SELF-EFFICACY	-.38	1.44	.41
Party where most use	-.33	1.22	.37
Close friend suggests	-.35	1.38	.20
Feel sad and bored	-.37	1.52	.13
Offered on school property	-.22	1.70	1.00
Friend's house w/o parents	-.29	1.36	.33

Note: All mean differences statistically significant ($p < .05$).

offered on school property, nonintenders think it is most difficult to say no when they are at a party where most of the people at the party are using it, whereas intenders think it is most difficult to say no when they are bored and feeling sad. Thus, despite the fact that self-efficacy is the weakest of the three psychosocial determinants of intentions to use marijuana almost every month, it does seem that it would be useful to try to increase intenders' beliefs that they could say no even when they are bored and/or feeling sad.

SUMMARY AND CONCLUSIONS

To summarize briefly, our analyses have important implications for developing media campaigns to prevent marijuana use among adolescents. First, despite having equally negative attitudes and subjective norms with respect to using marijuana "even once or twice" or "almost every month" in the next 12 months, never-users hold significantly different beliefs about the consequences of performing these two behaviors. Thus, at least among never-users, different interventions may be necessary to prevent "trial" and "regular" use. Unfortunately, because of our decision to ask ever-users only about "use almost every month," we do not know whether those who have ever used marijuana hold different behavioral, normative, or efficacy beliefs about using marijuana once or twice and using it almost every month. We do know, however, that ever users have very different intentions to perform these two behaviors, which suggests that, for ever-users, these behaviors are also quite different and will require different behavior change messages. Moreover, and equally important, ever-users and never-users hold very different behavioral and normative beliefs about "using marijuana almost every month for the next 12 months." Thus, different interventions may be necessary to prevent "regular" use in these two populations. These findings clearly support the assumption that to maximize potential effectiveness, interventions should be designed to change a given behavior in a given population.

Perhaps not surprisingly, the data clearly indicate that most adolescent never-users appear to have little or no intention to use marijuana. Recall that only 3% of never-users intend to use marijuana "even once or twice" in the next 12 months, and only 1% intend to use marijuana "nearly every month." Indeed, 80% of never-users say they "definitely will not" use marijuana even once or twice in the next 12 months and 93% say they definitely will not use it "nearly every month." This finding raises an important question about the utility of a campaign strategy that focuses on providing never-users information designed to weaken their intentions to use marijuana and/or to strengthen their intentions to avoid using marijuana. Should we be designing messages that attempt to change the intentions of the 3% of the never-users who currently hold positive intentions to use marijuana even once or twice, or should we be designing messages to help the 97% of never-users who already have negative intentions to act on those intentions?[4] As discussed earlier, very different interventions are necessary when people have formed an intention but are not acting on it than when they have not formed an intention. Given the large proportion of adolescents who have no intention to use marijuana, it could be argued that our primary task should not be to design messages to reduce non-users marijuana use intentions, but instead to identify factors that will help these adolescents maintain and act on their already existent negative intentions. It is our guess that messages designed to help people act on their intentions will look very different from those that have been directed at changing intentions by reducing either attitudes, norms, or self-efficacy concerning regular or trial use. In contrast, it does seem to be important to reduce ever-users' intentions to use marijuana "even once or twice" or "almost every month." Indeed, 44% of ever-users say they will use marijuana "once or twice" whereas 25.5%

---

[4] It could be argued that the 17% of never-users who report that they *probably* will not use marijuana even once or twice are still an important audience for an intention change strategy. However, one must still question whether the best strategy for this subgroup would be to design a message to strengthen this negative intention (i.e., move them to *definitely* will not use), or to design a message that will help the adolescent act on this intention.

say they will use it "nearly every month." In addition, only 31% say they definitely won't "try" marijuana and only 50% say they definitely won't use it "regularly." Given that a high percentage of ever-users intend to continue to use marijuana, it does seem that a message strategy focused on changing these intentions would be quite appropriate. And here, as we have tried to demonstrate, we can use theory to help us identify those factors that are most likely to influence these intentions. Recall, however, that the data analyses described in this chapter were based on data obtained from a sample of school-based adolescents, most of whom had probably never used marijuana, and very few of whom had any intention to use marijuana almost every month. Thus, these findings again raise the question of whether, in relatively young, school-based samples, it is better to help nonintenders act on their intentions or to try to convert intenders to nonintenders. In any case, because of the nature of our school-based sample, our findings should be considered as illustrative, and not be taken as recommendations for developing one or more messages to prevent "trial" or "occasional" users from becoming "regular" users. At best, the results presented here may be suggestive of messages that could be presented in a school setting to a mixed, but primarily nonusing, audience.

And although we are hesitant to put too much weight on these findings, they do raise some interesting questions. For example, consistent with earlier research, many external variables (e.g., sensation seeking, parental supervision, time spent with risky friends, etc.) were found to be significantly related to the adolescents' intentions to use marijuana. However, analyses showed that these variables influenced the intention only indirectly, through their influence on the underlying psychosocial determinants of that intention. Thus, it would seem more appropriate to design interventions to directly attack the underlying psychosocial variables than to attack the "external" variable per se. Moreover, although we found that all three psychosocial variables (i.e., attitudes, norms, and self-efficacy) did contribute to the formation of intentions to use marijuana almost every month, attitudes appear to be much more important determinants of this intention than either norms or self-efficacy. Recall, however, that although attitudes and norms were assessed with respect to the specific behavior of "using marijuana almost every month for the next 12 months," self-efficacy was assessed more generally with respect to "saying no" to marijuana use. Thus, the relative importance of self-efficacy as a determinant of intentions to regularly use marijuana may be underestimated. Nevertheless, the data suggest that messages designed to change beliefs about the consequences of using marijuana will be more effective than messages designed to increase social pressure or self-efficacy. Consistent with this, we saw that adolescents are already aware that their parents, grandparents, and teachers think they should not use marijuana, and we questioned the utility of trying to change beliefs about the proscriptions of the adolescent's girlfriend, boyfriend or other close friends.

With respect to self-efficacy, it does appear that there is room to try to increase intenders' beliefs that they can say no to drugs if they really want to. Indeed, one of the more surprising results in our data is the finding that intenders feel that it is hardest for them to say no to drugs when they are feeling sad or bored. This finding certainly raises questions about the often-expressed assumption that adolescent drug use is more of a "social" than a "private" behavior.

Finally, it is important to note that although almost all of the behavioral beliefs we considered did discriminate between intenders and nonintenders, a careful consideration of these beliefs suggests that only a limited number may be amenable to change. In particular, we would argue that the most effective messages are likely to be those focusing on increasing adolescents' perceptions that use of marijuana will have mental and self-esteem costs.

Clearly, to be effective, a message designed to change a given belief (be it behavioral, normative or self-efficacy) should, at a minimum, change the belief at which it was directed. However, it is important to remember that to produce change in intentions and behavior, changes in beliefs should lead to a change in attitudes, perceived norms, or self-efficacy. As we have argued previously however, the relative importance of these three psychosocial variables as determinants of intention will vary as a function of both the behavior and the population being considered. Thus, prior to developing an intervention it is necessary to demonstrate that the psychosocial variable being attacked has the potential to change intentions. Note that by using a theory to guide message development, one also has an analytic framework for determining why a given message was or was not effective in producing behavior change. This type of information is necessary if we are truly going to understand media and message effects.

REFERENCES

Ajzen I. (1985). From intentions to actions: A theory of planned behavior, in J. Kuhl & J. Bechmann (Eds.), *Action control: From cognition to behavior* (pp. 11-39). New York: Springer-Verlag.

Ajzen I. (1991). The theory of planned behavior. *Organizational Behavior and Human Decision Processes, 50*, 179-211.

Ajzen, I., & Fishbein, M. (1980). *Understanding attitudes and predicting social behavior.* Englewood Cliffs, NJ: Prentice-Hall.

Ajzen I., Madden, T. J. (1986). Prediction of goal-directed behavior: Attitudes, intentions, and perceived behavioral control. *Journal of Experimental Social Psychology, 22,* 453-474.

Bandura, A. (1977). Self-efficacy: Toward a unifying theory of behavioral change. *Psychological Review, 84,* 191-215.

Bandura, A. (1986). *Social foundations of thought and action: A social cognitive theory,* Englewood Cliffs, N.J.: Prentice-Hall.

Bandura, A. (1991). Self-efficacy mechanism in physiological activation and health-promoting behavior, in J. Madden IV (Ed.), *Neurobiology of learning, emotion and affect* (pp. 229-269). New York: Raven.

Bandura, A. (1994). Social cognitive theory and exercise of control over HIV infection. In R. J. DiClemente & J. L. Peterson (Eds.), *Preventing AIDS: Theories and methods of behavioral interventions* (pp. 25-59). New York, Plenum.

Becker, M. H. (1974). The health belief model and personal health behavior. *Health Education Monographs, 2,* 324-508.

Becker, M. H. (1988). AIDS and behavior change. *Public Health Reviews, 16,* 1-11.

Fishbein, M. (1995). Developing effective behavior change interventions: Some lessons learned from behavioral research. In T. E. Backer, S. L. David, & G. Soucy (Eds.), *Reviewing the behavioral sciences knowledge base on technology transfer* (NIDA Research Monograph No. 155, NIH Pub. No. 95-4035, pp. 246-261). Rockville, MD: National Institute on Drug Abuse.

Fishbein, M. (2000). The role of theory in HIV prevention. *AIDS Care, 12,* 273-278.

Fishbein, M. & Ajzen, I. (1975). *Belief, Attitude, Intention and Behavior: An Introduction to Theory and Research.* Reading, MA, Addison-Wesley.

Fishbein, M., Guenther-Grey, C., Johnson, W., Wolitski, R. J., McAlister, A., Rietmeijer, C. A., O'Reilly, K., and the AIDS Community Demonstration Projects. (1996). Using A Theory-Based Community Intervention to Reduce AIDS Risk Behaviors: The CDC's AIDS community demonstration projects. In S. Oskamp & S. C. Thompson (Eds.), *Understanding and preventing HIV risk behavior: Safer sex and drug use* (pp. 177-206). Thousand Oaks, CA: Sage

Fishbein, M., Middlestadt, S. E., & Hitchcock, P. J. (1991). Using information to change sexually transmitted disease-related behaviors: An analysis based on the theory of reasoned action, in J. N. Wasserheit, S. O. Aral, & K. K. Holmes (Eds.), *Research issues in human behavior and sexually transmitted diseases in the AIDS era* (pp. 243-257). Washington, DC, American Society for Microbiology.

Fishbein, M., Triandis, H. C., Kanfer, F. H., Becker, M. H., Middlestadt, S. E., & Eichler, A (2001). Factors influencing behavior and behavior change. In A. Baum, T. R. Revenson & J. E. Singer (Eds.), *Handbook of health psychology* (pp. 3-17). Mahwah, NJ: Lawrence Erlbaum Associates.

Fishbein, M., von Haeften, I., & Appleyard, J. (in press). The role of theory in developing effective interventions: Implications from Project SAFER. *Psychology, Health and Medicine.*

Fisher, J. D., & Fisher W. A. (1992). Changing AIDS-risk behavior. *Psychological Bulletin,111,* 455-474.

Gerrard, M., Gibbons, F. X., & Bushman, B. J. (1996). Relation between perceived vulnerability to HIV and precautionary sexual behavior. *Psychological Bulletin, 119,* 390-409.

Holden, G. (1991). The relationship of self-efficacy appraisals to subsequent health related outcomes: A meta-analysis. *Social Work in Health Care,16,* 53-93.

Hornik, R. & Woolf, K. D. (1999). Using cross-sectional surveys to plan message strategies. *Social Marketing Quarterly, 5,* 34-41.

Kanfer, F. H. (1970). Self-regulation: Research, issues, and speculations. In C. Neuringer & J. L. Michael (Eds.), *Behavior Modification in Clinical Psychology* (pp. 178-220). New York: Appleton-Century-Crofts.

Kraus, S. J. (1995). Attitudes and the prediction of behavior: A meta-analysis of the empirical literature. *Personality and Social Psychology Bulletin, 21,* 58-75.

National Institutes of Health. (1997). *Interventions to prevent HIV risk behaviors. Consensus development conference statement.* Bethesda, MD: National Institutes of Health.

Prochaska, J. O., & DiClemente, C. C. (1983). Stages and processes of self-change in smoking: Towards an integrative model of change. *Journal of Consulting and Clinical Psychology, 51,* 390-395.

Prochaska, J. O., & DiClemente C. C. (1986). Toward a comprehensive model of change, in W. R. Miller & N. Neather (Eds.), *Treating addictive behaviors: Processes of change* (pp. 3-27). New York, Plenum Press.

Prochaska, J. O., & DiClemente, C. C. (1992). Stages of change in the modification of problem behaviors. In M. Hersen, P. M. Miller, & R. Eisler (Eds.), *Progress in behavior modification, 28* (pp. 184-218). New York: Wadsworth.

Prochaska, J. O., DiClemente, C. C., & Norcross, J. C. (1992). In search of how people change: Applications to addictive behaviors. *American Psychologist, 47,* 1102-1114.

Prochaska, J. O., Redding, C. A., Harlow, L. L., Rossi, J. S., & Velicer, W. F. (1994). The transtheoretical model of change and HIV prevention: A review. *Health Education Quarterly, 21,* 471-486.

Rosenstock, I. M. (1974). The health belief model and preventive health behavior. *Health Education Monographs, 4,* 354-386.

Rosenstock, I. M., Strecher, V. J., & Becker, M. H. (1994). The health belief model and HIV risk behavior change. In R. J. DiClemente & J. L. Peterson (Eds.), *Preventing AIDS: Theories and methods of behavioral interventions* (pp. 5–24). New York: Plenum Press.

Sheppard, B. H., Hartwick, J., & Warshaw, P. R. (1988). The theory of reasoned action: A meta-analysis of past research with recommendations for modifications and future research. *Journal of Consumer Research, 15,* 325-343.

Strecher, V. J., McEvoy, D. B., Becker, M. H., & Rosenstock, I. M. (1986). The role of self-efficacy in achieving health behavior change. *Health Education Quarterly,* 73-91.

Triandis, H. C. (1972). *The analysis of subjective culture.* New York: John Wiley and Sons.

van den Putte, B. (1991). *20 years of the theory of reasoned action of Fishbein and Ajzen: A meta-analysis.* Unpublished manuscript, University of Amsterdam, Amsterdam, The Netherlands.

6

Attention, Persuasive Communication, and Prevention

Lewis Donohew, Philip Palmgreen, Elizabeth Lorch, Rick Zimmerman, and Nancy Harrington

University of Kentucky

Humans are not the consistently aware, thoughtful creatures we often assume them to be, at least not until we can engage them in some way and lure or jolt them into a higher level of awareness (Bardo, Donohew, & Harrington, 1998; Donohew, Lorch & Palmgreen, 1998). Thus, changing their health behaviors is a formidable task. On the basis of research to date, we take the position that the human decision-making process may or may not be "rational." Many individuals may be more likely to choose to be in situations or to engage in behaviors that are novel, reduce boredom, lead to disinhibition, or are thrilling or adventuresome. Beyond this, many of those who find themselves in these sorts of situations are less likely to act in ways that might be predicted by rational models of health-related behavior.

A central assumption of the research described in this chapter is that in order for health messages to be seriously attended, they must be capable of attracting and holding attention long enough for persuasive content, which might involve more rational decision-making (e.g., Ajzen & Fishbein, 1980) to be processed. This requires that they provide enough stimulation to generate a level of attention many implicitly assume is present all the time. Given growing evidence of the influence of biology on behavior, we posit a somewhat more primal human than is implicitly assumed in some of the theories of human behavior. Thus, for example, the presence or absence of immediate reward may play a greater role in changing behavior than is generally thought. The importance of immediate reward may signal a problem in changing health behaviors. Unlike the advertiser who sells people services or objects they often already want and that usually provide them an immediate reward, those engaged in health communication must convince audiences to not do things they want to do, and the principal reward for such behavior-avoidance of negative health consequences usually is long delayed. Yet, despite these difficulties, when the early history of prevention efforts is compared to the present, it is apparent that considerable advances have been made (Flay & Sobel, 1983; Rogers & Storey, 1987) in interventions involving both media and classroom approaches.

A crucial component of all prevention efforts is communication, and the development of a more advanced science of persuasive communication offers greater hope for success in altering behaviors and getting people to live healthy lives. Increasing the effectiveness of public health media campaigns has been a source of continuing interest because of their potential for reaching vastly greater audiences than normally are reached through other interventions. Increasing the effectiveness of school-based instructional programs also continues to have considerable appeal because such programs are delivered directly to target audiences.

The advances are due in part to the incorporation of more sophisticated theories of the persuasion process in campaign design, along with more rigorous techniques of formative, process, and summative evaluation, sharpened design methodologies, including more sophisticated audience segmentation and targeting, and more powerful statistical tools (Backer, 1990; Flora, Maccoby, & Farquhar, 1989; Perloff, 1993; Rogers & Storey, 1987). They have resulted in the detection of a variety of intervention effects. Design elements that have contributed to successful campaigns include professional quality messages, which can compete with product ads or curriculum components for the attention of audience members.

OVERVIEW

In this chapter, we describe a program of research that has evolved over a 15-year period. It includes both media and classroom approaches and has resulted in successful interventions in both. Although the research reported here was headed by principal investigators in communication whose primary concern was in further explanation of the human communication process, it includes researchers in a number of disciplines and subdisciplines. Among them are social psychologists, a physiological psychologist who used laboratory animals (white mice and rats) to study genetic and environmental bases of novelty seeking, a pharmacologist studying the chemical composition of brain slices from the novelty-seeking and novelty-avoiding animals, and an experimental psychologist using a human residential research laboratory. The resulting cooperative projects involved exploration of both the behavioral and biological bases for behaviors, and the testing of strategies for changing them.

As noted earlier, the program of research conducted by these investigators and funded by the National Institute on Drug Abuse, the National Institute on Alcohol Abuse and Alcoholism, the National Institute of Mental Health, and others, has focused on increasing the effective use of televised public service announcements (PSAs) in drug abuse prevention campaigns, and on increasing the effectiveness of classroom programs aimed at reducing risky sex and alcohol use. These studies have investigated:

1. The role of message sensation value in differentially influencing theresponses of high sensation seekers (HSS) and low sensation seekers among young adults.
2. The role of the sensation value of the television program context for antidrug PSAs in differentially eliciting attention from HSS and LSS.
3. The effectiveness of a message targeting strategy using message sensation value and program sensation value in a 5-month televiion antidrug PSA campaign to reach high HSS.
4. Effectiveness of a classroom-based curriculum in which theory and data from the media research program on sensation-seeking and message design were employed to adapt a nationally-respected curriculum, Reducing the Risk (RTR), to make it more appealing to HSS and to impulsive decision makers (IDM). Although the content of the curriculum was left essentially unchanged, its format was altered to make it more participatory and to make its materials more inviting to the students.

The results of these studies provide important direction for the design of prevention campaigns with regard to the critical issues of effective message design and placement.

Connection With Prevention Research

Higher needs for novelty and sensation, impulsive decision-making, or both have been connected by the investigators and others to drug and alcohol use, initiating sex at an early age, having multiple sexual partners, unprotected sex, and sex following use of alcohol and other drugs, with levels of one or both of these characteristics (e.g., Donohew, Helm,

Lawrence, & Shatzer, 1990; Donohew et al, 1998; Donohew et al., 2000; Langer, Zimmerman, Warheit, & Duncan, 1993; Palmgreen et al., 1995; Zuckerman, 1994). Research on sensation-seeking targeting and sensation value messages was adopted into the design of the proposed billion-dollar national antidrug media campaign of the Office of National Drug Control Policy (ONDCP).

The investigators established in previous research that adolescents and young adults who have higher needs for novelty and sensation (HSS) are more likely to become involved in risky situations and those who are IDM are more likely to engage in risky behaviors (Donohew et al., 1990, 2000). HSS may be more likely to choose to be in situations or to engage in behaviors that are novel, reduce boredom, lead to disinhibition, or are thrilling or adventuresome. Beyond this, IDM, if they find themselves in these sorts of situations, are less likely to act in ways that might be predicted by rational models of health-related behavior. Thus, an individual who is both an HSS and an IDM may be especially likely to drink alcohol before having sex to reduce anxiety about sexual activity, and may be especially likely as well not to use a condom in order to increase the sensation of the experience. On the other hand, an individual who is a low sensation seeker (LSS) and a rational decision-maker may be more likely to plan steps to avoid being in a situation where intercourse would occur, or might anticipate the need for a condom in case of a last-minute decision to have sex. Such a person also might be more likely to avoid alcohol use before a date with a possible sexual partner. Although either sensation-seeking or impulsive decision making could be expected to increase the probability that individuals involved would be more likely to take significantly greater health risks, the combination of these two characteristics makes them prime targets for health interventions.

In one HIV prevention study, for example (Donohew et al., 2000), involving 2949 ninth-grade students in 17 high schools in two Midwestern U.S. cities, strong associations were observed between sensation-seeking and impulsive decision-making and their separate and combined relationships and almost all of the indicators of sexual risk-taking, including intentions to have sex, ever had sex, number of lifetime sexual partners, been pregnant or caused a pregnancy, used alcohol, used a condom, used marijuana, had unwanted sex when drunk, had unwanted sex under pressure, said no to sex, used alcohol or partner used alcohol before sex, and used marijuana before sex.

CONCEPTS AND THEORIES

Needs for Novelty and Sensation

Attention to novelty in our ancient past probably was a fundamental survival behavior developed in the process of our evolution. Although the attention value of novelty no longer is as vital to survival, it continues to have major implications for human communication (Donohew et al., 1998) because humans appear to have a need for exploring novelty. The attention process is further affected by individual differences in reactivity to intense and novel stimulation as described by the sensation-seeking trait (Zuckerman, 1979,1983, 1988, 1994; Zuckerman, Kolin, Price, & Zoob, 1964; Zuckerman, Kuhlman, Joireman, Teta, & Kraft, 1993). In describing the phenomenon of novelty-seeking as a major driving force in human behavior, we (Bardo et al., 1996, p. 33) wrote:

> Numerous historical anecdotes are available to underscore the human attraction to novelty. Indeed, discovery of the "new world" may not have been possible had it not been for the innate human attraction to novelty. In the middle of the nineteenth century, Charles Darwin recognized that "it is human nature to value any novelty, however slight, in one's own possession (1859).

When viewed as an adaptive behavior, approach to novelty may promote survival of the species because it allows organisms to locate new sources of food and potential sources of danger.

Sensation-Seeking

Probably the most widely-researched concept employed to describe novelty seeking and attendant risk-taking is the concept of sensation-seeking (Zuckerman, 1979, 1983, 1988, 1994), which has been an integral component of the researches described in this chapter. Zuckerman (1994) described sensation-seeking as a trait defined by "the seeking of varied, novel, complex, and intense sensations and experiences, and the willingness to take physical, social, legal, and financial risks for the sake of such experience" (p. 27). HSS are receptive to stimuli that are intense, novel and arousing; stimuli producing lower levels of arousal may be considered "boring" and cause the HSS to seek alternative sources of stimulation. LSS tend to reject stimuli that are highly intense, preferring the familiar and less complex.

According to Zuckerman, sensation-seeking and sensation avoidance may represent adaptation to a dangerous environment in which novel stimuli can be either sources of reward or threats to survival. He has proposed that the search for novelty (Cloninger, Adolfson, & Svrakic, 1996; Cloninger, Pryzbeck, Svrakic, & Wetzel, 1994; Zuckerman, 1994) is a fundamental survival behavior, in which detection of novel stimuli leads to alerting the system for fight or flight (Franklin, Donohew, Dhoundiyal, & Cook, 1988).

One biological difference between HSS and LSS is in levels of blood platelet monoamine oxidase (MAO-B), the brain-specific enzyme that breaks down dopamine and other neurotransmitters (Arque, Unzeta,& Torrubia, 1988; Fowler, von Knorring & Oreland, 1980; Murphy, et al., 1977; Schooler, Zahn, Murphy & Buchsbaum, 1978). Schooler and colleagues (1978), among others, found a significant negative correlation between platelet MAO activity and scores on Zuckerman's Sensation-seeking Scale in both males and females, although males had lower MAO levels than females. Sensation-seeking has been connected with the mesolimbic dopamine pathway in work by Zuckerman and associates (Zuckerman, 1979, 1988, 1994) and with the male hormone testosterone. According to Bardo et al. (1996), the mesolimbic dopamine reward pathway presumably has evolved because it subserves behaviors that are vital to survival, and particularly because it is posited to be responsible for producing reinforcement (Glickman & Schiff, 1967; Vaccarino, Schiff, & Glickman, 1989). Bardo and associates (Bardo et al., 1993; Bardo & Hammer, 1991; Bardo, Neisewander, & Pierce, 1989) studied responses to novelty and selected drugs and their relationship to dopamine D1 and D2 receptors in animals. They suggested that novelty-seeking and drug-seeking behaviors may involve activation of a common neural substrate (in the mesolimbic dopamine system), supporting the possibility that novel or high-sensation stimulation may substitute for drug reward. Clearly, then, stimuli possessing stimulation-generating characteristics are likely to be sought over those that do not, especially by individuals with higher need for sensation. Work reported recently by teams conducting research at the National Institutes of Health and in Israel (Benjamin et al., 1996; Cloninger et al., 1996; Ebstein et al., 1996) connected novelty seeking and the D4 dopamine receptor gene (Vandenbergh, Zonderman, Wang, Uhl, & Costa, 1997). A substantial body of psychopharmacological and genetic research implicated the mesolimbic dopamine reward pathway as a critical link mediating drug reward (e.g., Koob, Le, & Creese, 1987; Wise & Rompre, 1989).

Impulsive Decision-Making

Beyond needs for novelty and sensation, but having considerable implications for design of health interventions is impulsivity, or an impulsive decision-making style, which has been viewed as being related to
sensation-seeking in a number of different ways. Several personality
researchers have viewed impulsivity and sensation-seeking as related
personality traits (Buss & Plomin,1975; Eysenck & Eysenck, 1977, 1978;
Zuckerman et al., 1993). In his review of the relationship between impulsivity and sensation-seeking, Zuckerman (1994) concluded that "while [it
is] not an equivalent or supraordinate of sensation-seeking, [it] is a highly
related trait, particularly in its nonplanning and risk-taking aspects." As
part of a broad personality test, the Zuckerman—Kuhlman Personality
Questionnaire, one of the five factors was composed of impulsivity and
sensation-seeking items and was labeled "impulsive sensation-seeking."
However, Zimmerman and Donohew (1996) suggested that, rather than
impulsivity and sensation-seeking being two components of the same
dimension, they are moderately correlated and only overlap somewhat.
Rather than viewing impulsivity as a trait variable, Zimmerman and Donohew (1996) view impulsive decision-making as one end of a continuum of
decision-making styles that vary from a consistent, rational decision-making style to a consistently impulsive decision-making style. Although conceptions of impulsivity suggest that impulsive individuals act
spontaneously, that is, without considering consequences, impulsive decision-making also focuses on the cues that these individuals do use to
make decisions. Zimmerman and associates propose that although rational decision-makers use beliefs about consequences of their actions,
impulsive decision-makers use noncognitive cues, including affective and
physiological cues (as opposed to merely ignoring consequences), to
make decisions. Zimmerman's 11-item decision-making style scale has
been shown to be moderately correlated with Eysenck and Eysenck's
(1977) narrow impulsivity scale (correlations of .31 to .65 in three samples
of 100-650 high school students) and more strongly related to risky sexual behavior (unpublished data). Internal consistency is comparable to
that of the Eysenck scale (generally in the .7 to .8 range), with a similar
1-year test-retest correlation in high school students (r_{tt} = .5).

In the program of research to be described here, impulsive decision-making has been a component only of the classroom interventions
but has been added to the media studies in the two-cities project currently
underway.

Risky Personality Types

Other researchers, employing additional indicators of "risky personality types," have collected longitudinal evidence supporting not only the existence of the type, but also that such types place themselves at greater health risks. Among longitudinal studies completed in the past 10 years, a 20-month Norwegian study of 553 adolescents found that sensation-seeking was a consistent and important longitudinal predictor of use of cannabis, alcohol, benzodiazepine, and cigarettes (Pederson, 1991).

Masse and Tremblay (1997) found in a study of 1,034 boys measured at ages 6 and 10 years that those high on novelty seeking and low on harm avoidance at age 6 (as measured by Cloninger's personality scale) exhibited earlier onset of substance use.

Caspi and associates (1997) conducted a considerably longer study in New Zealand, following a cohort from age 3 (n = 1,037) to age 21 (n = 961). At age 3 the participants in the study were rated on 22 behavioral characteristics. By age 18, the participants were administered the Multidimensional Personality Questionnaire (MPQ; Tellegen, 1982), and at age 21 they were measured on four health-risk behaviors: alcohol dependence, violent crime, risky sexual behavior, and dangerous driving habits. Those who exhibited each of these characteristics scored lower on scales indicating a need for safety and higher on scales indicating a need for novelty. Those possessing a "risky personality" configuration at age 18 had displayed similar temperament qualities at age 3 (Caspi & Silva, 1995). Drawing on other data gathered on the cohort at ages 5, 7, 9, 11, and 13, Caspi and associates (1997) suggested that "the origins of a personality type at risk for health behaviors may be found early in life and...the type stabilizes during adolescence" (p. 1061). In interpreting implications of the findings, they emphasized the importance of designing programs specifically to reach individuals on the basis of their different needs:

> The origins of a personality type at risk for health-risk behaviors may be found early in life and...individual differences in personality may influence steps in the persuasion process....Thus, different types of individuals may attend to, comprehend, accept, and retain different types of messages....If we know the personality characteristics of a target audience, it may be possible to tailor campaigns to zero-in on the characteristic motivations, attitudes, and feelings of the audience....Knowledge of the psychological characteristics that motivate you to engage in health-risk behaviors may thus help public health officials choose more effective campaigns that would motivate risk takers to minimize harm. (p.1061)

These recommendations are consistent with the approach taken in our research on communication and health campaigns during the past 15 years. We have reported (Donohew, Palmgreen, & Duncan,1980; Donohew et al., 1998; Donohew et al., 2000; Donohew, Lorch, & Palmgreen, 1991, 1994; Lorch et al., 1994; Palmgreen et al., 1991; Zimmerman & Donohew, 1996) that interventions designed to meet higher needs for novelty and sensation (which find biological expression in the mesolimbic dopamine reward pathway) considerably advance our ability to capture the attention of target individuals likely to engage in health-risk behaviors, enhance information processing, and motivate attitude and behavior change.

INDIVIDUAL DIFFERENCES MODEL OF INFORMATION EXPOSURE

These interventions are guided by an activation model of information exposure (Donohew et al., 1980, 1998; Donohew, Finn, & Christ, 1988) in which the level of need for novelty and sensation is a fundamental component in the process of attending, affecting the likelihood that a stimulus event in the form of a message will attract and hold the attention of any given individual. Messages are more likely to attract attention if they possess one or more characteristics signaling a need for an arousal or alertness response. This model has implications for the development of prevention programs.

Data

Our research has indicated that persons with high need for sensation tend to tolerate or even require stronger and more novel messages for attracting and holding their attention (Donohew, 1982; Donohew et al., 1980, 1989). Findings from our studies indicate that individual differences in need for sensation and, to a lesser extent, in current alcohol and other substance use play a major role in exposure to and comprehension of substance abuse messages, arousal (skin conductance), and attitudinal and behavioral intention responses to the messages (Donohew et al., 1990).

Theoretic Background

The activation theory of information exposure (Donohew et al., 1980) operates under the assumption that human beings are continuously involved in a search for stimulation, driven by pleasure centers of the mid-brain (Olds & Fobes, 1981). It has been known for more than a century that humans find arousal in moderate amounts to be pleasurable (Wundt, 1894). This response to moderate arousal soon became connected with optimal behavior in an inverted U-curve (Yerkes & Dodson, 1908). At the lower end of this curve, arousal is too low to motivate performance. Beyond this and up to an optimal point, arousal has positive motivating values. After that point is passed, its value tends to be negative and inversely related to performance (Berlyne,1971; Hebb, 1955; Zajonc, 1980).

The theory of information exposure is grounded in assumptions that individuals operate most effectively at some optimal level of arousal, which is presumed to differ across individuals—perhaps because individual differences exist in plasma catecholamine levels released from the sympathetic nervous system (Zuckerman, 1978, 1983, 1988). Arousal needs serve an important function in the mechanisms guiding exposure to information (Christ, 1985). Part of the motivation for exposure to a message involves need for physiological stimulation rather than cognitive need for information alone (Donohew et al., 1989; Finn, 1983, 1984). A central assumption of this model is that although individuals may have a cognitive reason for exposing themselves to a particular stimulus, such as a source of information, processes of which they are unaware may play a major role in the information they expose themselves to. Thus, the form of the message (i.e., its formal features, such as novelty, movement, etc., which we have mentioned before) plays a significant role in attracting individuals to a source of stimulation, and it plays an even more significant role in receivers' continued exposure to the source. The level of stimulation required to trigger these responses varies according to the level of need for stimulation (or need for sensation) of the individual. According to Judee Burgoon and her colleagues (Burgoon, Newton, Walther, & Baesler, 1989; Burgoon, Kelley, Newton, & Keeley-Dyreson, 1989) violation of nonverbal expectations—which are somewhat similar to what are called "formal features" in message research—divert attention to the new source of arousal and can produce greater credibility and persuasiveness (see Siegal and Burgoon, chap. 8, this volume).

We have observed that because HSS are attracted to novel, dramatic, and stimulating messages (Donohew, Palmgreen, & Lorch, 1991; Palmgreen & Donohew, in press), manipulation of message sensation value can be a successful way of surmounting cognitive and attitudinal barriers to prevention messages raised by those engaged in, or who are likely to become engaged in, risky sex practices. In addition, making impulsive decision-makers more aware of their special risks, as well as focusing on the sensation-value of alternative behaviors, may enable them to reduce their risky sexual behaviors while they persist in their impulsive decision-making style.

THE MODEL

The model is a major cornerstone of the program of research on persuasive communication and prevention, and provides theoretic guidance for each of the several studies conducted. It offers propositions about information choice behaviors, based on cognitive and activation needs. The model assumes that the reader or viewer of a media or interpersonal message may be largely unaware of the affective influences to continue or discontinue exposure.

The central assumption of the theory is that human beings have individual levels of need for stimulation at which they are most comfortable, and that attention is a function primarily of an individual's level of need for stimulation and the level of stimulation provided by a stimulus source.

From this it is deduced that if individuals do not achieve or maintain this state on exposure to a message, it is very likely that they will turn away and seek another source of stimulation that helps them achieve the desired state. If activation remains within some acceptable range, however, individuals are most likely to continue exposure to the information.

The theory has guided an extensive series of experiments and field studies on improving the effectiveness of public health campaigns (Donohew, 1990; Donohew et al., 1991; Donohew, Palmgreen, & Lorch, 1994; Donohew et al., 1998, 2000; Lorch et al., 1994; Palmgreen & Donohew, in press; Palmgreen et al., 1991, 1995; Zimmerman & Donohew, 1996). It posits that messages with high sensation value (HSV) are required to attract and hold the attention of individuals who are HSS. The sensation value of a message is defined by Palmgreen and Donohew (in press) as the ability to elicit sensory, affective, and arousal responses. Message sensation value "should be an important factor in attracting and holding the attention of individuals with varying degrees of need for sensation " (Lorch et al., 1994, p. 395). Thus, we have proposed that HSV messages should be more attractive to HSS, whereas low sensation value (LSV) messages should be preferred by LSS. The model has employed Zuckerman's Sensation-seeking Scale as a measure of need for stimulation. According to Zuckerman (1990), HSS "tend to give stronger physiological orienting responses than lows to novel stimuli of moderate intensity, particularly when such stimuli are of specific interest" (p. 313).

RESEARCH PROJECTS IN THE PROGRAM

Early Research

The first research projects, which provided the basic research which led to the more extensive projects to follow:

1. Identified characteristics of adolescents and young adults more likely to become early drug users (Donohew et al., 1990).
2. Developed a profile of stimuli that attract and hold their attention (Donohew et al., 1994).
3. Employing formative research, designed messages and interventions that have been highly successful in reaching them (Donohew et al., 1991; Lorch, et al., 1994; Palmgreen et al., 1995).

Findings from these studies thus have implications for other interventions, such as the design and presentation of school-based materials and programs that will have a higher likelihood of attracting, holding the attention of, and persuading students, particularly those who are at-risk. Characteristics of messages likely to meet these criteria have been identified in these studies, contributing further to this general knowledge base for intervention in the large-scale time-series media interventions and the multicity classroom interventions to follow, by identifying the processes involved in message-attitude-behavior interactions in audiences possessing various risk and protective factors.

Sensation-seeking, Drug Use, and Message Style

The first study to be considered (Donohew, 1988; Donohew et al., 1990) indicated highly significant differences in alcohol and drug use between HSS and LSS beginning with the onset of puberty and continuing through young adulthood (Donohew et al., 1988, 1990, 1994). In the study of junior and senior high school students, HSS were twice as likely as LSS to report use of beer and liquor during the past 30 days, three times as likely to have used marijuana, and seven times as likely to have used cocaine. In the laboratory portion of the study, HSS were more likely to expose themselves to messages presented in a more novel (narrative) format than to messages presented in other formats.

Formative Research on Message Sensation Value

Prior to designing messages or interventions likely to attract, hold the attention of, inform, and persuade audiences possessing characteristics similar to those just described, we first conducted extensive formative research that revealed characteristics of televised messages that have differential appeal for HSS and LSS young adults. The responses of HSS or LSS focus groups to a selection of product ads and PSAs demonstrated that HSS subjects reacted more positively to more novel and intense messages. With the help of focus groups, half made up of HSS only and half made up of LSS only, we were able to identify a number of characteristics of the videos that have had differential appeal to the two groups (Donohew et al., 1990, 1994; Lorch et al., 1994; Palmgreen, Donohew, Lorch, Hoyle, & Stephenson, in press). In addition to preferring more novel formats and unusual use of formal features (e.g., extreme close-ups and heavy use of sound effects), HSS subjects also responded more positively to high levels of suspense, tension, drama, and emotional impact than did LSS subjects.

HSS have greater preferences than LSS for messages that contain one or more of the following characteristics: (a) novel, creative, unusual; (b) complex; (c) intense (auditory and visual); (d) physically arousing (exciting, stimulating); (e) emotionally strong; (f) graphic; (g) ambiguous; (h) unconventional; (i) fast-paced; and (j) suspenseful. In televised PSAs and ads, there were the same kinds of differences just described on: (a) an absence of "preaching"; (b) less closure; (c) strong sound and visual effects; and (d) use of close-ups (Donohew, et al., 1991; Palmgreen et al., 1991).

Because of these preferences among message characteristics, HSS have been found to exhibit a greater preference than LSS for horror films, sexually explicit films, heavy metal as opposed to Top 40 rock music and music videos, graphic violence, offbeat and unconventional comedy, shows that violate social norms, and sports shows.

The foregoing discussion suggests, therefore, that the sensation value of a program or message—that is, the degree to which its formal and content features elicit sensory, affective, and arousal responses— should be an important factor in determining the appeal of a message. Messages with HSV should be more attractive to HSS, whereas LSV messages should be more appealing to LSS. Although the first research reported here dealt with testing of messages in a public service announcement (PSA) format, we later learned that characteristics found to be appealing to HSS in PSAs were appealing to HSS in an instructional setting as well, thereby making the instruction more effective.

Messages employing the characteristics just described have been highly successful with appropriate target audiences in laboratory settings and more recently in actual substance abuse prevention campaigns and risky sex and alcohol prevention instructional settings.

Laboratory Study: Persuasion to Call a Hotline

In one of the early laboratory studies, Donohew and colleagues designed an experiment to test the ability to differentially motivate HSS and LSS by employing messages that contained different levels of sensation value. Based on the earlier formative research, we developed two 30-sec televised antidrug PSAs. Both were built around the same concept, but varied in production features such that one included characteristics that theoretically would appeal to HSS and one included characteristics thought to be preferred by LSS individuals. Participants completed Zuckerman's (1979) Sensation-seeking Scale. A median split on the sum of the 37 non-drug-related items was used to define LSS and HSS, who then were randomly assigned to one of the experimental conditions (n = 165) or the control group (n = 42). HSS and LSS participants were shown HSV and LSV versions of a televised antidrug public service announcement (PSA). The behavioral intention of HSS to call a hotline was more affected by the HSV message (which was more dramatic and stimulating), whereas LSS were somewhat more persuaded by the LSV message (p = .057) (Donohew et al., 1991; Palmgreen et al., 1991). The most important result from a targeting perspective is the interaction effect between message sensation value and sensation-seeking on an index of intent to call the hotline. Values greater than 1.00 on the index indicate a stronger intention of the experimental group to call the hotline, relative to the appropriate comparison group. As hypothesized, the HSV message was more effective with HSS in inducing participants' intentions to call a hotline mentioned in the PSA, whereas the LSV message was more effective with LSS participants (p < .06) (see Donohew et al., 1991, Fig.2). HSS users of illicit drugs in the past 30 days showed the strongest impact on behavioral intention.

Laboratory Study: Influence of Programming in Which PSAs Are Embedded

Another experiment (Lorch et al., 1994) involved a more naturalistic setting, with participants seated individually in a living room, exposed to prevention-oriented PSAs in different program contexts, with a number of reading options available. Participants were seated facing a color television monitor and were told they would be shown several televised ads/ messages. The videotape began with 4 min of a story from "CBS Sunday Morning," and continued with two 30-sec commercials, the HSV or LSV PSA, then three more 30-sec ads, and a repeat of the PSA. Participants then completed measures of behavioral intention to call a hotline mentioned in the test PSAs, attitude toward drugs, and drug use scales. Control group participantsts participated in all procedures, except the antidrug PSAs were not included in the video content. HSS paid more attention to HSV programming (exciting drama or an off-beat sitcom) than to LSV programming (slow-paced drama or conventional sitcom). There were considerable differences, however, in the amount of watching by each. HSS attended considerably more to HSV programming than they did to LSV programming, $F(1,300) = 4.06$, $p < 05$. LSS, on the other hand, although preferring LSV programming, also watched HSV programming almost as much as LSVs. One conclusion of this research was that stimuli should be designed for HSS because that would not only be more likely to reach the audience members at highest risk, but it would attract much of the remaining audience as well.

Field Test of Targeting and Motivation to Call a Hotline

The next step was to test whether the procedures used to design and evaluate messages and program contexts in the laboratory could be implemented effectively with an actual televised campaign targeted at HSS young adults. Results of the experimental investigations were drawn on to design a drug abuse prevention campaign targeted at HSS through a campaign involving a combination of paid and free public service announcements and a hotline (Palmgreen et al.,1995).

The campaign was carried out in January-June 1992, in Lexington, Kentucky, and included five different spots. Each spot concluded with an appeal to call a hotline for more information about exciting alternatives to drug use. Callers to the hotline received a full-color, 20-page guidebook, "A Thrillseeker's Guide to the Bluegrass," which explained the concept of sensation-seeking and its connection to drug use, and listed a wide variety of activities available in Lexington/Fayette County and surrounding areas. Over the course of the campaign, 615 purchased spots and 887 donated spots were televised. Information obtained in the precampaign survey (discussed later in this chapter) on television program preferences of HSS was used by a professional media buyer to guide placement of the campaign PSAs. Evaluation of the campaign was based on pre- and postcampaign surveys, within-campaign surveys, and surveys of hotline callers. Data from these several sources converge on a conclusion that the campaign was successful in reaching the target audience of HSS with prevention messages.

The combination of novel and highly stimulating messages was highly successful in motivating members of the prime target audience to call a telephone hotline featured in the PSAs. Hotline survey findings showed that 73% of those calling scored above the sensation-seeking median of the population. This occurred despite earlier findings from this series of projects and others indicating that HSS watch less television than LSS and express considerably lower behavioral intentions to call a hotline to obtain substance abuse prevention information. It also should be noted that alcohol and other substance use was positively related to reported exposure to the campaign spots, and that 32% of the hotline survey respondents reported some use of illicit drugs in the past 30 days compared to 23% of the general population. Recall of the content of the messages also was considerably higher among HSS than among LSS, although the small number of LSS who also were drug users recalled the messages almost as well. LSS nonusers (the group least essential to target in a prevention campaign) showed the lowest recall.

A Causal Model of Sensation-seeking, Peers, and Drug Use

The objective of this study was to investigate the prospective influence of individual adolescents' sensation-seeking tendencies and the sensation-seeking tendencies of named peers on the use of alcohol and marijuana, controlling for a variety of interpersonal and attitudinal risk and protective factors (Donohew et al., 1999). Data were collected from a cohort of adolescents (n = 428; 60% female) at three points in time, starting in the eighth grade. Respondents provided information about sensation-seeking, the positivity of family relations, attitudes toward alcohol and drug use, perceptions of their friends' use of alcohol and marijuana, perceptions of influences by their friends to use alcohol and marijuana, and their own use of alcohol and marijuana. In addition, they named up to three peers with whom they were close friends. Data on sensation-seeking and use from the three peers were integrated with respondents' data to allow for tests of hypotheses about peer clustering and substance use.

Structural equation modeling analyses revealed direct effects of peers' sensation-seeking on adolescents' own use of both marijuana and alcohol 2 years later. An unexpected finding was that the individual's own sensation-seeking had indirect (not direct) effects on drug use 2 years later.

These findings indicate the potential importance of sensation-seeking as a characteristic on which adolescent peers cluster. Further, the findings indicate that, beyond the influence of a variety of other risk factors, peer sensation-seeking contributes to adolescents' substance use.

Messages and Behavior Change: A Two-Cities Time-Series Study

Despite encouraging results indicating success in targeting the primary audience, HSS, and attracting them to call a hotline, many important questions remained, not the least of which was, could such a campaign also change attitudes and marijuana use behaviors? Although a number of techniques had been found to be successful, there was little knowledge about the evolutionary process by which media messages began to change attitudes and behaviors in at-risk individuals. What are the causal lag periods involved? Are there more effective ways of designing and placing such messages? What amounts of expensive media time and space are needed to bring about desired change?

The study designed to answer these questions employed a controlled time-series design in two matched communities. Two 4-month televised antimarijuana campaigns targeted at HSS adolescents were conducted in one county with one 4-month campaign in the comparison county. Personal interviews were conducted with 100 randomly selected teens per month in each county for 32 months. The cohorts followed were initially in the 7th through 10th grades.

Regression-based interrupted time-series analyses indicated that all three campaigns reversed upward developmental trends in 30-day marijuana use among HSS ($p <. 002$), with one campaign producing an estimated 26.7% decline in in the relative proportion of HSS users over 12 months. As expected, LSS exhibited low levels of use and no campaign effects (Palmgreen et al., in press).

Televised campaigns with high reach and frequency which employ PSAs designed for and targeted at HSS adolescents can effect significant reductions in substance use among members of this high-risk population.

Alcohol and Risky Sex—An HSV/IDM Curriculum

The project involved 3,300 ninth-grade students in two Midwestern cities in an experimental design using both a mass media campaign (radio) and a classroom-based HIV prevention intervention aimed at reducing risky sexual behaviors, including alcohol use with sex. The radio campaign was developed using focus and reaction groups, and then was implemented in one of the cities, which was randomly selected, to increase awareness and salience of HIV-related prevention issues; students in the other city did not receive the media campaign. The radio campaign employed both purchased and donated time. Matched schools in both communities were randomly allocated to one of three conditions: Reducing the Risk (RTR), a skills based HIV prevention curriculum; an enhanced version of the Reducing the Risk (ERTR) curriculum targeting HSS and impulsive decision-making adolescents (and developed on the bases of surveys, focus groups, and reaction groups); or a no-RTR comparison group, in which students received their standard HIV prevention curriculum. Among the changes made in the ERTR version of the curriculum designed to appeal to persons requiring higher sensation value to become more involved in learning was the addition of trigger films, which were designed to enhance interest in topics under discussion. Talk-show formats were used for other discussions, with video cameras placed in the hands of student participants and proceedings videotaped and played back for discussion. Contests were held and prizes awarded on the basis of quality of participation. All programs involved formative research employing focus and reaction groups in their development, and all teachers were trained to administer the curriculum. In the subsequent years, booster classroom-based and/or media interventions were implemented in the respective cities. Students were followed-up over 3 years to assess the impact of the interventions on skills, behavioral intentions, and sexual risk taking behaviors.

Results of the Classroom Intervention. Analyses that had been completed at the time this chapter was being written revealed that the ERTR curriculum influenced the attitudes and behaviors of participating students relative to students in the no-curriculum condition, and in some cases relative to those in the regular RTR curriculum condition. The effect of the curriculum was measured in terms of its influence on rates of initiation of sexual intercourse among youth who were sexually inexperienced at baseline, and on rates of condom use among those who were or became sexually active at the time of follow-up. Overall, students in the ERTR curriculum were more likely than students in the control condition to remain abstinent (odds ratio = 1.45, p = .05). This effect was particularly pronounced for African-American HSS and African-American impulsive decision-makers. Impulsive African-Americans in our ERTR curriculum were nearly four times as likely to remain abstinent as those in the control conditions (odds ratio = 3.91, p = .02). Similarly, HSS African-Americans who were in the ERTR curriculum were twice as likely as their peers in control conditions to remain abstinent, although this effect did not reach statistical significance (odds ratio = 2.06, p = .12). Our ERTR curriculum also appeared to affect initiation rates for males and Whites in general. Both males and Whites in the ERTR condition were nearly twice as likely as their peers in the control condition to remain abstinent (odds ratio = 1.96, p = .02 for males; odds ratio = 1.98, p = .02 for Whites).

Of particular note are the relative effect sizes for those in the ERTR condition and those in the regular condition compared to controls. With the exception of one subgroup, the effect sizes for the ERTR condition were greater than those for the regular condition compared to controls. This effect was especially pronounced for HSS Whites (odds ratio = 2.92, p = .04).

Results of Radio PSA Campaign. In the media city, two of the six test PSAs were randomly allocated per classroom at survey follow-up. More than half of all participants reported hearing at least one of the test PSAs. The number of test PSA characteristics correctly recalled by students was significantly related to involvement in classroom activities in both the RTR and ERTR conditions. Those high in involvement recalled more test PSA characteristics than those reporting low classroom participation (p < .01). Nearly 90% of students in both classroom conditions correctly identified at least one test PSA characteristic. However, recall was unrelated to subsequent behavioral or efficacy outcomes.

Analysis of results of unaided recall data collected from all students in the project (i.e., both media and nonmedia communities) indicates that students in the media community recalled more test PSA characteristics than students in the nonmedia community (p < .05), and that HSS were more likely to recall hearing PSAs related to HIV prevention in both communities.

Sensation-Seeking, Impulsive Decision-Making, Sexual Behavior and Outcomes. Data from the first two waves of our current study show strong relationships of sensation-seeking and impulsive decision-making with risky sexual behaviors. Both variables were related to initiation of sexual activity. Dividing at the median (separately by race-gender groups), 47.9% of the HSS reported ever having sex, compared to only 36.9% of the LSS (p < .001). On a similar median split analysis for impulsive decision makers, 49% of the impulsive decision makers (IDMs) reported ever having sex at baseline while only 33.6% of the rational decision makers (LO IDM) had ever had sex (p <. 0001). The interactive effects suggest that the highest percentages of students who reported ever having sex at baseline were the HSS impulsive decision-makers (52.7%). This stands in sharp comparison to the percentage of LSS—LO IDM (31.1%).

The results for a question asking the respondents whether they had used alcohol before the last instance of sexual intercourse showed that sensation-seeking had a main effect (p < .001) with HSS having higher reported percentages than the LSS participants. Although there were no statistically significant main effect of decision-making style on alcohol use before sex, there was a significant interaction; there was no significant effect of sensation-seeking on alcohol use with sex for rational deci-sion-makers, but sensation-seeking was significant for impulsive deci-sion-makers. That is, among impulsive decision-makers, HSS were more likely to have used alcohol before the last time they had sexual inter-course (42.7%) than were LSS (28.4%). This suggests that having a more rational decision-making style may be a protective factor for the HSS for engaging in a risky sexual activity such as using alcohol before sex.

CURRENT STUDIES

Work presently underway includes a partial replication of the two cities study during the Office of National Drug Control Policy's National Youth Anti-drug Media Campaign and two studies of prevention of risky sex and HIV, one with particular emphasis on study of the role of alcohol. One of the latter studies is aimed at young people at even higher risk than in the previous media and classroom study: (a) students in alternative schools, (b) adolescent females living in inner-city housing developments, and (c) young men who have sex with other men.

Another project is an experimental study in which effects of need for sensation and need for cognition (Caccioppo & Petty; & Kao, 1984; Cac-cioppo, Petty, Feinstein, & Jarvis, 1996) are assessed in response to per-suasive messages about risky behaviors (drug abuse). Need for sensation has been found to be a risk factor in health behaviors, as noted earlier, whereas need for cognition is expected to be a protective factor. Given this, do HSS individuals who possess a high need for cognition seek—or are they more receptive to—messages that warn them about dangers of drug abuse, whereas do those who are low on need for cogni-tion tend to ignore the messages? Such a finding would have consider-able implications both for targeting and for message design in prevention campaigns.

ACKNOWLEDGMENTS

Research described in this chapter was supported by grant DA03462 from the National Institute on Drug Abuse (Lewis Donohew, PI), grant DA05312 from NIDA (Lewis Donohew, PI; Philip Palmgreen and Eliza-beth Lorch, co-PIs), grant DA06892-04 from the National Institute on Drug Abuse (Lewis Donohew, PI; Philip Palmgreen, Elizabeth Lorch, and Will-iam Skinner, co-PIs), grant AA10747 from the National Institute on Alcoholism and Alcohol Abuse (Lewis Donohew, PI, Rick Zimmerman, co-PI), grant DA04887 from the National Institute on Drug Abuse (Lewis Dono-hew, PI, Richard Clayton, co-PI), grant DA06892-08 from the National Institute on Drug Abuse (Lewis Donohew, PI; Philip Palmgreen, Elizabeth Lorch, and Rick Hoyle, co-PIs), grant DA12371 from the National Institute on Drug Abuse (Philip Palmgreen, PI; Lewis Donohew, Elizabeth Lorch, and Rick Hoyle, coinvestigators), grant MH61187 from the National Institute on Mental Health (Rick Zimmerman, PI; Lewis Donohew and Sonja Feist-Price (coinvestigators), grant AA10747-04 (Rick Zimmerman, PI; Philip Palmgreen, Lewis Donohew, Sonja Feist-Price, and Eric Ander-man, coinvestigators), and grant DA12490 from the National Institute on Drug Abuse (Lewis Donohew, PI; Nancy Harrington, Rick Zimmerman, Philip Palmgreen, and Derek Lane, coinvestigators).

REFERENCES

Ajzen, I., & Fishbein, M. (1980). *Understanding attitudes and predicting social behavior.* Englewood Cliffs, NJ: Prentice Hall.

Arque, J., Unzeta, M., & Torrubia, R. (1988). Neurotransmitter systems and personality measurements: A study in psychosomatic patients and healthy subjects. *Neuropsychobiology, 19*, 149-157.

Backer, T. (1990). Comparative synthesis of mass media health behavior campaigns. *Knowledge: Creation, Diffusion, Utilization, 11*, 315-329.

Bardo, M. T., Bowling, S. L., Robinet, P. M., Rowlett, J. K., Lacy, M., & Mattingly, B. A. (1993). Role of dopamine D-sub-1 and D-sub-2receptors in novelty-maintained place preference. *Experimental and Clinical Psychopharmacology, 1*, 101-109.

Bardo, M., Donohew, L., & Harrington, N.G. (1996). Psychobiology of novelty-seeking and drug-seeking behavior. *Brain and Behavior, 77,* 23-43.

Bardo, M. T., & Hammer, R. P. (1991). Autoradiographic localization of dopamine D1 and D2 receptors in rat nucleus accumbens: Resistance to differential rearing conditions. *Neuroscience, 45*, 281-290.

Bardo, M. T. Neisewander, J. L., & Pierce, R. C. (1989). Novelty-induced place preference behavior in rats: Effects of opiate and dopaminergic drugs. *Pharmacology, Biochemistry and Behavior, 32*, 683-689.

Benjamin, J., Li, L., Patterson, C., Greenberg, B., Murphy, D., & Hamer, D. (1996). Population and familial association between the D4 dopamine receptor gene and measures of novelty seeking. *Nature Genetics, 12*, 81-84.

Berlyne, D. (1971). *Aesthetics and psychobiology.* New York: Appleton-Century-Crofts.

Burgoon, J. K., Newton, D. A., Walther, J. B., & Baesler, E. J. (1989). Nonverbal expectancy violations and conversational involvement. Journal of Nonverbal Behavior, 13, 97-119.

Burgoon, J. K., Kelley, D. L., Newton, D. A., & Keeley-Dyreson, M. P. (1989). The nature of arousal and nonverbal indices. *Human Communication Research, 16,* 217-255.

Buss, A. H., & Plomin, R. (1975). *A temperament theory of personality development.* New York: Wiley.

Caccioppo, J., Petty, R., & Kao, C. (1984). The efficient assessment of need for cognition. *Journal of Personality Assessment, 48,* 306-307.

Caccioppo, J., Petty, R., Feinstein, J., & Jarvis, W. (1996). Dispositional differences in cognitive motivation: The life and times of individuals varying in need for cognition. *Psychological Bulletin, 119,* 197-253.

Caspi, A., Begg, D., Dickson, N., Harrington, H., Langley, J., Moffitt, T. E., & Silva, P. A. (1997). Personality differences predict health-risk behaviors in young adulthood: Evidence from a longitudinal study. *Journal of Personality and Social Psychology, 73,* 1052-1063.

Caspi, A., Harrington, H., Moffitt, T. E., Begg, D., Dickson, N., Langley, J. & Silva, P. A. (1997). Personality differences predict health-risk behaviors in young adulthood: Evidence from a longitudinal study. *Journal of Personality and Social Psychology, 73,* 1052-1063.

Caspi, A., & Silva, P. A. (1995). Temperamental qualities at age 3 predict personality traits in young adulthood: Longitudinal evidence from a birth cohort. *Child Development, 66,* 486-498.

Christ, W. G. (1985). The construct of arousal in communication research. *Human Communication Research, 11,* 575-592.

Cloninger, C. R., Adolfson, R., & Svrakic, N. M. (1996). Mapping genes for human personality. *Nature Genetics, 13,* 3,4.

Cloninger, C. R., Pryzbeck, I., Svrakic, D., & Wetzel, R. (1994). *The temperament and character inventory: A guide to its development and use.* St. Louis, MO: Center for the Psychobiology of Personality.

Darwin, C. (1859). *The origin of species by means of natural selection.* New York: A. L. Burt.

Donohew, L., Finn, S., & Christ, W. (1988). The nature of news revisited: The role of affect, schemes, and cognition. In L. Donohew, H. Sypher, & E. T. Higgin (Eds.), *Communication, social cognition, and affect* (pp. 195-218). Hillsdale, NJ: Lawrence Erlbaum Associates.

Donohew, L., Helm, D., Lawrence, P., & Shatzer, M. (1990). Sensation-seeking, marijuana use, and responses to drug abuse prevention messages. In R. R. Watson (Ed.), *Drug and alcohol abuse reviews* (pp. 77-93). Clifton, NJ: Humana Press.

Donohew, L., Hoyle, R., Clayton, R. R., Skinner, W., Colon, S. and Rice, R. E. (1999). Sensation-seeking and drug use by adolescents and their friends: Models for marijuana and alcohol. *Journal of Studies of Alcohol, 60,* 622-631.

Donohew, L., Lorch, E. P., Palmgreen, P. (1991). Sensation-seeking and targeting of televised antidrug PSAs. In L. Donohew, H. E. Sypher, & W. J. Bukoski (Eds.), *Persuasive communication and drug abuse prevention* (pp. 208-226). Hillsdale, NJ: Lawrence Erlbaum Associates.

Donohew, L., Lorch, E. P., Palmgreen, P. (1998). Applications of a theoretic model of information exposure to health interventions. *Human Communication Research, 24,* 454-468.

Donohew, L., Palmgreen, P., & Duncan, J. (1980). An activation model of information exposure. *Communication Monographs, 47,* 295-303.

Donohew, L., Palmgreen, P., & Lorch, E. P. (1994). Attention, sensation-seeking, and health communication campaigns. *American Behavioral Scientist, 38,* 310-332.

Donohew, L., Palmgreen, P., Lorch, E. P., Rogus, M., Helm, D., & Grant, N. (1989). *Targeting of televised antidrug PSAs.* Paper presented at the annual meeting of the International Communication Association, San Francisco, June.

Donohew, L., Zimmerman, R., Cupp, P., Novak, S., Colon, S. & Abell, R. (2000). Sensation-seeking, impulsive decision making, and risky sex: Implications for risk-taking and design of interventions. *Personality and Individual Differences, 28,* 1079-1091.

Ebstein, R., Novick, O., Umansky, R., Priel, B., Osher, Y., Blaine, D., Bennett, E., Nemanov, L., Katz, M., & Belmaker, R. (1996). Dopamine D4 receptor (D4DR) exon III polymorphism associated with the human personality trait of novelty seeking. *Nature genetics, 12,* 78-80.

Eysenck, S. B. G., & Eysenck, H. J. (1977). The place of impulsiveness in a dimensional system of personality description. *British Journal of Social and Clinical Psychology, 16,* 57-68.

Eysenck, S. B. G., & Eysenck, H. J. (1978). Impulsiveness and venturesomeness: Their position in a dimensional system of personality description. *Psychological Reports, 43,* 1247-1255.

Finn, S. (1983). An information theory approach to reader enjoyment of print journalism (Doctoral dissertation, Stanford University-1982). *Dissertation Abstracts International, 43,* 2481A-2482A.

Finn, S. (1984). Information-theoretic measures of reader enjoyment. *Written Communication, 2,* 358-376.

Flay, B. & Sobel, J. (1983). The role of mass media in preventing adolescent substance abuse. NIDA Research Monograph 47. In T. J. Glynn, C. G. Leukefeld, & J. P. Ludford (Eds.), *Preventing adolescent drug abuse: Intervention strategies* (pp. 5-35). Rockville, MD: National Institute on Drug Abuse.

Flora, J., Maccoby, N., & Farquhar, J. (1989). Communication campaigns to prevent cardiovascular disease: The Stanford community studies. In R. E. Rice & C. Atkin (Eds.), *Public Communication Campaigns* (pp. 233-252). Newbury Park, CA: Sage.

Fowler, C., von Knorring, L., & Oreland, L. (1980). Platelet monoamine oxidase activity in sensation seekers. *Psychiatric Research, 3,* 273-279.

Franklin, J., Donohew, L., Dhoundiyal, V., & Cook, P. L. (1988). Attention and our ancient past: The scaly thumb of the reptile. *American Behavioral Scientistist, 31,* 312-326.

Glickman, S. E., & Schiff, B. B. (1967). A biological theory of reinforcement. *Psychological Review, 74,* 81-109.

Hebb, D. (1955). Drives and the CNS (conceptual nervous system). *Psychological Review, 62*, 243-254.

Koob, G., Le, H., & Creese, I. (1987). The D1 dopamine receptor antagonist SCH 23390 increases cocaine self-administration in the rat. *Neuroscience Letters, 79*, 315-320.

Langer, L., Zimmerman, R., Warheit, G. J., & Duncan, R. C. (1993). An examination of the relationship between adolescent decision-making orientation and AIDS-related knowledge, attitudes, beliefs, behaviors, and skills. *Health Psychology, 12*, 227-234.

Lorch, E. P., Palmgreen, P., Donohew, L., Helm, D., Baer, S. A., & Dsilva, M. U. (1994). Program context, sensation-seeking, and attention to televised anti-drug public service announcements. *Human Communication Research, 20*, 390-412.

Masse, L., & Tremblay, R. (1997). Behavior of boys in kindergarten and the onset of substance abuse during adolescence. *Archives of General Psychiatry, 54*, 62-68.

Murphy, D., Belmaker, R., Buchsbaum, M., Martin, N., Ciaranello, R., & Wyatt, R. J. (1977). Biogenic amine related enzymes and personality variations in normals. *Psycholgie Medicale, 7*, 149-157.

Olds, M. E., & Fobes, J. (1981). The central basis of motivation: Intracranial self-stimulation studies. *Annual Review of Psychology, 32*, 523-574.

Palmgreen, P., & Donohew, L. (in press). Effective mass media strategies for drug abuse prevention campaigns. In W.J. Bukoski & Z. Sloboda (Eds.), *Handbook of drug abuse theory, science and practice.* New York: Plenum.

Palmgreen, P., Donohew, L., Lorch, E., Hoyle, R., & Stephenson, S. (in press). Television campaigns and adolescent marijuana use: Tests of sensation-seeking targeting. *American Journal of Public Health.*

Palmgreen, P., Donohew, L., Lorch, E., Rogus, M., Helm, D., & Grant, N. (1991). Sensation-seeking, message sensation value, and drug use as mediators of PSA effectiveness. *Health Communication, 3*, 217-234.

Palmgreen, P., Lorch, E.P., Donohew, L., Harrington, N.G., Dsilva, M., & Helm, D. (1995). Reaching at-risk populations in a mass media drug abuse prevention campaign: Sensation-seeking as a targeting variable. *Drugs and Society, 8*, 29-45.

Pederson, W. (1991). Mental health, sensation-seeking and drug use patterns: A longitudinal study. *British Journal of Addiction, 86*, 195-204.

Perloff, R. (1993). *The dynamics of persuasion.* Hillsdale, NJ: Lawrence Erlbaum Associates.

Rogers, E., & Storey, J. (1987). Communication campaigns. In C. Berger & S. Chaffee (Eds.), *Handbook of communication science* (pp. 817-846). Newbury Park, CA: Sage.

Schooler, C., Zahn, T., Murphy, D., & Buschbaum, M. (1978). Psychological correlates of monoamine oxidase in normals. *Journal of Nervous and Mental Disorders, 166*, 177-186.

Vaccarino, F. J., Schiff, B. B., & Glickman, S. E. (1989). Biological view of reinforcement. In S. B. Klein & R. R. Mowrer (Eds.), *Contemporary learning theories* (pp.111-142). Hillsdale, NJ: Lawrence Erlbaum Associates.

Vandenbergh, D. J., Zonderman, A. B., Wang, J., Uhl, G. R., & Costa, U., Jr. (1997). *No association between novelty seeking and dopamine D4 receptor (D4DR) exon II seven repeat alles in Baltimore longitudinal study of aging participants* [Online]. Available: http://lpewww.grc.nia.nih.gov/lpc/lpcpub/inpress/dr-1997-06.html.

Wise, R., & Rompre, P. (1989). Brain dopamine and reward. *Annual Review of Psychology, 40*, 191-225.

Wundt, W. (1894). *Grundzuge der physiologischen psychologie*. Leipzig: Engelman.

Yerkes, R. M., & Dodson, J. D. (1908). The relation of stimulus to rapidity of habit formation. *Journal of Comparative and Neurological Psychology, 18,* 459-482.

Zimmerman, R., & Donohew, L. (1996, November). *Sensation-seeking, impulsive decision-making, and adolescent sexual behaviors.* Paper presented at the American Public Health Association, New York.

Zimmerman, R. S., & Vernberg, D. (1994) Models of preventive health behavior: Comparison, critique, and meta-analysis. In G. Albrecht (Ed.), *Advances in Medical Sociology, Health Behavior Models: A reformulation.* JAI Press.

Zuckerman, M. (1979). *Sensation-seeking: Beyond the optimal level of arousal.* Hillsdale, NJ: Lawrence Erlbaum Associates.

Zuckerman, M. (Ed.) (1983). *Biological bases of sensation-seeking, impulsivity, and anxiety.* Hillsdale, NJ: Lawrence Erlbaum Associates.

Zuckerman, M. (1988). Behavior and biology: research on sensation-seeking and reactions to the media. In L. Donohew, H. E. Sypher, & E. T. Higgins (Eds.), *Communication, social cognition, and affect* (pp. 173-194). Hillsdale, NJ: Lawrence Erlbaum Associates.

Zuckerman, M. (1991). *The psychobiology of personality.* New York: Cambridge University Press.

Zuckerman, M. (1994). *Behavioral expressions and biosocial bases of sensation-seeking.* Cambridge, UK: Cambridge University Press.

Zuckerman, M., Kolin, E., Price, L., & Zoob, I. (1964). Development of a sensation-seeking scale. *Journal of Consulting Psychology, 28,* 477-482.

Zuckerman, M., Kuhlman, D. M., Joireman, J., Teta, P., & Kraft, M. (1993). A comparison of three structural models for personality: The big three, the big five and the alternative five. *Journal of Personality and Social Psychology, 65*, 757-768.

Zajonc, R. B. (1980). Feeling and thinking: Preferences need no inferences. *American Psychologist, 35*, 151-175.

7

Sex, Drugs, and Attitudinal Ambivalence: How Feelings of Evaluative Tension Influence Alcohol Use and Safe Sex Behaviors

Joseph R. Priester

University of Michigan

Attitudes generally are defined as people's global evaluative responses to other people, places, activities, products, and ideas (Eagly & Chaiken, 1995; Petty, Priester, & Wegener, 1994; Petty & Wegener, 1998). The importance of attitudes lies in their ability to shape and guide behavior (Allport, 1935). Attitudes can be powerful predictors of behavior (Ajzen & Fishbein, 1977, 1980; Fazio, 1995; Fazio, Powell, & Herr, 1983; Fazio, Powell, & Williams, 1989; Fazio & Williams, 1986; Fishbein & Ajzen, 1975; Petty & Cacioppo, 1986; Petty, Haugtvedt, & Smith, 1995). As such, an effective strategy for changing the behavior of an individual is to change that person's attitude. Thus, the goal of many antidrug campaigns is to change young people's attitudes toward drugs, such that drugs are seen as bad rather than good. It is hoped that, as a consequence, those young people will be less likely to use drugs as a function of their changed attitude.

Attitudes typically have been conceptualized (as well as measured) as lying along a bipolar continuum, from negative reactions at one end of the continuum to positive reactions at the other. Thus, within this perspective, an adolescent's attitude toward marijuana could range from extreme dislike (resulting in avoidance and withdrawal) to extreme liking (resulting in attraction and consumption). But are attitudes, especially those attitudes toward such complex social issues as drug use and sexual behavior, so unambiguous? Are attitudes always simply positive or simply negative reactions? Is it that young people feel either favorably or unfavorably toward drugs? Or is it possible that young people sometimes feel both positively and negatively toward drugs? In fact, recent research

(Breckler, 1994; Cacioppo & Berntson, 1994; Cacioppo, Gardner, & Berntson, 1997; Priester & Petty, 1996, 2001; Thompson, Zanna, & Griffin, 1995) suggests that attitudes can be more complex in nature. Attitudes can, and often do, possess both positive and negative components. Such attitudes are referred to as ambivalent. The key aspect of ambivalence is that individuals experience tension in their evaluations. Rather than merely feeling positive or negative toward an attitude object, individuals feel conflict in their evaluative reaction. The goal of the research presented in this chapter is to examine and understand the influence of these feelings of evaluative tension on health-risk related behaviors, such as alcohol use and safe sex behavior.

AMBIVALENCE

Intrapersonal Conflict

Traditionally, evaluative tension has been conceptualized as resulting from the positive and negative reactions that an individual possesses toward an attitude object (Brown & Farber, 1951; Kaplan, 1972; Scott, 1966, 1969). For example, if a person believes both that the practice of safe sex is good because it reduces the likelihood of contracting HIV (human immunodeficiency virus), and at the same time feels that the practice of safe sex diminishes the pleasure associated with sex, that person has conflicting thoughts and feelings toward safe sex. And it was the intrapersonal conflict between an individual's positive and negative evaluative responses that until recently was hypothesized to result in feelings of evaluative tension.

Interpersonal Conflict

Priester and Petty (2001), as well as McGregor, Newby-Clark, and Zanna (1999), noted that the feelings of evaluative tension predicted by the positive and negative reactions to an attitude object did not account for a preponderance of the variance associated with the psychological experience of ambivalence. That is, conflicting reactions did not seem sufficient to explain the subjective experience of evaluative tension. Priester and Petty (1996) hypothesized that one reason for this inability was that there may exist other influences on feelings of evaluative tension in addition to the individual's positive and negative reactions. They explored this possibility by investigating the influence of interpersonal attitudinal conflict on feelings of subjective ambivalence (i.e., evaluative tension). Priester and

Petty (2001) hypothesized that when important others held attitudes that were in conflict with an individual, this interpersonal attitudinal conflict could result in increased feelings of evaluative tension above and beyond the feelings of ambivalence resulting from a person's own positive and negative reactions. For example, imagine a young women who holds many positive and no negative thoughts and feelings about the practice of safe sex. As such, she would be described as possessing an attitude relatively free of intrapersonal conflict. However, imagine further that this woman's sexual partner holds extremely negative attitudes toward the practice of safe sex. Conceptualizations of evaluative tension based on the notion that ambivalence is the result of conflicting intrapersonal reactions would predict that the woman should feel minimal subjective ambivalence. Priester and Petty (2001) hypothesized and found support for the notion that interpersonal attitudinal discrepancy, such as that hypothetically experienced by the woman, contributes to feelings of evaluative tension independently of intrapersonal sources of conflicting reactions. Specifically, their research found that individuals experience greater feelings of evaluative tension when their attitudes are in conflict, rather than in agreement, with liked others, and, further, that individuals experience greater feelings of evaluative tension when their attitudes are in agreement, rather than in conflict, with disliked others.

At one level, this research can be viewed as providing evidence that feelings of evaluative tension are the result not only of intrapersonal conflict, but also of interpersonal attitudinal conflict. As such, this research explains the relatively moderate relationship between intrapersonal conflict and feelings of evaluative tension. However, this research not only provides insight into the reason for the relative low correlations of intrapersonal conflict with the psychological experience of evaluative tension, but also provides insight into *why* individuals may be particularly likely to experience evaluative tension for controversial social issues, such as alcohol use and safe sex. Even when their own intrapersonal reactions are not in conflict, they may yet experience feelings of evaluative tension owing to the interpersonal influences of their friends, peers, and parents. In short, feelings of evaluative tension can be the result of intrapersonal and/or interpersonal conflict.

Ambivalence Across the Attitude Scale

Historically, attitude researchers focused their concern of ambivalence on the ambiguity associated with midscale (i.e., neutral) responses. Given the bipolar perspective on attitudes, when an individual provides a midscale response, it is impossible to know whether this response indicates no positive or negative reactions to the attitude object (i.e., the individual feels indifferent) or whether this response indicates both positive and negative reactions to the attitude object (i.e., the individual feels ambivalent; see Edwards, 1946; Klopfer & Madden, 1980). Thus, ambivalence was often construed as an issue restricted to "neutral" responses.

In fact, empirically it does appear as if attitude extremity and ambivalence are negatively related, such that as attitudes become more extremely positive or negative, they are associated with less evaluative tension. However, even though evaluative tension is most likely to occur for neutral responses, ambivalence can occur across the entire attitude scale. Imagine an attitude measure ranging from −3 (equal to negative) to +3 (equal to positive). One could provide a +3 response on such a scale for different reasons. An unambivalent response would occur because the individual feels many and only positive reactions, and important others agree with the individual. In contrast, an ambivalent response could occur because, although the individual feels many positive reactions, he or she also feels slight negativity. As such, the person would feel ambivalence because of intrapersonal attitudinal conflict. Alternatively, an individual might personally feel only positive reactions but know that close friends felt negatively. As such, the person would feel ambivalence because of interpersonal attitudinal conflict. The key point is that evaluative tension can be experienced for extreme, as well as neutral, responses. Research has demonstrated that individuals can feel evaluative tension toward such extremely positively evaluated events such as their own upcoming weddings (Otnes, Lowrey, & Shrum, 1997).

AMBIVALENCE STUDY: ALCOHOL USE AND SAFE SEX

The goal of the research presented in this chapter is to examine how feelings of evaluative tension (i.e., ambivalence) influence health-risk-related behaviors. Prior research raises the possibility that ambivalence moderates the influence of attitudes on behavior (e.g., Costello, Rice, & Schoenfeld, 1974; Moore, 1973; Sparks, Hedderley, & Shepherd, 1992). We investigate whether young people who feel greater evaluative conflict toward the use of alcohol and the practice of safe sex are guided by their attitudes to a lesser extent than those young people who feel less evaluative tension. In short, the question that guides the present research is whether attitudinal ambivalence attenuates the influence of attitudes on behavior. A related goal of this research is to explore the possibility of identifying individuals and/or groups who are vulnerable to acting in ways that increase their risk to health related problems. That is, are individuals of high evaluative tension toward drinking and safe sex more prone to act in riskier ways than individuals of low levels of evaluative tension?

To examine these questions, a study was conducted in which 193 undergraduate students completed a series of self-report measures on attitudes, subjective feelings of ambivalence, and reports on past behavior, as well as behavioral intentions, toward a number of topics and issues, including the use of alcohol and the practice of safe sex.

Alcohol Use

Evaluative Measures. To assess attitudes toward the use of alcohol, participants completed a single, bipolar measure anchored with −3 equal to *unfavorable* and +3 equal to *favorable.* To assess the evaluative tension associated with the use of alcohol, participants responded to three 11-point scales, with 0 equal to "I feel no behavioral indecision," "my thoughts and feelings are completely one-sided," and "I feel no conflict in my thoughts and feelings" and 10 equal to "feel maximum behavioral indecision," "completely mixed thoughts and feelings," and "maximum conflict in my thoughts and feelings." These three indicators were chosen to assess the three possible bases of evaluative tension. Attitudes traditionally have been conceptualized as being comprised of three distinct bases – affective, behavioral, and cognitive (Ostrom, 1969).   The three measures used in this study were designed to assess evaluative tension related to the affective, behavioral, and cognitive bases of the attitudes (see Priester & Petty, 1996, 2001).

Behavioral Measures. To assess past alcohol use, participants were asked, "How often do you consume alcohol?" and "How much alcohol do you consume?" To assess behavioral intentions, they were asked, "How often do you plan to consume alcohol in the next week?" and "How much alcohol do you plan to consume during the next week?" These four measures were highly associated; thus, one behavioral measure was created by averaging the four responses of each participant.

Results. Preliminary analyses revealed that attitudes toward alcohol use ranged from −3 to +3, with the mean response slightly above the scale midpoint ($M = 0.5$). Feelings of evaluative tension were not significantly correlated with attitudes toward alcohol use ($r = -.02$). Further analyses revealed a wide range of (high and low) levels of evaluative tension, at each level of attitude. As such, the use of alcohol provides a good test of whether evaluative tension moderates the influence of attitudes on behavior.

It should be recalled that the primary question guiding this research was whether evaluative tension associated with an attitude moderates that attitude's influence on behavior. To examine this question, a regression analysis was conducted, examining the influence of attitudes, evaluative tension and the attitudes x evaluative tension interaction on behavior. This regression analysis yielded a significant main effect of attitudes on behavior. Not surprisingly, this main effect revealed that attitudes influenced behavior such that the more positively one evaluated the use of alcohol, the more likely that person was to consume alcohol.

Of greater importance, the regression analysis also yielded a significant attitudes x evaluative tension interaction on behavior. To decompose this interaction, a tertiary split was performed on the Evaluative Tension scores, such that those individuals with scores less than 1.34 were classified as low, those individuals with scores greater than 3.34 were classified as high, and those with scores in-between were classified as moderate. To examine the interaction, the correlations between attitudes and behaviors were calculated within each of the three groups. These correlations are depicted in Figure 7.1. As can be seen, the attitudes x evaluative tension interaction on behavior is due to the difference in the relationships between attitudes and behavior for those individuals reporting high levels of evaluative tension versus those reporting moderate and low levels of evaluative tension. Specifically, the attitudes of the individuals of low or moderate levels of evaluative tension were much more highly associated with attitudinally congruent behavior than the attitudes of those individuals reporting high levels of evaluative tension. In short, attitudes influenced alcohol use when those attitudes were relatively free of evaluative tension. They were not as influential when they were associated with evaluative tension.

Discussion. At their most basic, the analyses of the alcohol use data provide support for the notion that feelings of evaluative tension moderate the influence of attitudes on behavior. Those individuals who report relatively low levels of evaluative tension are guided by their attitudes in their use of alcohol. Those individuals with little evaluative tension who report positive attitudes are more likely to consume alcohol and those individuals who report negative attitudes are less likely to consume alcohol. In contrast, predicting the alcohol usage of those individuals who report relatively high levels of evaluative tension is problematic: Those with high evaluative tension who report positive attitudes are not as likely to consume alcohol, whereas those with high levels of evaluative tension who report negative attitudes are not as likely to avoid it.

This finding raises an important point for the purposes of antidrug campaigns. Many antidrug campaigns are designed to change the attitudes of young people toward drugs (e.g., alcohol). It is hoped that by changing attitudes toward drugs, the behavior of the young people will

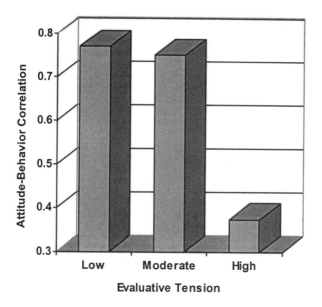

FIGURE 7.1 Correspondence of alcohol-related attitudes and alcohol use as a function of evaluative tension.

correspondingly change. The present research suggests that attitude change, per se, may not be sufficient to produce such behavioral changes. Specifically, if it is the case that the changed attitude is associated with evaluative tension, then this anti-drinking attitude may not be as likely to guide subsequent behavior; antidrug attitudes may not result in reduced consumption of alcohol if those attitudes are associated with high levels of evaluative tension. Thus, what looks like a successful outcome (an attitude changed in the desired direction) may not be associated with the desired behavioral changes.

The influence of evaluative tension also raises the counterintuitive insight that campaigns that appear relatively unsuccessful may in fact lead to desired behavioral changes. Specifically, it is possible that a campaign might result in attitudes that appear unchanged from the traditional bipolar attitude perspective. That is, individuals may still report positive attitudes toward the use of drugs and alcohol. If, however, the campaign has increased the evaluative tension associated with these positive attitudes, it is possible that there will emerge changes in the behavior in the desired direction. That is, individuals may be less likely to consume drugs and alcohol even though they report positive attitudes, because of the influence of the evaluative tension on the attitude's capacity to guide subsequent behavior. As such, evaluative tension potentially plays a crucial role in understanding the efficacy of antidrug campaigns.

Alternative Explanation: The Relationship Between Evaluative Tension and Attitude Extremity. Before such implications can be accepted, it is important to explore an alternative explanation to the findings of the alcohol use data that would render such inferences misguided. Examination of the relationship between evaluative tension and attitudes toward alcohol use reveals that, although evaluative tension is not associated with attitudes, evaluative tension is associated with attitude extremity. That is, as attitudes move away from the neutral response (i.e., become more extreme), the evaluative tension associated with those attitudes is reduced ($r = -.5$). This relationship between evaluative tension and attitudes toward alcohol use is presented in Figure 7.2.

Recall that it was inferred, based on the evaluative tension x attitudes interaction on the use of alcohol, that feelings of evaluative tension attenuated the influence of attitudes on behavior. Given the relationship between attitude extremity and evaluative tension, however, a cogent alternative explanation to this interpretation emerges. Rather than evaluative tension being causally related to the attenuation of the influence of attitudes on behavior, it may instead be the case that extreme attitudes (which are associated with less evaluative tension) are better able to influence and guide behavior than less extreme attitudes (which are associated with greater evaluative tension). This alternative explanation receives support from research demonstrating that attitude extremity is related to attitude strength, such that more extreme attitudes are stronger than less extreme attitudes (Judd & Brauer, 1995). In short, this alternative explanation suggests that evaluative tension may be primarily a midpoint (i.e., neutral) phenomenon, such that attitudes that are changed away from the midpoint are more likely to guide behavior, whereas attitudes near the midpoint are less likely to do so.

If this alternative explanation is accepted, then the implications outlined in the discussion of the alcohol use data are unwarranted. As long as antidrug campaigns produce extreme attitudes against drugs and alcohol, these attitudes are likely to influence and guide behavior, and the concern of evaluative tension attenuating these attitudes is rendered moot.

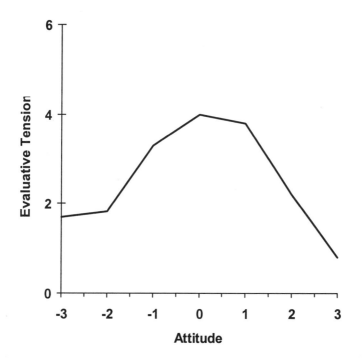

FIGURE 7.2 Association between feelings of evaluative tension and attitude.

Safe Sex

Fortunately, the relationship between safe sex attitudes and evaluative tension is quite different from that involving attitudes toward the use of alcohol. Preliminary analyses found that attitudes toward safe sex practices are highly and negatively correlated with feelings of evaluative tension ($r = -.60$). Specifically, 90 of 97 low and moderate ambivalence participants reported attitudes of +3 (i.e., the most extremely positive attitude possible), and 35 of 96 high ambivalence participants report similar attitudes of +3. This naturally occurring relationship between attitudes and evaluative tension toward safe sex practices provides an opportunity to examine the alternative explanation to the findings for alcohol use. By examining the behavior of only those individuals who report the most positive attitudes possible toward safe sex along with their feelings of evaluative tension, it is possible to examine the influence of evaluative tension on an attitude's capacity to guide behavior free from the influence of attitude extremity. If the results of the alcohol data were due to attitude extremity, there should emerge no influence of evaluative tension on safe sex behavior, because only those individuals with equally extreme attitudes are being examined. In contrast, if the results of the alcohol data were due to feelings of evaluative tension, there should emerge an influence of evaluative tension on safe sex behaviors. That is, we are able to ask whether the influence of an (extreme) attitude on behavior varies as a function of evaluative tension.

Evaluative Measures. The measures used to assess attitudes toward and evaluative tension associated with safe sex practices were identical to those used to assess attitudes toward, and evaluative tension associated with, the use of alcohol.

Behavioral Measures. Participants provided measures of their past behavior and behavioral intentions. To assess past behavior, participants were asked, "How often do you currently practice safe sex?," "How often do you currently abstain from sexual intercourse for purposes of safe sex?," and "How often do you (or your partner) use a condom for purposes of safe sex?" To assess behavioral intention, participants were asked if they planned to perform the three behaviors assessed for past behavior in the future. As an additional indicator of behavior, participants returned to the laboratory 1-week later and provided self-reports of their behavior the week following the initial session. That is, they indicated the extent to which they engaged in any unprotected sexual intercourse during the past week (this item was reverse-coded), and whether they abstained from sexual intercourse or used a condom during the past week. Factor analyses provided evidence that these nine measures were single-factored. As such, the measures were standardized and averaged to yield one indicator of safe sex behavior.

Unlike the use of alcohol, safe sex is by definition a social behavior, in which the assistance and cooperation of another individual is required. As such, the question arises as to whether feelings of evaluative tension influence the extent to which individuals engage in social influence attempts. To measure these social influence attempts, all participants were asked, "How often do you try to convince others to practice safe sex?"

Data Analysis Strategy. To examine the influence of evaluative tension independently of attitude extremity, only those participants who provided the most extremely positive attitude response possible were included in data analyses. Thus, 125 participants (90 of whom possessed low or moderate evaluative tension and 35 of whom possessed high evaluative tension) were used. All participants possessed equally positive (and extreme) attitudes toward safe sex. As such, it would be expected that all participants should generally practice safe sex behaviors. The question of whether evaluative tension influences these attitudes' capacity to guide behavior is best examined by comparing the relationship between safe sex behavior and feelings of evaluative tension associated with attitudes toward safe sex. If evaluative tension does influence safe sex attitudes' ability to guide behavior, then there should emerge a negative relationship between feelings of evaluative tension and safe sex practices, such that as feelings of evaluative tension increase, safe sex practice decreases.

Results. Recall that the primary question guiding these analyses was whether evaluative tension associated with an extremely positive attitude influences the extent of attitude-congruent behavior resulting from these attitudes. To examine this question, correlational analyses were conducted examining the relationship between evaluative tension and the behaviors of interest. The first correlational analysis examined the relationship between feelings of evaluative tension associated with safe sex attitudes and the extent to which individuals attempted to convince others to engage in safe sex behaviors. This analysis yielded a statistically significant negative correlation ($r = -.16$), suggesting that as feelings of evaluative tension increase, social influence attempts decrease. A tertiary split was performed on the evaluative tension scores associated with safe sex attitudes, such that those individuals with scores less than .1 were classified as low, those individuals with scores greater than 1.34 were classified as high, and those with scores in-between were classified as moderate. The number of social influence attempts as a function of level of evaluative tension is illustrated in Figure 7.3. As can be seen, those individuals reporting high levels of evaluative tension in their extremely positive safe sex attitudes are less likely to attempt to convince others to practice safe sex than those individuals reporting low and moderate levels of evaluative tension in their extremely positive safe sex attitudes. Evaluative tension associated with safe sex attitudes undercuts the attitude's capacity to guide social influence attempts, even when the attitudes are as extremely positive as possible.

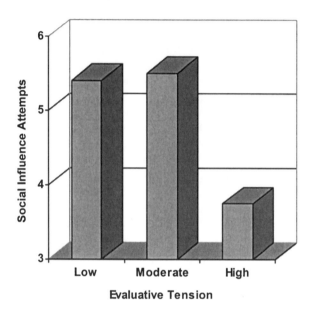

FIGURE 7.3 Social influence attempts as a function of evaluative tension.

The second correlational analysis examined the relationship between feelings of evaluative tension associated with safe sex attitudes and the extent to which individuals behaved in a manner congruent with their extremely positive safe sex attitudes. This analysis also yielded a significant negative correlation (r = -.20). As feelings of evaluative tension increase, safe sex behavior decreases. To better illustrate this relationship, the extent of safe sex behavior was examined as a function of level of evaluative tension. This relationship is presented in Figure 7.4. As can be seen, those individuals reporting high levels of evaluative tension in their extremely positive safe sex attitudes are less likely to practice safe sex than those individuals reporting low and moderate levels of evaluative tension in their extremely positive safe sex attitudes. Evaluative tension associated with safe sex attitudes undercuts the attitude's capacity to guide safe sex behavior, even when the attitudes are as extremely positive as possible.

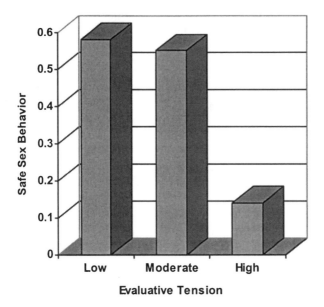

FIGURE 7.4 Safe sex behavior as a function of evaluative tension.

Discussion. Recall that the alternative explanation arising from the alcohol use analyses raised the question of whether the influence uncovered was due to evaluative tension, as hypothesized, or to attitude extremity. Because evaluative tension and attitude extremity were highly associated for the alcohol use data, it was difficult to determine which variable accounted for the moderation of attitudes on behavior. The safe sex data demonstrated a different relationship between attitude extremity and evaluative tension, such that many individuals possessed extremely positive attitudes toward safe sex, even when those attitudes were associated with evaluative tension. This relationship between attitude extremity and evaluative tension provided an opportunity to examine the cogency of the alternative explanation arising from the alcohol use data. Specifically, it was possible to examine the influence of evaluative tension on behavior for those attitudes associated with extremely positive attitudes. As such, in these analyses, all attitudes are extremely positive. Thus, any differences in safe sex behavior as a function of evaluative tension provides support for the interpretation that evaluative tension influences an attitude's ability to guide subsequent behavior.

The results of the safe sex data provided support for the hypothesis that, indeed, evaluative tension influences the relationship of attitudes on behavior. Individuals who possessed extremely positive attitudes associated with high evaluative tension were less likely to attempt to convince others to engage in safe sex behaviors than those individual who possessed extremely positive attitudes associated with low or moderate evaluative tension. And those individuals who possessed extremely positive attitudes associated with high evaluative tension were less likely to engage in safe sex behaviors than those individuals who possessed extremely positive attitudes associated with low or moderate evaluative tension. These results provide evidence that evaluative tension plays an important role in safe sex behavior.

GENERAL DISCUSSION

Implications

These findings suggest the advantage of including measures of evaluative tension, in addition to traditional measures of attitudes, when assessing the effectiveness of campaigns intended to change attitudes and influence behavior. Reliance on attitude measures alone may provide misleading inferences as to the success or failure of any such campaign. For example, a campaign might result in persuasion, as measured by attitudes, and be termed a success. If, however, individuals feel evaluative tension in their changed attitudes, these attitudes are not as likely to guide future behavior. In short, the campaign may result in more positive attitudes but fail to influence behavior. A conclusion that such a campaign was a success is questionable, if not wrong. Similarly, a campaign might not appear to change already extreme attitudes and be termed a failure. If, however, individuals feel less evaluative tension in their unchanged attitudes, these attitudes are more likely to guide future behavior. In short, the campaign may have not changed attitudes, but may have resulted in attitudes that are more likely to guide future behavior. The inclusion of measures of evaluative tension, in addition to traditional measures of attitudes, will provide greater insight into the efficacy of antidrug campaigns.

Evaluative Tension as a Segmentation Tool

This research suggests that evaluative tension can be used as a variable to segment groups and individuals according to their vulnerability to health-risk related behaviors. Reflect on the safe sex findings. Were one to judge vulnerability by the attitudes expressed, all of the +3 individuals (i.e., those individuals who expressed as much agreement with safe sex as possible) would be viewed as relatively impervious toward unsafe sex practices. However, by assessing ambivalence in addition to attitudes, it is possible to identify those individuals who, although possessing extremely positive attitudes toward safe sex practices, are more likely to engage in unsafe sex practices. Evaluative tension provides a measure by which the likelihood of an individual acting in accord with his or her attitudes can be assessed, and as such provides a tool by which to segment individuals and groups according to their vulnerability toward engaging in unsafe sex practices.

Ambivalence Reduction

The observation that ambivalence can be used to identify groups and individuals who are vulnerable to engaging in health-risk related behaviors raises an important issue: once these individuals are identified, what can be done to reduce their vulnerability? Once we have identified individuals who feel ambivalent, by what means can that ambivalence be reduced? This is an important issue that deserves considerable research. One step toward addressing this issue is to include measures of evaluative tension in addition to other, more standard, measures in persuasion studies. By incorporating evaluative tension, persuasion researchers will have a better understanding of how different persuasion processes influence evaluative tension.

Beliefs, Attitudes, and Attitude Components as Keys to Behavioral Change

At one point, the goal of health-risk-related campaigns was to identify and change beliefs. It was thought that once people understood the dangers associated with their behaviors, and once they understood their susceptibility to these negative outcomes, they would change their behavior. Research provided evidence, however, that changing beliefs was not sufficient to change behavior. Beliefs sometimes seemed to predict behavior change, at other times predicted the opposite behavior, and often did not predict behavior at all (Kinder, Pape, & Walfish, 1980; Rundall & Bruvold,

1988). In part because of these findings, campaigns evolved to focus on changing people's attitudes. Attitude change was more likely to result in the desired behavioral changes than belief change. The present research provides support for the notion that attitude change is not sufficient to influence behavior. Specifically, understanding more specific attitudinal components, such as evaluative tension (and attitude strength; Petty & Krosnick, 1995), helps provide even better understanding of who is likely to engage in health-risk-related behavior. As such, evaluative tension deserves a place within both the theoretical study of attitudes and persuasion, and within public campaigns designed to influence and change health-risk-related behaviors.

ACKNOWLEDGMENTS

This research was supported by National Institute of Health traineeship T32 MH19728, a Graduate Student Alumni Research Award, and a grant from the University of Michigan Business School.

REFERENCES

Ajzen, I., & Fishbein, M. (1977). Attitude-behavior relations: A theoretical analysis and review of empirical research. *Psychological Bulletin, 84*, 888-918.

Ajzen, I., & Fishbein, M. (1980). *Understanding attitudes and predicting social behavior.* Englewood Cliffs, NJ: Prentice-Hall.

Allport, G. W. (1935). Attitudes. In C. Murchison (Ed.), *Handbook of social psychology* (pp. 798-844). Worcester, MA: Clark University Press.

Breckler, S. J. (1994). A comparison of numerical indexes for measuring attitude ambivalence. *Educational and Psychological Measurement, 54*, 350-365.

Brown, J. S., & Farber, I. E. (1951). Emotions conceptualized as intervening variables B With suggestions toward a theory of frustration. *Psychological Bulletin, 48*, 465-495.

Cacioppo, J. T., & Berntson, G. G. (1994). Relationship between attitudes and evaluative space: A critical review, with emphasis on the separability of positive and negative substrates. *Psychological Bulletin, 115*, 401-423.

Cacioppo, J. T., Gardner, W. L., & Berntson, G. G. (1997). Beyond bipolar conceptualizations and measures: The case of attitudes and evaluative space. *Personality and Social Psychology Review, 1*, 3-25.

Costello, R. M., Rice, D. P., & Schoenfeld, L. S. (1974). Attitudinal ambivalence with alcoholic respondents. *Journal of Consulting and Clinical Psychology, 42*, 303-304.

Eagly, A. H., & Chaiken, S. (1993). *The psychology of attitudes.* Fort Worth, TX: Harcourt Brace.

Edwards, A. L. (1946). A critique of "neutral" items in attitude scales constructed by the method of equal appearing intervals. *Psychological Review, 53*, 159-169.

Fazio, R. H. (1995). Attitudes as object-evaluation associations: Determinants, consequences, and correlates of attitude accessibility. In R. E. Petty & J. A. Krosnick (Eds.), *Attitude strength: Antecedents and consequences* (pp. 247-282). Mahwah, NJ: Lawrence Erlbaum Associates.

Fazio, R. H., Powell, M. C., & Herr, P. M. (1983). Toward a process model of attitude-behavior relation: Accessing one's attitude upon mere observation of the attitude object. *Journal of Personality and Social Psychology, 44*, 723-735.

Fazio, R. H., Powell, M. C., & Williams, C. J. (1989). The role of attitude accessibility in the attitude-to-behavior process. *Journal of Consumer Research, 16*, 280-288.

Fazio, R. H. & Williams, C. J. (1986). Attitude accessibility as a moderator of the attitude-perception and attitude-behavior relations: An investigation of the 1984 presidential election. *Journal of Personality and Social Psychology, 51*, 505-514.

Fishbein, M., & Ajzen, I. (1975). *Belief, attitude, intention, and behavior: An introduction to theory and research*. Reading, MA: Addison-Wesley.

Judd, C. M., & Brauer, M. (1995). Repetition and evaluative extremity. In R. E. Petty & J. A. Krosnick (Eds.), *Attitude strength: Antecedents and consequences* (pp. 43-72). Mahwah, NJ: Lawrence Erlbaum Associates.

Kaplan, K. J. (1972). On the ambivalence-indifference problem in attitude theory and measurement: A suggested modification of the semantic differential technique. *Psychological Review, 77*, 361-372.

Kinder, B. N., Pape, N. E., & Walfish, S. (1980). Drug and alcohol education programs – A review of outcome studies. *International Journal of the Addictions, 15*, 1035-1054.

Klopfer, F. J., & Madden, T. M. (1980). The middlemost choice on attitude items: Ambivalence, neutrality, or uncertainty? *Personality and Social Psychology Bulletin, 6*, 97-101.

McGregor, I., Newby-Clark, I. R., & Zanna, M. P. (1999). "Remembering" dissonance:Simu ltaneous accessibility in inconsistent elements moderates epistemic discomfort. In E. Harmon-Jones & J. Mills (Eds.), *Cognitive dissonance: Progress on a pivotal theory in social psychology* (pp. 325-353). Washington, DC: American Psychological Association.

Moore, M. (1973). Ambivalence in attitude measurement. *Educational and Psychological Measurement, 33*, 481-483.

Ostrom, T. M. (1969). The relationship between the affective, behavioral, and cognitive components of attitude. *Journal of Experimental Social Psychology, 5*, 12-30.

Otnes, C., Lowrey, T. M., & Shrum, L. J. (1997). Toward an understanding of consumer ambivalence. *Journal of Consumer Research, 24*, 80-93.

Petty, R. E., & Cacioppo, J. T. (1986). *Communication and persuasion: Central and peripheral routes to attitude change*. New York: Springer-Verlag.

Petty, R. E., Haugtvedt, C. P., & Smith, S. M. (1995). Elaboration as a determinant of attitude strength: Creating attitudes that are persistent, resistant, and predictive of behavior. In R. E. Petty and J. A. Krosnick (Eds.), *Attitude strength: Antecedents and consequences* (pp. 93-130). Mahwah, NJ: Lawrence Erlbaum Associates.

Petty, R. E., & Krosnick, J. A. (1995). *Attitude strength: Antecedents and consequences.* Mahwah, NJ: Lawrence Erlbaum Associates.

Petty, R. E., Priester, J. R., & Wegener, D. T. (1994). Cognitive processes in attitude change. In R. S. Wyer & T. K. Srull (Eds.), *Handbook of social cognition* (2nd ed., Vol. 2, pp. 69-142). Hillsdale, NJ: Lawrence Erlbaum Associates.

Petty, R. E., & Wegener, D. T. (1998). Attitude change: Multiple roles for persuasion variables. In D. Gilbert, S. Fiske, & G. Lindzey (Eds.), *The handbook of social psychology* (4th ed., pp. 323-390). New York: McGraw-Hill.

Priester, J. R., & Petty, R. E. (2001). Extending the bases of subjective attitudinal ambivalence: Interpersonal and intrapersonal antecedents of evaluative tension. *Journal of Personality and Social Psychology, 80,* 19-34.

Priester, J. R., & Petty, R. E. (1996). The gradual threshold model of abivalence: relating the positive and negative vases of attitudes to subjective ambivalence. *Journal of Personality and Social Psychology, 71,* 431-449.

Rundall, T. G., & Bruvold, W. H. (1988). A meta-analysis of school-based smoking and alcohol use prevention programs. *Health Education Quarterly, 15,* 317-334.

Scott, W. A. (1966). Brief report: Measures of cognitive structure. *Multivariate Behavioral Research, 1,* 391-395.

Scott, W. A. (1969). Structure of natural cognitions. *Journal of Personality and Social Psychology, 12,* 261-278.

Sparks, P., Hedderley, D., & Shepherd, R. (1992). An investigation into the relationship between perceived control, attitude variability and the consumption of two common foods. *European Journal of Social Psychology, 22,* 55-71.

Thompson, M. M., Zanna, M. P., & Griffin, D. W. (1995). Let's not be indifferent about (attitudinal) ambivalence. In R. E. Petty & J. A. Krosnick (Eds.), *Attitude strength: Antecedents and consequences* (pp. 361-386). Mahwah, NJ: Lawrence Erlbaum Associates.

8

Expectancy Theory Approaches to Prevention: Violating Adolescent Expectations to Increase the Effectiveness of Public Service Announcements

Jason T. Siegel and Judee K. Burgoon

University of Arizona

The facts are these: In 1999, more than 11 million Americans used marijuana (Substance Abuse and Mental Health Services Administration [SAMHSA], 1999). Almost half of all high schools students surveyed used marijuana on at least one occasion, and more than 25% of high school students who were questioned reported using marijuana 30 days prior to being surveyed (Kann et al., 2000). Illicit drug use costs taxpayers upward of $110 billion a year (Harwood, Fountain, & Livermore, 1998). In addition to impairing cognitive functioning, marijuana use is associated with increased risk of dropping out of high school, driving under the influence, engaging in crime, and destroying property. And, it is linked to chronic bronchitis and reproductive system problems (Block, Farnham, Braverman, & Noyes, 1990; Brey, Zarkin, Ringwalt, & Qi., 2000; Brook, Balka, & Whiteman, 1991; Ellickson, Bui, Bell, & McGuigan, 1998; Nahas & Latour, 1992; Osgood, Johnston, O'Malley, & Bachman, 1988; Polen et al., 1993; SAMHSA, 1998a, 1998b; Spunt, Goldstein, & Fendrich, 1994; Tashkin et al., 1990; Tommasello, 1982; Yamada, Kendix, & Yamada, 1996;).

The goal is simple: Persuade people not to do drugs. Seems easy enough in principle. Unfortunately, even with $3 billion being spent by the Partnership for a Drug- Free America on media time alone, the amount of people who use illegal substances is not decreasing. As discussed throughout this volume, the utilization of theory-driven campaigns must be considered if public service announcements (PSAs) are going to be a worthwhile force in the war on drugs. As stated by O'Keefe and Reid (1990), "Centering a campaign around a theoretical approach not only allows a broad base of knowledge to be brought to bear on the problem, but it also provides a guiding model or structure that can help the sometimes complex and disorganized components of contemporary campaigns" (pp. 76-77). Similar thoughts were put forth by Atkins and Freimuth (1989):

> Health educators have not typically used systematic approaches at the pre-production stage, as mass media campaigns efforts often proceed in the absence of a research foundation. Instead, messages tend to be produced in a haphazard fashion based on creative inspiration of copywriters and artists patterned after the normative standards of the health campaign genre. (p. 132)

This chapter focuses on three theories: Expectancy States Theory (EST), Expectancy Violations Theory (EVT), and Language Expectancy Theory (LET). Each theory offers its own contribution in understanding how PSA effectiveness can be increased. Although the theoretical framework to be proposed within this chapter is applicable across a variety of prevention contexts, to keep this chapter within a feasible scope, the applied context is limited to decreasing the usage of marijuana among adolescents. First, a brief explanation of EST is presented, followed by an explanation as to why creators of mass-media PSAs must be aware of how perceptions of past campaigns will influence the effectiveness of current campaigns. Next, EVT is introduced, followed by an explanation as to how the framework of EVT can be utilized to increase the attention paid to PSAs by adolescents. Lastly, following an explanation of LET, LET in combination with EVT is utilized as a framework for explaining how PSA messages can be constructed to achieve maximum effectiveness.

Defining Expectancies. Before considering the theories, we need to define expectations as used in these theories. Readers of this volume might be more familiar with the term *expectancy* as utilized in expectancy-value theories (e.g., Mitchell, 1982; Vroom, 1964) and Fishbein and Ajzen's theory of reasoned action (1975). Expectancy in that context focuses on how a person's expectations regarding one's own actions influence self-behavior. However, as utilized by the theories to be discussed in this chapter, *expectancy* denotes in the simplest sense the anticipated behavior of other individuals or groups (J. K. Burgoon & Walther, 1990). *Violations* refer to actions that deviate from expectations. Thus, EVT and LET address how communicative acts of an individual or group can confirm and/or disconfirm previously held expectations and the effects that violations have on how the individual or group is evaluated (e.g., J. K. Burgoon, 1978; M. Burgoon & Miller, 1985). Placing this distinction into a mass media drug prevention realm, expectancy-value theories focus on adolescents' beliefs about the benefits and costs of doing drugs and would structure messages according to self expectations and intentions. Expectancy violation theories, as discussed in this chapter, focus on adolescents' expectations related to antidrug messages and how violating these expectations can increase or decrease message effectiveness.

EXPECTANCY STATES THEORY

Expectancy States Theory (EST) addresses how individuals develop expectations concerning the potential of other group members to make quality contributions to the group (Berger, Conner, & Fisek, 1974; Berger, Wagner, & Zelditch, 1985). Although the theory has a great deal to say about many aspects of group performance and group interaction, the facets with the most potential applicability to responses to PSAs concern how expectations are formed and how those enable individuals to achieve influence.

Berger and Conner (1974), interested in how power and prestige roles emerge in groups, posited that groups form hierarchies based on external status characteristics and the perceived quality of each group member's contributions during group interactions. Individuals possessing such valued characteristics as task competency, special skills, past accomplishments, physical attractiveness, in-group membership, or the "right" sex or ethnicity have associated *performance expectations* (Cohen, 1972; Cohen & Sharan, 1980; Kelsey, 1998; Lockheed & Hall, 1976; Rashotte & Smith-Lovin, 1997; Tammivarra, 1982; Webster & Driskell, 1983). These expectations confer an *expectation advantage,* whereas possession of devalued characteristics (e.g., a reputation for poor performance) creates an expectation disadvantage. An expectation advantage means not only that such individuals are expected to contribute favorably or unfavorably to successful task completion but that they are also given more opportunities to do so. Once the hierarchy is formed, those who have earned higher expectations from fellow group members is given more opportunities to speak and initiate problem-solving performances, receive more positive feedback, be more impervious to disagreements and negative feedback, and generally have greater power to influence the group (Berger & Conner, 1974).

Additionally, a performance output, regardless of its quality, will be highly evaluated if produced by a group member held in high esteem; a performance output, regardless of its quality, will be poorly evaluated if produced by a group member in low esteem. Such bias will lead to a self-stabilization of the group hierarchy, because those in power will have their contributions viewed with a positive bias, whereas those without power will have their ideas laced with a negative bias (see Berger, Rosenholtz, & Zelditch, 1980, for a review). In other words, once a group decides that a member is likely to have little to contribute, future contributions will be evaluated not according to what the contribution consists of, but according to who made it. It has also been found that once a member is regarded in high esteem for one behavior, the high regard the member has earned will spread to additional types of behavior in typical "halo effect" fashion.

This theoretical explanation has found substantial empirical support in accounting for group influence (see Berger et al., 1985, for a review). Although at first glance EST may not appear as germane to the mass media prevention realm, the basic premises of EST provide an excellent framework for exploring the potential effect that past prevention campaigns have on present prevention efforts. Berger, Cohen, Snell, and Zelditch (1962) stated that the most important feature of EST is the ability for the theoretical construct to allow the researcher "to generalize and integrate, through underlying abstract concepts, other concepts that describe otherwise disparate features of a process" (p. 35). Looking at mass media viewers as equivalent to a large group and PSAs as equivalent to the communication of the group member whose performance can be evaluated, we can begin to see some explanatory possibilities.

Although one would be hard pressed to find literature suggesting that present campaigns need to overcome the effect that past campaigns have had on the credibility attributed to antidrug messages by adolescents, EST would recommend such an approach. First, consider the stabilization of expectations that result from repeated exposures. Following EST, viewers of present mass media antidrug messages will be biased in their evaluation, depending on the viewers' perceived contributions of past mass media antidrug messages. If viewers perceive past PSAs as noncredible and of little value, then new messages will be viewed with a negative bias (Berger, Conner, & McKeown, 1974). Furthermore, even if viewers view a PSA as providing a quality contribution (i.e., quality information about the effects of drugs on sex drive), if a negative bias already exists, then the contribution may be discounted as an exception—a "special event"—and future messages will still be viewed with a negative bias (Berger, Conner, & McKeown, 1974).

Following such logic, creators of PSAs wishing to utilize EST to assess whether bias may already exist for or against PSAs will have to answer several questions: Are adolescents aware of antidrug PSAs? In other words, are adolescents aware that mass media PSAs are part of their media consumption experience? Do adolescents perceive that PSAs make quality contributions? Do adolescents trust PSAs? If the answers to these questions are "yes," it can be assumed that adolescents will continue to view PSAs with a positive bias. As discussed earlier, if adolescents perceive PSAs of little value, then PSAs will hold little or no power to influence.

Present drug prevention efforts have tallied up a bill of over $3 billion in media exposure since 1987 (Partnership for a Drug-Free America, 1999) and 45% of today's adolescents claim to see or hear antidrug commercials at least once a day (Partnership Attitude Tracking Survey, 1999). Such data leave little doubt concerning whether or not adolescents are aware that antidrug messages are a part of their mass media consumption experience. However, the vital question concerns how adolescents perceive past messages.

Unfortunately, recent research has found teenagers to be untrusting of PSAs (Skinner & Slater, 1995). Nelson (1970) claimed that many adolescents have learned that a lot of drugs aren't as dangerous as parents have led them to believe. Feingold and Knapp (1977) found that high school students who were repeatedly exposed to anti-amphetamines/barbiturates messages shifted from having generally negative attitudes to significantly less negative attitudes. Furthermore, Skinner and Slater (1995) found that the more at-risk for drug use an adolescent is, the less credible he or she will find antidrug messages. Among others, Hanneman (1973) found trustworthy, personal informants to be more important sources of drug information than media. Twenty years and $3 billion in media time purchases later, Hemmelstein (1995) also found that adolescents' perception of drug risk was highly correlated with their perceptions of friends' acceptance.

Applying Berger and Conner's (1966) framework, we might look at the mass media and its adolescent viewers as comprising a large social group in which adolescents at-risk for drug use have granted their friends expectation advantages, which should confer on them greater opportunities to perform and exert influence. Comparatively, considering that past research has shown teenagers untrusting of antidrug mass media messages, PSAs and their originators should have expectation disadvantages, that is, perceptions that they have little to contribute. It is not surprising, then, that research has shown antidrug PSAs to be unsuccessful at bringing about desired attitude or behavior change in young people (Black, 1988; Flay & Sobel, 1983; Schoenbachler & Ayers,1996).

Specifically, the National Institute on Drug Abuse recently conducted a study of 45,000 students in 433 different schools (Johnston, O'Malley, &

Bachman, 2000) and found that marijuana is still the most widely used illicit drug (Johnston et al., 2000). Every year marijuana is used on at least one occasion by 17% of 8th graders, by 32% of 10th graders, and by 38% of 12th graders (Johnston, O'Malley, & Bachman, 2000). Additionally, only 46% of 8th graders, 33% of 10th graders, and 24% of 12th graders believe people who smoke marijuana occasionally are putting themselves at great risk.

Even more disturbing is the realization that since 1991, the percentage of students in the 8th grade who have tried marijuana has increased from 10% to 22% in 1999; 10th grade lifetime prevalence has increased from 23% to 40% over the same span; and, 12th grade lifetime prevalence has increased from 37% to 50% (Johnston et al., 2000). Annual prevalence rates have shown corresponding increases. Additionally, disapproval toward people who try marijuana has declined: From 1991 to 1999, 8th grade students' stated disapproval toward people who try marijuana once or twice declined from 85% to 71%; 10th graders showed a similar drop from 75% to 56%; and 12th graders showed a decline from 69% to 49% (Johnston et al., 2000).

Following the EST framework, it seems quite feasible that antidrug PSAs are on the bottom of the power/prestige pecking order in the adolescent world. EST would suggest that all future antidrug mass media attempts are going to be framed in a negative light due to the PSAs' lack of past contributions. Given antidrug messages' low status, the messages will be paid little attention and will not be influential in the decision making process (Ridgeway & Berger, 1986). This might explain why antidrug PSAs have been found to lead adolescents to become more curious about illicit drugs (Wagner & Sundar, 1999) and to decrease adolescent viewers' sense of the dangers of drug use.

The implication of EST is that creators of mass media antidrug campaigns have a difficult road ahead of them. Before even one message of a new antidrug campaign airs, the audience members may already mistrust the message (Skinner & Slater, 1995) while placing far more trust in their friends when it comes to drug use (Hemmelstein, 1995). Furthermore, EST predicts that once the power and prestige order is formed, it becomes quite stable (Berger, Wagner, & Zelditch, 1985) and can only be changed by the presence of an exogenous factor or by a change in the initial conditions of the group action. The major question that health educators must answer is, how can they persuade adolescents to pay attention to messages that they perceive as not credible and void of any positive contributions?

Additionally, as discussed earlier, once a member is regarded in high esteem for one behavior, the high regard the member has earned will spread to additional types of behavior. In regards to mass media PSAs, one has to consider if past PSAs in all arenas (i.e., tobacco, alcohol, birth control, AIDS) influence how adolescents view drug messages. Can, for example, an unsuccessful tobacco campaign have carryover, decreasing the effectiveness of future antidrug campaigns?

Following EST, these guidelines are presented for creators of mass media antidrug PSAs:

1. Be aware that past campaigns have influenced how adolescents perceive present campaigns.
2. Be aware that adolescents will likely view present campaign efforts with a negative bias.
3. Be aware that adolescents do not trust and will not place much credence in mass media antidrug PSAs.
4. Be aware that past campaigns in other areas, such as tobacco, can influence how future antidrug campaigns are perceived.

Additionally, future research needs to ask the following questions:

1. Do the rules of EST generalize to the mass media?
2. What specific expectations do adolescents hold for the contributions of mass media antidrug PSAs? How strong are these expectations?
3. Do adolescents trust antidrug PSAs? If not, why not?
4. Do adolescents differentiate between antidrug PSAs and other health PSAs?

EXPECTANCY VIOLATIONS THEORY

The paramount assumption of nonverbal expectancy violations theory is that communication participants develop expectancies about how others behave (J. K. Burgoon, 1991; J. K. Burgoon & Jones, 1976; J. K. Burgoon, Newton, Walther, & Baesler, 1989). Although the term *expectancy* is commonly left undefined in much psychological and communication literature, in EVT it refers to cognitions about the anticipated communication of specific others. Put differently, expectancies comprise cognitive, affective, and conative components and include judgments of what behaviors are possible, feasible, appropriate, and typical for a particular setting, purpose, and set of participants. In the absence of any individuating information, expectancies derive from social norms and roles. When actors are familiar with targets due to firsthand interaction, observation, or third-party information, then expectations become target-specific, reflecting a combination of the social norms and particularizing information. Although the original theory focused narrowly on personal space and related proxemic violations, it has since been expanded not only to a wide range of nonverbal phenomena but is readily applicable to verbal phenomena. For this reason, the *nonverbal* appellation has been dropped.

Expectancies derive from a large number of actor, relationship, and context factors that jointly determine what behavioral pattern is anticipated (predictive expectancy) and regarded as appropriate (prescriptive expectancy). For example, public figures are expected, in the predictive sense, to maintain a poised demeanor when speaking in public and to avoid embarrassing mannerisms or ungrammatical language (prescriptive expectancy).

The same factors that combine to yield expectations also affect another key concept in the theory—*communicator reward valence*. Also referred to simply as communicator valence, this concept captures how well the communicator is regarded by targets. As such, it taps into the same concept in EST of expectation advantages that create power and prestige orders (although the two theories developed independently and communicator valence is broader than expectation advantages). In both theories, actors have valences associated with them that permit them to be arrayed on a reward continuum from highly rewarding to highly unrewarding as message sources. EVT does not specifiy the algorithms by which the factors producing expectations and communicator valence are combined or weighted; it merely begins with the assumption that at the point of communicating, actors have associated expectations for their communicative behavior and an associated valence. Communicator valence not only should exert a direct effect on how credible, attractive, and persuasive they will be but should also moderate the impact of any expectancy violations.

Regarding the impact of expectancy violations, EVT posits the counterintuitive position that violating social norms and expectations may sometimes be a superior strategy to conformity for achieving such communication outcomes as attraction, credibility, relational satisfaction, helping behavior, and persuasion (Baxter & Bullis, 1986; J. K. Burgoon, 1978, 1983, 1993; J. K. Burgoon, Coker, & Coker, 1986; J. K. Burgoon & Hale, 1988; J. K. Burgoon & Jones, 1976; J. K. Burgoon, Segrin, & Dunbar, in press; J. K. Burgoon, Stacks, & Woodall, 1979).

The process begins with an actor engaging in a violation, such as intruding on another's personal space, engaging in an intimate touch, or reducing conversational involvement to a detached, remote level. Violations, like all manner of novel and unexpected stimuli, are thought to be attention-gaining and, in many cases, physiologically arousing. Specifically, violations can create a "stop, look, and listen" sort of reaction that leads to a heightened arousal, leading receivers of the communication to direct focal attention to the message and its source (e.g., J. K. Burgoon, 1978; LePoire & J. K. Burgoon, 1994). Although initial definitions of arousal incorporated both cognitive and psychological components of arousal, the theory has been revised to downplay arousal per se and emphasize the attentional shift that is produced (J. K. Burgoon & Hale, 1988), that is, to the "alertness or orienting response that diverts attention away from the ostensive purpose of the interaction and focuses it toward the source of the arousal-the initiator of the violation" (p. 62). Put differently, violations can galvanize attention toward the unexpected aspects of messages and their sources, thus bringing these message and actor features into the foreground.

The arousal is thought to activate a two-part interpretation and evaluation appraisal process in which perceivers (a) attempt to make sense of the violation and (b) evaluate the desirability of the violation. For example, if an older, apparently conservative, formally dressed adult were depicted smoking marijuana, adolescents would probably regard this as unexpected behavior and find themselves engaging in more active interpretive and attributional processes to answer such questions as, why is this person smoking and what does it mean? In cases of ambiguities about the meaning of the behavior, EVT posits that communicator valence will influence what interpretations are made. For highly regarded actors, positive interpretations are likely to be selected (e.g., "maybe he is using it for medicinal purposes); for poorly regarded communicators, less benign interpretations are likely (e.g., "he's trying to be cool"). The act is also evaluated for its desirability. Again, communicator valence may moderate the evaluation, with highly regarded actors having a higher probability (but not a guarantee) that their behavior will be judged more favorably than that of poorly regarded actors. Thus, an athlete who is popular with teens can get away with expressing disdain for smoking, whereas a politician cannot. In other words, the same act will be judged differently, depending on the valence of the person committing it.

The combination of the interpretation of a violation and its evaluation determine whether a violation qualifies as positive or negative. Positive violations are posited to produce more favorable outcomes than conforming to expectations, even when the behavior is a positive confirmation. Negative violations are thought to produce more unfavorable outcomes than behavioral confirmations, even negative ones (although this latter claim has come into question of late). To use an extended example, an adult media spokesperson who mimics adolescents' disheveled and baggy clothing, adopts "teen speak," and conveys a blasé attitude through demeanor and language may be viewed as engaging in a violation. If the combined nonverbal and verbal style is interpreted as rebelling against authority, and rebellious behavior is evaluated favorably, this will qualify as a positive violation and should be an effective means of persuading youth. If, however, these same behaviors are seen as trying too hard to be "hip" and as a blatant attempt to identify with teenagers, it may be evaluated as insincere and manipulative and, therefore, a negative violation. In such instances, it will backfire, producing even less persuasion than if the adult spokesperson had maintained his or her expected (stereotypical) nonverbal and verbal style.

Research has shown that behaviors that violate previously held expectations influence interaction outcomes in a plethora of situations: daily exchanges (e.g., Langer, 1978), intercultural encounters (e.g., Gudykunst, 1985; Gudykunst & Kim, 1984), physician-patient interactions (e.g., Birk & M. Burgoon, 1989), small group negotiation (e.g., J. K. Burgoon, Stacks, & Burch, 1982), sales encounters (e.g., J. K. Burgoon & Aho, 1982), employment interviews (e.g., Imada & Hackel, 1977), and relationship development (e.g., Kelley & Read, 1990). J. K. Burgoon et al. (in press) after reviewing the empirical findings in support of EVT (e.g., J. K. Burgoon, 1983, 1995; J. K. Burgoon & Hale, 1988; J. K. Burgoon & Le Poire, 1993; J. K. Burgoon, LePoire, & Rosenthal, 1995; J. K. Burgoon et al., 1989; Le Poire & J. K. Burgoon, 1994; LePoire & Yoshimura, 1999), concluded that although the findings do not universally support the theory, they do warrant the following conclusions:

1. Expectancies do guide behavior and have persistent effects on interaction.
2. Communicator reward valence exerts both main and interaction effects on communication patterns and outcomes such that highly regarded communicators (e.g., those having higher socioeconomic status, reputed intelligence and expertise, purchasing power, physical attractiveness, similarity to partner, or giving positive feedback) elicit more involved and pleasant communication from interaction partners and receive more favorable postinteraction evaluations (e.g., on credibility, attractiveness, and persuasiveness) than those who are poorly regarded; and actors with higher reward valence have more favorable meanings ascribed to their nonverbal behavior than those with lower reward valence.
3. Some violations, such as deviations from normative conversational distances and use of touch, are ambiguous or polysemous and susceptible to reward valence moderating their effects; other violations, such as gaze aversion and substantial increases or decreases in con-

versational distance, have fairly consensual social meanings that directly affect their status as positive or negative violations.

4. Nonverbal violations heighten attention and create orienting responses.

5. Nonverbal violations often (although not always) alter responses relative to confirmations such that positive violations produce more desirable communication patterns and outcomes, and negative violations produce less desirable ones, than behavioral confirmations.

Referring to earlier discussion concerning EST, it is predicted that once the power and prestige order is formed it becomes quite stable (Berger et al., 1985) and can only be changed by the presence of an exogenous factor or by a change in the initial conditions of the group action. This begs the question: If adolescents' expectations of PSAs can be violated, can it lead to an orienting response that will cause the adolescent to give greater focus to the message?

Although EVT has not been applied to the interaction between adolescent viewers and mass media advertisements, the examples offered here should make it plain that the theory has potential applicability to media sources and messages. It seems plausible, for instance, that violations from the mass media can cause the same increase in heart rate, decrease in pulse volume, and shift toward the cause of the violation as occur with interpersonal violations (Le Poire & J. K. Burgoon, 1996). For example, Flay (1986) stated that ads that are more novel and varied should have greater impact. If, following the premises of EST, adolescents have come to expect little or no contributions from mass media antidrug messages, a violation of expectations may be exactly what is needed.

Unfortunately, we do not know at this time what it would take to violate adolescents' expectations of antidrug PSAs. Research is needed in this area. What do adolescents expect from PSAs? What would it take to violate their expectations? Obviously, past EVT research in interpersonal contexts does not offer direct answers. However, past advertising research does suggest that if we can violate the adolescents' expectations and cause an orienting response, this extra attention paid to the PSA can lead to increased campaign effectiveness.

Klapper (1960) and Katz (1988), among others, have suggested that a major mediator of media effects concerns individual selectivity; that is, individual predispositions to attend or not to attend to messages on particular issues. Relations among brand perceptions, ad perceptions, attitude toward the ad, and brand attitudes vary depending on the level of advertising message involvement (involvement with the communication) and advertising execution involvement (involvement with the contextual, non-content aspects of the ads, such as source and executional characteristics) evoked at the time of ad exposure (Lutz, 1985; Lutz, MacKenzie, & Blech, 1983; MacKenzie & Lutz, 1989). Attention to the commercials has been cited as an obvious prerequisite to any PSA effects on knowledge, attitude, and behavior (Lorch et al., 1994). Hu and Mitchell (1981) found that the more a viewer is involved in the viewing of a PSA, the greater is the viewer's ability to recall the PSA. In short, if research can determine what it would take to violate adolescents' expectations of PSAs, and to have those violations committed by message sources whom are known to be positively valenced, the effectiveness of the campaign can be greatly increased.

Following EVT, these guidelines are presented for creators of mass media antidrug PSAs:

1. By violating the adolescents' expectations an orienting response will be created. This will lead to the adolescents focusing on the source of the violation—the PSA!
2. Once the adolescents focus on the PSA they will seek to make sense of the violation and to evaluate it.
3. Attention paid to these novel or unexpected PSAs should amplify their effectiveness relative to PSAs that are expected.

Additionally, future research needs to ask the following questions:

1. Is it possible to violate adolescents' expectations of antidrug PSAs?
2. Will violating adolescents' expectations via PSAs have the same effect as nonverbal violations of expectations?

LANGUAGE EXPECTANCY THEORY

Language Expectancy Theory (LET) is an axiomatic theory, focusing on the effects of linguistic variations on message persuasiveness. This theory is based on a rather simple assumption: Language is a rule-governed system and people develop expectations concerning the language or message strategies employed by others in persuasive attempts (M. Burgoon, 1989, 1990, 1995; M. Burgoon, Jones, & Stewart, 1975; M. Burgoon & Miller, 1985).

Much like EVT, LET posits that violations can either be positive or negative (M. Burgoon, 1989, 1990). However, LET differs from the other theories presented in that LET has already been applied to the mass media realm. Specifically, LET has been found to explain the success of negative attack campaigns in politics (Pfau, Parrott, & Lindquist, 1992), compliance and satisfaction with physicians' instructions (M. Burgoon, Birk, & Hall, 1991), effectiveness of communication strategies designed to improve both initial and long-term medical adherence (Klingle, 1993; Klingle & M. Burgoon, 1995), and adherence to sun safety recommendations (Buller et al., 2000).

LET proposes that people develop cultural and sociological expectations concerning the type of language to be used in specific contexts depending on the situation and the communicator. Specifically, LET looks at expectations regarding persuasive communications and whether the type of language utilized will lead to greater acceptance or rejection of the persuasive message. When expectations concerning language use in a particular context are negatively violated, receivers will react by either not being influenced by the speaker or, in the worst case, being persuaded in the opposite direction of the speaker's advocated position. When the communicator positively violates expectations regarding appropriate persuasive communication behavior, the communicator's message will have increased persuasive strength.

Positive violations can be obtained in two ways: (a) when the enacted behavior is better or more preferred than that which was expected in the situation, or (b) when negatively evaluated sources conform more closely than expected to cultural values, societal norms, or situational exigencies. Change occurs in the first case because enacted behavior is outside the normative bandwidth in a positive direction and such behavior prompts attitude and or behavioral changes. In the second condition, a person who is expected to behave incompetently or inappropriately conforms to cultural norms and/or expected social roles, resulting in an overly positive evaluation of the source and subsequently, of change advocated by that actor. Negative violations of expectations result from language choices or the selection of message strategies that lie outside the bandwidth of socially acceptable behavior in a negative direction. The result is no attitude and/or behavioral changes, or changes in the direction opposite to that intended by the actor.

Negatively evaluated speakers only need to conform to more closely expected social norms, cultural values, or situational requirements to receive an overly positive evaluation. To receive a similar overly positive evaluation, a neutral or positively evaluated speaker will have to positively exceed the normative bandwidth of expectations. By committing either the former or the latter positive violation, persuasive effectiveness can be enhanced. On the flip side, an overly negative evaluation, which will result in no attitude change in the best scenario and attitude change in the opposite direction in the worst, occurs when the speaker selects a message strategy or language choice that lies on the negative exterior of socially acceptable behavior.

Similar to EST, where group members in high status will have greater power of influence, LET proposes that communicators with high credibility have a greater range of language strategies and compliance-gaining techniques to choose from than communicators with low credibility. Specifically, LET proposes that highly credible sources can be more successful using low intensity appeals and more aggressive compliance-gaining messages than communicators of low credibility using either strong or mild language or more prosocial compliance-gaining strategies. It is further proposed that communicators perceived as low in credibility or those unsure of their perceived credibility will usually be more persuasive if they employ appeals low in instrumental verbal aggression or elect to use more prosocial compliance-gaining message strategies.

Three additional propositions of LET are as follows:

1. People in this society have normative expectations about appropriate persuasive communication behavior that are gender specific, such that males are usually more persuasive using highly intense persuasive appeals and compliance-gaining message attempts, while females are usually more persuasive using low-intensity appeals and unaggressive compliance-gaining messages.

2. People in this society have normative expectations about the level of fear-arousing appeals, opinionated language, language intensity, sequential message techniques, and compliance-gaining attempts varying in instrumental verbal aggression appropriate to persuasive discourse.

3. Fear arousal that is irrelevant to the content of the message of the harmful consequences of failure to comply with the advocated position mediates receptivity to different levels of language intensity and compliance-gaining strategies varying in instrumental verbal aggression. Receivers aroused by the induction of irrelevant fear or suffering from specific anxiety are most receptive to persuasive messages using low intensity and verbally unaggressive compliance-gaining attempts but are unreceptive to intense appeals or verbally aggressive suasory strategies.

Recent research utilizing LET has demonstrated both the ecological validity and utility of the theory in a number of health behavior contexts, including a sun safety health campaign (Buller, Borland, & M. Burgoon, 1998), tobacco prevention campaigns (Grandpre, Alvaro, M. Burgoon, Miller, &

Hall, in press) and doctor-patient interactions (M. Burgoon & J. K. Burgoon, 1990; M. Burgoon et al., 1991; Klingle & M. Burgoon, 1995).

At first glance, it may appear that LET perfectly lays out approaches for mass media antidrug PSAs. However, there is one significant problem: We cannot assume that speakers whom adults find credible will be perceived as credible by adolescents. The success of using LET as a framework requires creators of advertising campaigns to be aware of which sources of information are credible not just to adolescents but to the adolescents who are at greatest risk for drug use. Additionally, just because adolescents find a speaker credible does not imply that adolescents will find the speaker credible in all contexts. For example, Serena Williams may be a highly credible source for tennis issues, but may not be held in high regard for adolescents at risk for doing drugs. As stated by Schoenbachler and Whittler (1996), "Although PSAs were implemented to discourage drug consumption, little is known about how young people respond to those messages" (p. 37).

McPeek and Edwards (1975) conducted an experiment that perfectly highlights this point. Students listened to an antidrug message; the message was attributed either to a seminarian or a hippie. The hippie was found to be more credible and more persuasive than the seminarian. Would the hippie always be seen as more credible than the seminarian? Obviously not, but when it came to the effects of drugs, the hippie was far more trusted, doubtless because the message served as a positive violation of the expectation, set by the speaker's appearance, that he would advocate drug use.

CONCLUDING THOUGHTS

The three theories we have presented here demonstrate the import that social (as compared to self) expectations can hold in determining the impact of persuasive messages generally and PSAs specifically. However, PSA creators must use EST, LET, and EVT with caution. The wrong advertisement at best will be ignored and at worst will cause a boomerang effect. Before money is spent on airtime, it is essential to know the effect that the commercials will have, and not just on any kids but on the target audience to be persuaded. Answering the critical questions requires pretest and evaluation research. We conclude with some guidance on the questions to be addressed and the methods that might be used to answer them.

First, research must answer what specific expectations and evaluations adolescents hold for mass media antidrug PSAs. We have argued that adolescents' reactions toward PSAs are typically dismissive and negative. The first step in utilizing the proposed approach must include pretest surveys or focus-group interviews to assess adolescents' awareness of, expectations for, evaluation of, and trust in past PSA media campaigns. Additionally, the strength of these attitudes must be taken into account. Weakly held expectations and evaluations should be more malleable than strongly held ones.

Moreover, campaigns do not occur in a vacuum. Not only might past drug campaigns influence how present PSAs are viewed, but also past PSAs for alcohol, drunk driving, and AIDS may influence how these ads are perceived. Perceptions concerning the potential for a quality contribution on the part of a PSA will influence how the adolescent viewer processes the advertisement. One component of pretest assessment efforts should address whether adolescents differentiate antidrug PSAs from other PSAs such as those that are antitobacco. In other words, research should determine how topic-specific or generalized the expectations and evaluations are.

Another key part of the pretest assessment effort, if campaigns are to be successfully targeted, is to conduct research on diverse samples of adolescents. Research shows that rebellious kids react differently to messages than nonrebellious kids (Alvaro et al., 2000). Special emphasis should be given to ethnic differences and how those differences might affect reactions to a given ad. Researchers looking at various social and ethnic groups have determined that assessing social, environmental, and psychological factors, even among groups that are considered to be homogeneous, is essential for a substance abuse intervention to be successful at changing behaviors (Longshore, 1997; Resnicow, Soler, Braithwaite, Ahluwalia, & Butler, 2000; Trimble, 1990-1991).

Second, a critical piece of the testing effort must be directed to how PSAs can capture and hold adolescents' attention. If, as posited by this chapter and past research (Feingold & Knapp, 1977; Hanneman, 1973; Skinner & Slater, 1995), adolescents do not put much stock in PSAs, a major challenge will be creating something akin to the an orienting response. Research must test to see if television commercials can create an orienting response and, if so, how best to violate expectations in PSA so as to maximize the likelihood of eliciting such a response. The goal is simple: direct the adolescents' attention toward the antidrug PSA. A glamorous celebrity or rock musician who might be otherwise be suspected of using drugs, for example, may be an unexpected spokesperson for an antidrug PSA capable of creating the desired orienting response.

One approach would be to measure physiological reactions on a small bench sample to see what prior ads or features of ads create arousal and an orienting response (see, e.g., Le Poire & Burgoon, 1996), then test newly created PSAs for their capacity to galvanize attention among teens. As discussed throughout, we cannot rely on intuition to determine what incidents might bring about such a response. What appeals to adults may not be the same thing that piques the interest of young people. Thus, pilot testing and follow-up evaluation research must replace or at least supplement the "creative instincts" that have guided past efforts. There is no reason to spend millions of dollars on a campaign with the hope that a satisfactory orienting response has been created, when pilot testing among homogeneous subsets of adolescents can dissolve the majority of guesswork for a fraction of the cost.

A third question to be answered asks, what features of PSAs are likely to function as positive violations? More specifically, what nonverbal behaviors, message content, and contextual features should spokespeople or other figures in PSAs employ to create the novelty, incongruity, and surprise value needed for a message to be a violation? And what are needed to ensure that any violation is a positive rather than a negative one? Compared to creating a typical, expected message, a positive violation can increase the persuasive strength of a PSA, but a negative violation can significantly impair message effectiveness (J. K. Burgoon et al., in press; M. Burgoon, 1989, 1990).

According to EVT, unexpected actions that have favorable meanings associated with them, are judged as desirable, and/or emanate from attractive sources are the best bets for being positive violations. Once again, of paramount importance is the sizing up of the interpretations and evaluations associated with depicted behaviors and messages in addition to the credibility and attractiveness of those enacting them. Speakers whom adolescents find credible will have a greater range of language strategies and compliance-gaining techniques to choose from than communicators whom adolescents believe lack credibility. However, a speaker who would be viewed as credible in one realm may not be credible in another. For example, as discussed earlier, although Serena Williams would be a credible source in terms of athletic training, it's doubtful that many adolescents find Serena Williams to have credible information concerning drug use. Only after identifying not only which spokespeople are favorably regarded by adolescents within the drug realm but also which ones adolescents are least likely to expect to give an antidrug message can solid research-based decisions be made.

There is no question that the theoretically-driven model put forth necessitates some significant pilot testing before a PSA is aired and also necessitates subsequent evaluative research to determine its effectiveness. The payoff for the extra effort "up front" should be a successful antidrug PSA that not only saves money in the long run but also has greater potential to persuade the target demographic. The pay-off for conducting follow-up research is to pinpoint what features of commercials are most and least effective and which audiences are most persuaded. Although the same messages that appeal to adolescents unfortunately may not be immediately appealing to nonadolescents, who frequently prejudge PSAs on personal standards, if advertisers let theory and research guide their decision-making, the resultant ads should generate enough spillover to convert a wider audience than is being reached at present.

ACKNOWLEDGMENTS

The research discussed in this chapter was funded by the National Institute on Drug Abuse (grant DA12578, William Crano & Michael Burgoon, principal investigators). All conclusions and interpretations are those of the authors and do not necessarily reflect those of the funding agencies.

REFERENCES

Alvaro, E. M., Siegel, J. T., Grandpre, J. R., Burgoon, M., Miller, C. H., & Hall, J. R. (May, 2000). *Adolescent reactance and anti-smoking campaigns III: At-risk youth.* Paper presented at the annual meeting of the National Communication Association, Seattle, WA.

Atkin, C. K., & Freimuth, V. (1989). Formative evaluation research in campaign design. In R. E. Rice & C. K. Atkin (Eds.), *Public communication campaigns* (pp. 131-150). Newbury Park, CA: Sage.

Baxter, L. A., & Bullis, C. (1986). Turning points in developing romantic relationships. *Human Communication Research, 4,* 469-493.

Berger, J., Cohen, B. P., Snell, J. L., & Zelditch, M. (1962). *Types of formalization in small-group research.* Boston: Houghton Mifflin.

Berger, J., & Conner, T. L. (1966). *Performance expectations and behavior in small groups.* Stanford, CA: Stanford University Laboratory for Social Research.

Berger, J., & Conner, T. L. (1974). Performance expectations and behavior in small groups: A revised formulation. In J. Berger, T. L. Conner, & M. H. Fisek (Eds.), *Expectation states theory: A theoretical research program* (pp. 100-125). Cambridge, MA: Winthrop Publishers, Inc.

Berger, J., Conner, T. L., & Fisek, M. H. (Eds.). (1974). *Expectancy states theory: A theoretical research program.* Cambridge, MA: Winthrop.

Berger, J., Conner, T. L., & McKeown, W. L. (1974). Evaluations and the formation and maintenance of performance expectations. In J. Berger, T. L. Conner, & M. H. Fisek (Eds.), *Expectation states theory: A theoretical research
program* (pp. 27-52). Cambridge, MA: Winthrop.

Berger, J., Rosenholtz, S. J., & Zelditch, M. (1980). Status organizing processes.
Annual Review of Sociology, 6, 479-508.

Berger, J., Wagner, D. G., & Zelditch, M. J. (1985). Introduction: Expectancy sates
theory: Review and assessment. In J. Berger & M. J. Zelditch (Eds.), *Status,
rewards, and influence: How expectations organize behavior.* San Francisco,
CA: Jossey-Bass.

Birk, T., & Burgoon, M. (1989). *The effects of instrumental verbal aggression and
physician gender on compliance in the medical context.* Unpublished manuscript, University of Arizona.

Black, G. (1991). Changing attitudes toward drug use: The effect of advertising. In
E. L. Donohew, H. E. Sypher, & W. J. Bukoski (Eds.), *Persuasive communication and drug abuse prevention.* Hillsdale, NJ: Lawrence Erlbaum Associates.

Block, R. I., Farnham, S., Braverman, K., & Noyes, R. (1990). Long-term marijuana use and subsequent effects on learning and cognitive functions related
to school achievement: Preliminary study. *National Institute on Drug Abuse:
Research Monograph Series, 101*, 96-111.

Brey, J. W., Zarkin, G. G., Ringwalt, C., & Qi, J. (2000). The relationship between
marijuana initiation and dropping out of high school. *Health Economics, 9*, 9-
18.

Brook, J. S., Balka, B. B., Whiteman, M. (1999). The risks for late adolescence of
early adolescent marijuana use. *American Journal of Public Health, 89*, 1549-
1554.

Buller, D. B., Borland, R., & Burgoon, M. (1998). Impact of behavioral intention on
effectiveness of message features: Evidence from the Family Sun Safety
Project. *Human Communication Research, 24*, 433-453.

Buller, D. B., Burgoon, M., Hall, J. R., Levine, N., Taylor, A. M., Beach, B. H.,
Melcher, C., Buller, M. K., Bowen, S. L., Hunsaker, F. G., & Bergen, A.
(2000). Using language intensity to increase the success of a family intervention to protect children from ultraviolet radiation: Predictions from language
expectancy theory. *Preventive Medicine: An International Journal Devoted to
Practice & Theory, 30*, 103-1147.

Burgoon, J. K. (1978). A communication model of personal space and violations:
Expectation and an initial test. *Human Communication Research, 4*, 129-142.

Burgoon, J. K. (1983). Nonverbal violations of expectations. In J. M. Wiemann &
R. P. Harrison (Eds.), *Nonverbal interaction* (pp. 77-112). Beverly Hills, CA:
Sage.

Burgoon, J. K. (1991). Relational message interpretations of touch, conversational
distance, and posture. *Journal of Nonverbal Behavior, 15*, 233-259.

Burgoon, J. K. (1993). Interpersonal expectations, expectancy violations, and
emotional communication. *Journal of Language and Social Psychology, 12*,
30-48.

Burgoon, J. K. (1995). Cross-cultural and intercultural applications of expectancy violations theory. In R. L. Wiseman (Ed.), *Intercultural communication theory: International and Intercultural Communication Annual* (Vol. 19, pp. 194-214). Thousand Oaks, CA: Sage.

Burgoon, J. K., & Aho, L. (1982). Three field experiments on the effects of violations of conversational distance. *Communication Monographs, 49,* 71-88.

Burgoon, J. K., Coker, D. A., & Coker, R. A. (1986). Communicative effects of gaze behavior: A test of two contrasting explanations. *Human Communication Research, 12,* 495-524.

Burgoon, J. K., & Hale, J. L. (1988). Nonverbal expectancy violations: Model elaboration and application to immediacy behaviors. *Communication Monographs, 55,* 58-97.

Burgoon, J. K., & Jones, S. B. (1976). Toward a theory of personal space expectations and their violations. *Human Communication Research, 2,* 131-146.

Burgoon, J. K., & Le Poire, B. A. (1993). Effects of communication expectancies, actual communication, and expectancy disconfirmation on evaluations and their communication behavior. *Human Communication Research, 20,* 75-107.

Burgoon, J. K., Le Poire, B. A., & Rosenthal, R. (1995). Effects of preinteraction expectancies and target communication on perceiver reciprocity and compensation in dyadic interaction. *Journal of Experimental Social Psychology, 31,* 287-321.

Burgoon, J. K., Newton, D. A., Walther, J. B., & Baesler, E. J. (1989). Nonverbal expectancy violations and conversational involvement. *Journal of Nonverbal Behavior, 13,* 97-120.

Burgoon, J. K., Segrin, C., & Dunbar, N. E. (in press). Nonverbal communication and social influence. In M. Pfau & J. P. Dillard (Eds.), *The persuasion handbook: Theory and practice.* Thousand Oaks, CA: Sage.

Burgoon, J. K., Stacks, D. W., & Burch, S. (1982). The role of interpersonal rewards and violations of distancing expectations in achieving influence in small groups. *Communication, 11,* 114-128.

Burgoon, J. K., Stacks, D. W., & Woodall, W. G. (1979). A communicative model of violations of distancing expectations. *Western Journal of Speech Communication, 43,* 153-167.

Burgoon, J. K., & Walther, J. B. (1990). Nonverbal expectancies and the consequences of violations. *Human Communication Research, 17,* 232-265.

Burgoon, M. (1995). Language expectancy theory: Elaboration, explication, and extension. In C. R. Berger & M. Burgoon (Eds.), *Communication and social influence processes* (pp. 29-52). East Lansing:: Michigan State University Press.

Burgoon, M. (1989). Messages and persuasive effects. In J. Bradac (Ed.), *Message effects in communication science* (pp. 129-164). Newbury Park, CA: Sage.

Burgoon, M. (1990). Language and social influence. In H. Giles & P. Robinson (Eds.), *Handbook of language and social psychology* (pp. 51-72). London: Wiley & Sons.

Burgoon, M., Birk, T. S., & Hall, J. R. (1991). Compliance and satisfaction with physician-patient communication: An expectancy theory interpretation of gender differences. *Human Communication Research, 18*, 177-208.

Burgoon, M., & Burgoon, J. K. (1990). Compliance-gaining and health care. In J. P. Dillard (Ed.), *Seeking compliance: The production of interpersonal influence messages* (pp. 161-188). Scottsdale, AZ: Gorsuch Scarisbrick.

Burgoon, M., Jones, S. B., & Stewart, D. (1975). Toward a message-centered theory of persuasion: Three empirical investigations of language intensity. *Human Communication Research, 1*, 240-256.

Burgoon, M., & Miller, G. R. (1985). An expectancy interpretation of language and persuasion. In H. Giles & R. N. St. Clair (Eds.), *Recent advances in language communication and social psychology*. London: Lawrence Erlbaum.

Cohen, E. G. (1972). Interracial interaction disability. *Human Relations, 25*, 9-24.

Cohen, E. G., & Sharan, S. (1980). Modifying status relations in Israeli youth: An application of expectation states theory. *Journal of Cross-Cultural Psychology, 11*, 364-384.

Ellickson, P., Bui, K., Bell, R. M., & McGuigan, K. A. (1998). Does early drug use increase the risk of dropping out of high school? *Journal of Drug Issues, 28*, 357-380.

Feingold, P. C., & Knapp, M. L. (1977). Antidrug abuse commercials. *Journal of Communication, 27*, 20-28.

Fishbein, M., & Ajzen, I. (1975). *Belief, attitude, intention, and behavior: An introduction to theory and research*. Reading, MA: Addison-Wesley.

Flay, B. (1986). Efficacy and effectiveness trials (and other phases of research) in the development of health promotion programs. *Preventive Medicine, 15*, 451-474.

Flay, B. R., & Sobel, J. L. (1983). The role of mass media in preventing adolescent substance abuse. In T. J. Glynn, C. G. Leukefeld, & J. P. Ludford (Eds.), *Preventing adolescent drug abuse: Intervention strategies* (Vol. 47, pp. 5-36). Rockville, MD: National Institute on Drug Abuse.

Grandpre, J., Alvaro, E. M., Burgoon, M., Miller, C., & Hall, J. R. (in press). Adolescent reactance and anti-smoking campaigns: A theoretical approach. *Health Communication*.

Gudykunst, W. B., & Kim, Y. Y. (1984). *Communicating with strangers*. Reading, MA: Addison-Wesley.

Gudykunst, W. B. (1985). The influence of cultural similarity, type of relationship, and self-monitoring on uncertainty reduction processes. *Communication Monographs, 52*, 203-217.

Hanneman, G. J. (1973). Communicating drug abuse information among college students. *Public Opinion Quarterly, 37*, 171-191.

Harwood, H., Fountain, D., & Livermore, G. (1998). *The economic costs of alcohol and drug abuse in the United States, 1992*. National Institute of Drug Abuse and National Institute on Alcohol Abuse and Alcoholism. Rockville, MD: U.S. Department of Health and Human Services. Available online: http://165.112.61/EconomicCosts/Intro.html.

Hemmelstein, N. (1995). Adolescent marijuana use and perception of risk. *Journal of Alcohol and Drug Education, 41,* 1-15.

Hu, T., & Mitchell, M. E. (1981). *Cost effectiveness evaluation of the 1978 media drug abuse prevention television campaign.* Rockville, MD: National Institute on Drug Abuse.

Imada, A. S., & Hackel, M. D. (1977). Influence of nonverbal communication and rater proximity on impressions and decision in simulated employment interviews. *Journal of Applied Psychology, 62,* 285-300.

Johnston, L. D., O'Malley, P. M., & Bachman, J. G. (2000). *The monitoring of the future: National results on adolescent drug use.* (Rep. No. 00-4690). Bethesda, MD: National Institute on Drug Abuse.

Kann, L., Kinchen, S. A., Williams, B. I., Ross, J. G., Lowry, R., Grunbaum, J., & Kolbe, L. J. (2000). Youth risk behavior surveillance--United States, 1999. *MMWR Surveillance Summaries, 49*(SS05), 1-96.

Katz, E. (1988). On conceptualizaing media effects: Another look. In S. Oskamp (Ed.), *Television as a social issue. Applied social psychology annual* (Vol. 8, pp. 361-374). Beverly Hills, CA: Sage.

Kelley, D. L., & Read, V. S. (1990, October). *Changes in relational expectations and relational behaviors across family life-cycle.* Paper presented at the annual meeting of the Speech Communication Association, Chicago.

Kelsey, B. L. (1998). The dynamics of multicultural groups: Ethnicity as a determinant of leadership. *Small Group Research, 29,* 602-623.

Klapper, J. T. (1960). *The effects of mass communication.* Glencoe, IL: Free Press.

Klingle, R. S. (1993). Bringing time into physician compliance gaining research: Toward a reinforcement expectancy theory of strategy effectiveness. *Health Communication, 5,* 283-308.

Klingle, R. S., & Burgoon, M. (1995). Patient compliance and satisfaction with physician influence attempts: A reinforcement expectancy approach to compliance-gaining over time. *Communication Research, 22,* 148-187.

Langer, E. J. (1978). Rethinking the role of thought in social interactions. In J. H. Harvey, W. Ickes, & R. F. Kidd (Eds.), *New directions in attribution research.* (pp. 36-58). Hillsdale, NJ: Lawrence Erlbaum.

Le Poire, B. A., & Burgoon, J. K. (1994). Two contrasting explanations of involvement violations: Expectancy violations theory and discrepancy arousal theory. *Human Communication Research, 20,* 560-591.

Le Poire, B. A., & Burgoon, J. K. (1996). Usefulness of differentiating arousal responses within communication theories: Orienting response of defensive arousal within theories of expectancy violation. *Communication Monographs, 63,* 208-230.

Le Poire, B. A., & Yoshimura, S. M. (1999). The effects of expectancies and actual communication on nonverbal adaptation and communication outcomes: A test of interaction adaptation theory. *Communication Monographs, 66,* 1-30.

Lockheed, M. E., & Hall, K. P. (1976). Conceptualizing sex as a status characteristic: Applications to leadership training strategies. *Journal of Social Issues, 32,* 111-124.

Longshore, D. (1997). Treatment motivation among Mexican American drug-using arrestees. *Hispanic Journal of Behavioral Sciences. 19*, 214-229

Lorch, E. P., Palmgreen, P., Donohew, L., Helm, D., Baer, S. A., & Dsilva, M. U. (1994). Program context, sensation-seeking, and attention to televised anti-drug public service announcements. *Human Communication Research, 20,* 390-412.

Lutz, R. J. (1985). Consumer psychology. In E. M. Altmaier & M. E. Meyer (Eds.), *Applied specialties in psychology* (pp. 275-304). New York: Random House.

Lutz, R. J., MacKenzie, S. & Blech, C. (1983). The role of attitude toward the ad as a mediator of Advertising Effectiveness: A test of competing explanations. *Journal of Marketing Research, 23*, 130-143.

MacKenzie, S. B. & Lutz, R. J. (1989). An empirical examination of the structural antecedents of attitude toward the ad in an advertising pretesting context. *Journal of Marketing, 53*, 48-65.

McPeek, R. W., & Edwards, J. D. (1975). Expectancy disconformation and attitude change. *Journal of Social Psychology, 96*, 193-208.

Mitchell, T. R. (1982). Expectancy influences in social interaction. In N. T. Feather (Ed.), *Expectations and actions: Expectancy value models in psychology* (pp. 293-312). Hillsdale, NJ: Lawrence Erlbaum Associates.

Nahas, G., & Latour, C. (1992). The human toxicity of marijuana. *Medical Journal of Australia, 156*, 495-497.

Nelson, P. (1970). Information and consumer behavior. *Journal of Political Economy, 78*, 311-329.

O'Keefe, G. J., & Reid, K. (1990). The uses and effects of public service advertising. In L. A. Grunig, & J. E. Grunig (Eds.), *Public relations research annual* (Vol. 2, pp. 67-91). Hillsdale, NJ: Lawrence Erlbaum Associates.

Osgood, D. W., Johnston, L. D., O'Malley, P. M., & Bachman, J. G. (1988). The generality of deviance in late adolescence and early adulthood. *American Sociological Review, 53*, 81-83.

Partnership for a Drug-Free America. (1999). *Partnership attitude tracking survey, Spring 1999, Teens in Grades 7 through 12.* New York: Author.

Pfau, M., Parrott, R., & Lindquist, B. (1992). An expectancy theory explanation of the effectiveness of political attack television spots: A case study. *Journal of Applied Communication Research, 20*, 235-253.

Polen, M. R., Sidney, S., Tekawa, I. S., Sadler, M., & Friedman, G. D. (1993). Health care use by frequent marijuana smokers who do not smoke tobacco. *Western Journal of Medicine, 158*, 596-601.

Rashotte, L. S., & Smith-Lovin, L. (1997). Who benefits from being bold: The interactive effects of task cues and status characteristics on influence in mock jury groups. In B. Markovsky, & M. J. Lovaglia (Eds.), *Advances in group processes.* (pp. 235-255). Greenwich, CT: JAI Press, Inc.

Resnicow, K., Soler, R., Braithwaite, R. L., Ahluwalia, J. S., & Butler, J. (2000). Cultural sensitivity in substance use prevention. *Journal of Community Psychology, 28*, 271-290.

Ridgeway, C. L., & Berger, J. (1986). Expectations, legitimation, and dominance behavior in task groups. *American Sociological Review, 51*, 603-617.

Schoenbachler, D. D., & Ayers, D. J. (1996). Adolescent response to antidrug public service announcements: A segmentation approach. *Journal of Applied Business Research, 12*, 9-22.

Schoenbachler, D. D., & Whittler, T. E. (1996). Adolescent processing of social and physical threat communications. *Journal of Advertising, 25*, 37-54.

Skinner, E. R., & Slater, M. D. (1995). Family communication patterns, rebelliousness, and adolescent reactions to antidrug PSAs. *Journal of Drug Education, 25*, 343-355.

Spunt, B., Goldstein, H. B., & Fendrich, M. (1994). The role of marijuana in homicide. *International Journal of the Addictions, 29*, 195-213.

Substance Abuse and Mental Health Services Administration (1998a). *Driving after drug or alcohol use: Findings from the 1996 National Household Survey on Drug Abuse* (Analytic Series A-8). Rockville, MD: Office of Applied Studies, U.S. Department of Health and Human Services.

Substance Abuse and Mental Health Services Administration (1998b). *Analyses of substance abuse and treatment issues* (Analytic Series A-7). Rockville, MD: Office of Applied Studies, U.S. Department of Health and Human Services.

Substance Abuse and Mental Health Services Administration (2000). *Summary of Findings from the 1999 National Household Survey on Drug Abuse (NHSDA)*. Rockville, MD: Office of Applied Studies, Department of Health and Human Services.

Tashkin, D. P., Fligiel, S., Wu, T., Gong, H., Barbers, R. G., Coulson, A. H., Simmons, M. S., & Beals, T. F. (1990). Effects of habitual use of marijuana and/or cocaine on the lung. In C. N. H. Chaing, R.L. (Ed.), *Research Findings on Smoking of Abused Substances* (pp. 65-75). Rockville, MD: U.S. Department of Health and Human Services.

Tammivarra, J. S. (1982). The effects of task structure on beliefs about competence and participation in small groups. *Sociology of Education, 55*, 212-222.

Tommasello, A. C. (1982). Marijuana effects on sprem and testosterone. *Pharmalert, 13*, 1-4.

Trimble, J. E. (1990-1991). Ethnic specification, validation prospects, and the future of drug use research. *International Journal of the Addictions, 25*, 149-170.

Vroom, V. H. (1964). *Work and motivation*. New York: Wiley.

Yamada, T., Kendix, M., & Yamada, T. (1996). The impact of alcohol consumption and marijuana use on high school graduation. *Health Economics, 5*, 77-92.

Wagner, C. B., & Sundar, S. S. (1999, May). *The curiosity-arousing function of antidrug PSAs*. Paper presented at the annual meeting of the International Communication Association, San Francisco, CA.

Webster, M., & Driskell, J. E. (1983). Beauty as states. *American Journal of Sociology, 89*, 140-165.

9

Intermediate Outcomes from a Life Skills Education Program with a Media Literacy Component

Marvin Eisen

The Urban Institute

THE CONTEXT OF THE STUDY: WHY OUTCOME EVALUATIONS OF DRUG EDUCATION PROGRAMS HAVE BECOME IMPORTANT

Teenage drug usage remains a serious problem in the United States, despite efforts by public policymakers, health officials, educators, and prevention scientists to reduce it. Against the backdrop of a generalized decline in cigarette smoking, alcohol consumption, and substance usage in the U.S. population since the 1960s and 1970s, adolescent substance use appears to have stabilized at relatively high rates (Department of Health and Human Services [DHHS], 2000; Substance Abuse and Mental Health Services Administration [SAMHSA], 1999). National data from the 1999 Monitoring the Future (MTF) surveys show that almost 35% of 12th and 18% of 8th graders smoked cigarettes in the last 30 days, with more than 3% of 8th graders smoking at least one-half pack a day; 51% of 12th and 24% of 8th graders reported alcohol use in the last 30 days, with about 31% and 15%, respectively, reporting binge drinking (5+ drinks a day) in the last 14 days; 23.1% of senior and 9.7% of junior high students had used marijuana in the last month; and 2.6% of the older and 1.3% of the younger students had used cocaine in the last month (National Institute of Drug Abuse [NIDA], 1999). Moreover, MTF data point to a worrisome upsurge in almost all categories of substance use among 8th graders between 1994 and 1999: 30-Day prevalence rates are up about 3% for cigarettes, 2% for binge drinking, 6.5% for marijuana use, and 1% for cocaine use (NIDA, 1999).

Perhaps the most alarming trend is the recent evidence that the average age at first substance use for tobacco products has fallen to 12, for alcohol to 13, and for marijuana to 13½ years (SAMHSA, 1999). Early initiation of substance use is a major marker of "high-risk" behaviors (e.g., Mott & Haurin, 1988; Warren et al., 1997). Early initial use is associated with poorer general health, lower educational attainment, and less future economic productivity. It is also associated with higher chronic use rates, greater levels of consumption, and more difficulty quitting or maintaining nonabusing levels of usage (DHHS, 1990, 2000). Ultimately, society pays a substantial price to provide health and social services to persons who initiate drug use during their teen years and continue excessive use through adulthood (DHHS, 1993).

Because of strong public demand for remedial action, school-based programs intended to prevent or delay substance abuse now reach about 90% of middle and high school students (NIDA, 1998). Many of these programs are funded through the federal Safe and Drug Free Schools Act. Many school districts use these federal funds to purchase or subsidize drug education teacher training and curriculum materials in the belief that the training and programs will help deter, delay, or reduce their students' drug-related behavior.

Unfortunately, the school administrators charged with making decisions about which programs to use rarely know whether program efficacy information is available, how to get it, or how to assess it. As a result, decisions on prevention programming are often made on the basis of intuition, professional social networking, and the effective marketing efforts of commercial program developers and publishers.

In fact, until recently there has been little governmental interest in prevention program accountability and performance measurement. Consequently, there have been only limited efforts to demonstrate and document the effectiveness of prevention programs funded through that act. Now, because of increasing substance use among early adolescents, as well as several highly visible and tragic incidents of school violence, impending regulations would restrict Safe and Drug Free Schools funding to programs that can document relatively stringent evidence-based behavior change criteria (Department of Education [DOE], 1998).

This recent push for identification and implementation of "proven" programs may unfortunately be premature. Those prevention concepts and techniques that have shown experimental promise in school settings have rarely undergone large-scale field tests such, as the Midwestern Prevention Program (MPP) (Pentz et al., 1989), the Minnesota Heart Health Program (MHHP) (Perry, Kelder, Murray, & Klepp., 1992), and Life Skills Training (LST), (Botvin, Baker, Dusenbury, Botvin, & Diaz, 1995), and consequently have virtually no market penetration (Eisen, Pallitto, Brad-ner, & Bolshun, 2000). At the same time, the actual effectiveness of intu-ition-based popular prevention programs such as D.A.R.E. has yet to be established (e.g., Ennett, Tobler, Ringwalt, & Flewelling, 1994; Lynam, et al., 1999).

What has brought us to this current state of affairs where there are virtually no widely available empirically supported curricula? First, early interventions, despite their grounding in academic social psychology, proved to be ineffective. Most of these programs were based on social influence principles, were short (5 to 10 sessions) classroom interven-tions, and registered only short-term successes (6- to 24-month delays or reductions in tobacco and marijuana use, and less impact on alcohol use). Even with some booster sessions, notable effects of their interven-tion programs completely decayed after a few years (e.g., Ellickson, Bell, & McGuigan, 1993).

Researchers regrouped and two primary schools of thought emerged. The first framed school-based programs within a comprehensive commu-nity prevention approach that not only provided facts, and attempted to raise students' consciousness about negative external influences (includ-ing mass media) and to directly counteract them through teaching refusal skills and correcting inflated perceptions of substance use by peers, par-ents, and adults in the community, but also attempted to instill values and direct behaviors through the proactive use of mass media in the target communities. The promise of this approach was reflected in the results of the MPP, the MHHP, and the Mass Media Intervention and School Pro-grams (Flynn et al., 1994), and the recent work of Donohew and his col-leagues (see Donohew, Palmgreen, Lorch, Zimmerman, & Harrington, Chap. 6, this volume).

More recently, variants of these social-influence-based interventions have begun to focus specifically on the hypothesized mediational effects of various program components, program implementation factors, target audiences, and specific drugs targeted, in producing positive results. For example, Donaldson and his colleagues (Donaldson, Graham, & Hansen, 1994; Flay, Miller, Hedeker, & Siddiqui,1995) assessed the relative impor-tance of refusal skills training and normative education, including the cor-rection of erroneous perceptions of drug use acceptability and prevalence among peers. Sussman and his colleagues examined the relative effec-tiveness of changes in perceptions of harm, refusal skills, and social norms with respect to cigarette smoking and smokeless tobacco, and a variety of legal and illegal drugs in both universal and indicated settings (Dent et al., 1995; Sussman et al., 1993; Sussman, Dent, Stacy, Sun, & Craig, 1998). Taken together, these studies do not reveal a consistent pattern of findings across settings, target audiences, or substances, or even the primacy of any single intervention component across studies.

The second major approach to drug prevention focused on self-contained school interventions designed to help students translate their knowledge and attitudes into positive actions by enhancing their interpersonal skills and social competencies in so-called "life skills education" programs. For example, Botvin, Baker, Dusenbury, Tortu, and Botvin (1990) used a cognitive-behavioral approach that teaches both domain-specific skills such as understanding media influences and generic social skills such as anxiety management and assertiveness in his LST program. His data indicate delayed or reduced use of tobacco and marijuana, as well as lower prevalence of heavy alcohol use over a 3-year period. Results from a 6-year follow-up substantiate the initial reductions in drug and polydrug use (Botvin et al., 1995).

Although university researchers refined social influence and social cognition intervention approaches over the last two decades, two of the three most popular elementary and middle school curricula in the United States, D.A.R.E. and Here's Looking at You 2000 (HLAY), were developed primarily by practitioners. They contain few of the behavior change approaches and techniques that characterize the academic programs. Both D.A.R.E. and HLAY have been evaluated extensively; neither program's effectiveness in deterring or reducing drug use has been substantiated (e.g., Gerstein & Green, 1993; Lynam et al., 1999). Consequently, neither would presently qualify as an evidence-based intervention under the Safe and Drug Free Schools Act draft criteria (DOE, 1998). The third widely used program, the Lions-Quest *Skills for Adolescence* (SFA) curriculum (Quest International, 1992), is only now undergoing rigorous evaluation. However, unlike these other popular programs, SFA appears to rest on a firm foundation of empirically-supported concepts, program elements, and delivery mechanisms. *Skills for Adolescence* is a multicomponent life skills education program developed for middle school use by Quest International, a nonprofit foundation affiliated with the Lions Club International (Quest International, 1992). The program has been available commercially since 1988, and school districts around the country have sent more than 10,000 teachers to Quest International certified training workshops as part of their school--community drug prevention efforts. The most recent (third) edition contains a substantially revised and expanded 20+ session drug education unit embedded in a 103-session life-skills curriculum. In contrast to D.A.R.E. districts must purchase SFA. Clearly, school administrators believe SFA to be an effective life skills training and drug prevention program.

Until recently, however, there was no rigorous multisite, multiyear outcome evaluation of SFA to empirically test this belief. In the fall of 1996 the author and his colleagues, Gail L. Zellman of RAND and David M. Murray, now of the University of Memphis, received a 5-year grant from NIDA to conduct a randomized community trial of SFA. The overall goal was to compare the effectiveness of SFA against "standard" school-based drug prevention programs in preventing or delaying the onset of students' tobacco, alcohol, and controlled substance use.

The SFA program utilizes a comprehensive array of strategies to teach social competency and refusal skills to middle-schoolers. There is an emphasis on home/school/community partnerships. The curriculum teaches cognitive-behavioral skills for building self-esteem and personal responsibility, communicating effectively, making better decisions, resisting social influences and asserting rights, and increasing drug use knowledge and consequences. Following the consensus from major evaluations and meta-analyses, SFA program elements and processes utilize social influence and social-cognitive approaches to prevention, including life skills and resistance-skills training, as well as enhancement of perceptions of the harmful nature of drugs (e.g., Botvin et al., 1995; Tobler, in press; Tobler, Lessard, Marshall, Ochshorn, & Roona, 1999).

The seven major SFA units are intended to be taught in approximately 100 class sessions, including multiple sessions on improving peer relationships, strengthening family bonds, and (life) goals setting. In addition, SFA features a brief three-session "media literacy" program element that explicitly focuses on combating the external influences of media and advertising through the development and presentation of written and role-playing counterarguments, but does not contain a mass media intervention component.

The evaluation was designed to determine whether the SFA program had the following longer-term effects:

1. To prevent or significantly delay the initiation of "gateway" (tobacco, alcohol, marijuana) drug use during the study period,
2. To reduce the overall frequency of any substance use among those who do initiate use,
3. To prevent or delay the progression to more "advanced" substance use (e.g., binge drinking, regular smoking, and experimental or regular marijuana use) or to "hard" drug use following initiation relative to schools' usual drug prevention programming.

This chapter reports intermediate (baseline through intervention year) study findings.

METHODS

Overview of Experimental Design

The study employed a randomized community trial, as identifiable social groups rather than individuals were allocated to study conditions. More specifically, it employed a nested cohort design (Murray, 1998) with a single intervention condition and a single comparison condition. In this design, identifiable social groups are allocated to study conditions, and members of the groups are followed over time to assess the impact of the intervention; the same individuals are observed at each measurement occasion.

Thirty-four middle schools were recruited from four school districts in three major metropolitan areas during the spring and summer of 1997. A baseline survey was conducted with all consented sixth graders in each school in the spring of 1998. The schools were then pair-matched within each district on sixth-grade prevalence of any recent (previous 30 days) use of tobacco, alcohol, or any illicit drug, based on pre-test survey data. Schools were randomized to study conditions from within pairs during the summer of 1998 to reduce threats to internal validity (Murray, 1998). The study cohort in the 17 intervention schools received SFA as seventh graders during the 1998-1999 school year, whereas their counterparts in the 17 comparison schools received their usual drug education programming. The cohort was surveyed two additional times over the period of 2 years: (a) at the end of the seventh grade in the spring of 1999 (post-test); and (b) at the end of the eighth grade in the spring of 2000 (1-year follow-up).

Sampling Plan and School Recruitment

The goal of the sampling plan was to draw a sample of metropolitan areas, public school districts, and middle or junior high school students that represented the diversity of the U.S. population while maintaining a level of simplicity that allowed the study to go forward without undue logistical problems and cost. This goal was operationalized via a two-stage cluster-sampling plan (Kish, 1965). In the first stage, 4 of the 10 largest metropolitan areas ranked by population size were selected at random.

Within each of the selected areas (Los Angeles--Long Beach, California; Detroit--Wayne County, Michigan; Washington, DC--Baltimore, Maryland; and Boston, Massachusetts), a complete enumeration of those public schools within independent school districts was prepared that met the following eligibility criteria in the 1996-1997 school year: (a) contained grades 6—8 or 7—9; (b) had an enrollment of 200 or more students in the 8th or 9th grade; and (c) was not currently using SFA.

In the second stage, districts with at least four schools that met these criteria were screened for interest in participation. Within each interested district, all eligible schools were invited to send staff to an informational meeting regarding the nature and purposes of the study, the sampling procedures, and the costs and benefits of participation. The explanation included a description of the survey procedures, the intervention program, and the randomization procedure. Initially, to participate in the study, a school had to agree in writing to:

1. Participate in either condition and to accept the results of the randomization, regardless of its assignment.
2. Complete all data collection activities.
3. Implement at least 60% of the 100+ session SFA Classroom Curriculum, including the 20+ session Drug Education Unit, during the seventh-grade school year (1998-1999).

We anticipated relatively high agreement rates because all participating schools would receive high-quality teacher training, curriculum materials, and implementation assistance for a well-known life skills education program at no cost. Experimental schools would receive these benefits immediately, whereas schools randomized to the control condition would receive them once the study cohorts' final follow-up data were collected. However, we were not able to persuade a single school district in 4 of the 10 largest metropolitan areas of the United States to use the 103-session curriculum as written—even with virtually all training, curriculum materials, and student workbook costs to be paid by us. In nearly all cases, sheer burden imposed by the number of sessions was given as the reason. As a consequence, we modified and pared down the SFA Classroom Curriculum to a required 40 sessions and continued our recruitment efforts.

Ultimately, one Los Angeles district (with 12 of 82 middle schools participating), one Washington—Baltimore district (with 8 of 28 schools participating), and two Detroit—Wayne County districts (with 10 of 44 and 4 of 4 schools participating, respectively) agreed to participate in the evaluation project. Thus, in the first stage, major metropolitan areas were randomly selected for recruitment activities; then in the second stage, within metro areas, school districts meeting eligibility criteria self-selected into school-level informational meetings. When at least 4 of the eligible schools (within a district) agreed to participate, that district and its interested schools were taken into the study sample for a total of 34 middle schools.

Student Participants

Active parental consent to participate in the SFA evaluation was a study requirement. Prior to baseline data collection, school districts provided the names and addresses of the parents/guardians of each student for an informed-consent mailing to participate in the evaluation surveys. Consent was obtained from 7,424 sixth-grade students (71% of the eligible population) across the 34 study schools. About 60% of the sample was from the Los Angeles metro area, 22% from Detroit, and 18% from Washington—Baltimore. Females comprised 52% of the sample; Hispanic-Americans 34%, African-Americans 18%, Asian-Americans 7%, and 66% lived with both parents. The mean age of the sample was 11 at baseline (see Table 9.1).

Table 9.1
Demographic Characteristics and Drug Prevalence
Rates for 6th Grade Students, Baseline

Variable	N	%
Study Sites		
Los Angeles Metro	4415	59.5
Detroit Metro	724	9.8
Detroit Suburban	927	12.5
Washington Suburban	1358	18.3
Sex		
Female	3835	51.7
Male	3585	48.3
Age (as of 5/1/1998)		
Younger than 11	38	0.5
11	3790	51.1
12	3344	45.1
13	218	2.9
14	12	0.2
Missing	22	0.3

Table 9.1 (cont'd)

Variable	N	%
Race/Ethnicity		
Asian-American	526	7.1
American Indian	104	1.4
African-American	1310	17.6
Hispanic-American	2517	33.9
White	1909	25.7
Combination (of above groups)	514	6.9
Other	468	6.3
Missing	76	1.0
Living Arrangements		
Live With Both Parents or Guardians	4894	65.9
Live With Mother Only	1807	24.3
Live With Father Only	282	3.8
Live With Neither Parent	341	4.6
Missing	100	1.3
Education Aspirations		
Not Graduate H.S.	143	1.9
Graduate H.S.	439	5.9
Go to College	330	4.4
Graduate College	2797	37.7
College Plus	3115	42.0
Missing	600	8.1

SFA Program Content and Implementation

The 40-session curriculum included 3 on the challenges involved in entering the teen years, 4 on building self-confidence and communication skills, 5 on managing emotions in positive ways, 8 on improving peer relationships (including resisting peer pressure), and 20 on living healthy and drug free.

Most schools had difficulties even with the abridged version, noting that 40 sessions represented a major share of any one-semester class. To bring some consistency and uniformity to the classroom teacher observations, which were an integral part of the process evaluation, 8 of the 40 required sessions were deemed "Key Sessions." Teachers were asked to be sure to teach these sessions, some of which would be observed. Each Key Session focused on a key element, component, or a technique associated with successful drug prevention programming (e.g., developing resistance skills and increasing the perception of harm in using specific substances). The eight Key Sessions specifically included "Stepping Up to Good Decisions" (decision-making), "Communicating With 'What, Why, and How' Messages" (communication skill-building), "ASK: Three Steps to Saying 'No'" (refusal skill-building), "Filtering Facts From Fiction" (media literacy), "What the Ads Don't Tell You" (media literacy), "Avoiding Trouble" (refusal skill-building), "Refuse to Use" (refusal skill-building and perception of harm), and "Marijuana: The Drug That Keeps Hanging On" (perception of harm).

Teachers generally expressed satisfaction with the SFA curriculum, despite some resistance to teaching all of the required class sessions. Many noted that the curriculum was a pleasure to teach, and that most students responded well to it. The curriculum is highly regularized, with a similar structure and sequence of activities in each session. This structure, with specific examples from one of the Key Sessions on media literacy includes the following.

Quotation. Each session begins with a quotation and a set of related questions that introduce the key idea or goal of the session. As students discuss what the quote means, they develop expectations for the session. For example, the first session on media literacy ("Filtering facts from fiction") begins with the following quotation by Descartes: "It is not enough to have a good mind. The main thing is to use it well." Discussion of the quotation encourages students to develop ways of becoming "life smart" about societal influences that promote drug usage, employ their minds to solve the complexities of their environment, and take care of themselves and others in the process.

New Information/Skills. In this part of each session, lasting approximately 10 minutes, the teacher presents new material and skills, as well as models their appropriate use. This phase is generally a whole-group activity. In the "Filtering Facts" session, the teacher uses the time to demonstrate to the students how their daily decisions are often shaped by the influences surrounding them, such as family, friends, culture, religion, their own values, and the media. Training emphasizes that it is important for the teacher to distinguish between the positive and the negative nature of some of these influences, and to discuss with the students how pressures to conform may lead to harmful consequences, such as drug use. Students are specifically asked to think of the reasons why some people (and entities such as advertisers) might encourage others to use drugs, as well as to provide examples of how certain societal influences may either promote or discourage the use of drugs. Among the influences discussed are entertainment, celebrities, friends, laws, family, and religious values. Furthermore, students explore the meaning of "mixed messages" as they relate to drug use, and provide examples of how society frequently sends "mixed messages" to young people, leading them to underestimate the potential harm of cigarettes, alcohol and illegal drugs. Students are given specific situations in which "mixed messages" may arise (e.g., a sport event sponsored by a cigarette or beer company, or older teenagers daring younger teens to drink with them). For each of the situations, the students are asked to interpret the message, the rationale of a person or an entity sending the message, and the real facts surrounding the potentially harmful activity involved.

Activity. In this phase of each session, which lasts 10—30 minutes, students work individually or cooperatively to practice the new skills or apply the new knowledge just presented under the teacher's guidance. In some sessions they demonstrate what they have learned to classmates or another audience. For example, students work in groups to help design ways in which to help others overcome the existing prodrug influences. Specifically, they create a newsletter the contents of which are designed to discourage others from using drugs.

Closure Questions. In this part of the session, which typically lasts just 5 minutes, the teacher facilitates the students' analysis of what happened in the session, and the significance of the new information and skills for themselves and others. Some of the closure questions that the teacher raises during the "Filtering Facts" session include the influence of prodrug "mixed messages," the meaning of being "life smart," the importance of becoming aware of the surrounding influences, and the different ways in which young people can encourage each other to remain or become drug-free.

Beyond the Classroom. In this part of the session, the teacher presents an assignment that will help students gain confidence and mastery of the skills they have just learned and practiced. At the end of this media literacy session, students may be asked to bring alcohol or tobacco ads from local newspapers to the next class, or to discuss some of the social influences that affect drug use with their parents or other adults. Students report what they learned from these activities at the next class.

Notebook Entry. Each session ends with a 3-minute notebook entry, during which students may reflect on how the skills they have learned and practiced in the session affect them personally. This particular media literacy session uses this time to have the students list three positive societal influences that can support them to stay drug-free.

SFA Teacher Training and Provision of Curriculum Materials

Prior to seventh-grade implementation in the experimental schools in the fall of 1998, teachers selected to receive SFA training attended a 3-day workshop conducted by Quest-certified trainers. At the workshop, the teachers were provided with teacher manuals and other necessary curriculum materials. The certified trainers were independent contractors, not Quest International employees, but rather were engaged by The Urban Institute for the project. The purposes of the workshop were to:

1. Provide teachers with detailed explanations and practice sessions for teaching SFA.
2. Learn and practice specific skill-building exercises such as cooperative learning, team building, communication skills, problem solving, and peer relationships.
3. Reinforce the importance of maintaining fidelity to the previously agreed-upon (i.e., required) unit-by-unit and session-by-session sequence of the intervention implementation.
4. Provide an overview of the process evaluation approach and classroom data collection requirements and procedures to be used in the process evaluation.

Survey Data Collection

All consented students were surveyed annually from the sixth through the eighth grade; all seventh-grade students attending the experimental schools were offered the SFA curriculum regardless of their evaluation consent status. Annual surveys were group administered in classrooms by trained interviewers using standard protocols and questionnaires adapted or developed for this evaluation. The annual questionnaires were translated into Spanish, and students could choose to complete the surveys in either English or Spanish. With few exceptions, the data collectors were blind to each school's treatment condition.

Additional in-school makeup sessions were conducted for students who were absent initially. Consented students who were not surveyed in school for any reason were sent makeup questionnaires and were offered free movie passes or comparable cash prizes for completing the surveys.

Outcome Evaluation Measures

Drug Use Prevalence Rates. Tobacco, alcohol, and illegal drug use were assessed through a set of standard items which were modified, when necessary, following pretesting with the target population. The three cigarette smoking and two smokeless-tobacco questions have been established by the National Cancer Institute as standard items. Standard questions adapted from the MTF surveys on the incidence, prevalence, and personal effects of alcohol, marijuana, cocaine, and other illegal/illicit substances such as inhalants are also included on the questionnaire (NIDA, 1999).

Hypothesized Mediating and Moderating Measures

Drug Use Behavioral Intentions. Students' behavioral intentions to use tobacco, alcohol, marijuana, and cocaine in the next few months (anchored to concrete dates such as summer vacation or the start of the school year) were measured with items originally adapted from MTF. The time frame was reduced on these items because early adolescents have notoriously short future time perspectives (Eisen & Zellman, 1986).

Social Influence and Interpersonal Perceptions. Standard questions assessing students' normative beliefs about the prevalence of substance use by best friends, friends in general, and same-grade peers were adapted from questions used in MTF.

Drug Knowledge and Perceptions of Harm. Measures included several items on the perception of harm modified from MTF, as well as new items on the perception of helpfulness of drugs in terms of relaxation and facilitation.

Sensation-Seeking. Several items adapted from Zuckerman's Sensation-Seeking Scales for adults (e.g., Zuckerman, 1986), such as "doing dangerous things just for fun," were included.

Demographics. Gender, age, race/ethnicity, family structure/household composition, and other demographic factors related to adolescent smoking were included.

The questionnaire was translated into Spanish, back-translated to English, and wording was revised as necessary. The Spanish version was available at baseline and seventh-grade data collection so that students choose the one they preferred.

Analysis Plan

The main focus of the sixth-to-seventh grade (intermediate posttest) analysis was to assess the relationships among the implementation of SFA, moderating variables (e.g., demographics and sensation-seeking), and self-reported drug use outcomes. Initiation and changes in drug use from the spring of 1998 to the spring of 1999 were analyzed separately for baseline nonusers (universal level) and users (selective level) target audiences because we were especially interested in differences, if any, in SFA primary and secondary effectiveness. For baseline non-users, differences between SFA and control groups were assessed on lifetime (ever) and recent (last 30 days) use rates of alcohol, binge drinking (three or more drinks at one time), cigarettes, marijuana, and "any other" drugs, including inhalants, using 5- to7-point ordinal response categories (e.g., *never* or *none* to *more than 100 cigarettes [more than 5 packs]*). For baseline users, only differences in recent use of those substances were evaluated.

Preliminary analyses were conducted to verify the effects of pair-matching schools on baseline drug use prior to randomization and to assess attrition effects at the seventh-grade follow-up. Then, we moved to a series of analysis of covariance (ANCOVA) model analyses to assess changes in drug use incidence and prevalence, as well as changes in drug use-related knowledge, attitudes, perceptions, affect, and behavioral skills (see Figure 9.1).

The nested cohort design differs from the usual experiment because the units of assignment and observation are different. In this study, school was the unit of assignment and the student was the unit of observation. Persons within clusters such as schools tend to be more like one another than they are like persons in other clusters (Kish, 1965), and this within-cluster (or intraclass) correlation adds an additional component to the variability of the intervention group means over that attributable either to the individual participants or to the interventions themselves (Murray, 1998). Unless this extra variation is accounted for in the analysis, the evaluation of treatment effects will be positively and often substantially biased (Murray, 1998).

We accounted for the extra variation using SAS PROC MIXED (SAS Institute, Inc., 1997), a mixed-model regression program especially suited to analysis of data from designs involving nested random effects, including group-randomized trials (Murray, 1998). In these analyses, the pairs, schools and students, are treated as random effects whereas the intervention condition is treated as a fixed effect. Potential confounders were included as fixed effects when needed because randomization of a limited number of schools to each condition cannot guarantee baseline comparability on all factors, even with matching prior to randomization. When appropriate, baseline use of other relevant substances (e.g., ones hypothesized to be subject to earlier initiation) was included. For these latter analyses, a latent status approach was used to examine experimental versus control transition rates concerning progression from baseline

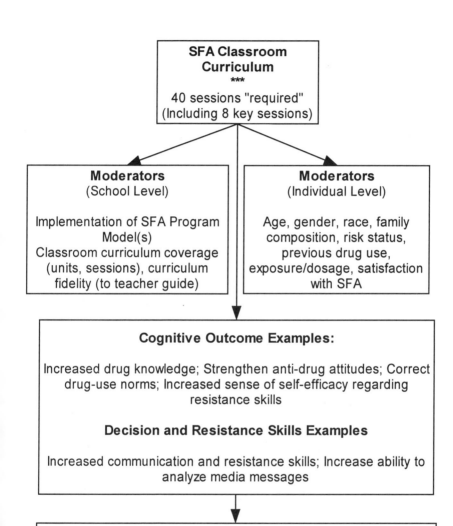

FIGURE 9.1 Skills for Adolescents (SFS) program evaluation model.

use to more advanced use (e.g., from nonbinge drinking to binge drinking) or to an illegal substance (e.g., from cigarettes to marijuana) over the follow-up period (Spoth, Reyes, Redmond, & Shin, 1999). Possible effect modifications due to racial/ethnic group and gender were assessed by adding terms to represent the interaction between condition and strata to the fixed effects and by adding terms to represent the interaction between strata and school nested within conditions to the random effects.

In all these analyses, the degrees of freedom (df) for the person-level covariates are removed from the df for the person-level error term and so do not reduce df available for the school-level error term. We chose to use these procedures in the analysis of the primary outcomes (ordinal indicators of lifetime and recent substance use, recoded to No/Yes) that have binomial distributions at the observation-level, based on earlier findings that this analysis is quite robust to violations of normality assumptions (Hannan & Murray, 1996). Comparisons of least square means (adjusted for demographic and psychosocial variables) were evaluated at $p < .05$, one-tailed, with $df=1/32$, because directional hypotheses were stated. This plan provides valid tests of the effects of interest and the statistical basis for generalizing findings to other schools and students like those included in the study (Murray, 1998).

RESULTS

Baseline Equivalence and Attrition

Baseline analysis indicated an overall 30-day prevalence rate of 14% for a composite measure of "any drug use" and that the 17 SFA (14%) and 17 control (14%) schools were equivalent with respect to self-reported drug use prior to the seventh-grade SFA intervention program. The composite measure was a combination of 30-day prevalence rates for any of five major substances: alcohol (9.5%), cigarettes (7.4%), marijuana (3%), and any other illicit drug(s), including cocaine and inhalants (2.3%) (see Table 9.2).

Intermediate posttest data were collected from 6,239 students (84% of the consented baseline sample) in the spring of 1999. Multivariate analysis of sixth- to seventh-grade attrition indicated only one significant difference in baseline drug use between students who did or did not complete seventh-grade surveys: Those who reported no recent marijuana use at baseline were more likely to complete the follow-up survey (85% vs. 78%, $p < .001$). There was one between-school district difference (fewer completers from the Detroit metro district), as well as several

TABLE 9.2
Baseline Drug Usage

Activity	N	%
Used Alcohol in Last 30 Days		
Yes	703	9.5
No	6687	90.1
Missing	34	0.5
Smoked Cigarettes in Last 30 Days		
Yes	257	3.5
No	6931	93.4
Missing	236	3.2
Used Marijuana in Last 30 Days		
Yes	225	3.0
No	6948	93.6
Missing	251	3.4
Used Cocaine/Crack in Last 30 Days		
Yes	78	1.1
No	7022	94.6
Missing	324	4.4
Used Any Other Illicit Drug in Last 30 Days		
Yes	171	2.3
No	6825	91.9
Missing	428	5.8

demographic and psychosocial variables associated with study retention: being non-Hispanic-American; coming from a two-parent household; not having taken a makeup survey at baseline; and reporting fewer friends who smoke cigarettes.

Sixth- to Seventh-Grade Intervention Outcomes

Outcome analyses were conducted using an "intent to treat" approach; that is, all students were retained in the analyses based on their school assignment to condition, unless they officially transferred to (or from) an SFA school before the intervention started (i.e., between the sixth and seventh grade).

For Baseline Nonusers. Recent cigarette smoking was lower in SFA schools (2.9%) than control schools (3.8%, $F = 4.17$, $p < .025$), as was lifetime marijuana use (SFA = 9.5%, control = 11.6%, $F = 3.42$, $p < .04$)

with salient demographic and psychosocial variables controlled (see Table 9.3). There also were condition by ethnicity interactions on two drinking behaviors (recent alcohol use, $p < .02$, and recent binge drinking, $p < .004$). The interaction pattern showed fewer Hispanic-Americans in the SFA schools who engaged in these behaviors than Hispanic Americans in control schools, while there were slightly more non-Hispanics in the SFA schools involved in drinking than there were in the control schools. There were no significant differences on either lifetime or recent use of other illicit substances.

Post hoc contingency table analyses provided some indication of what was driving the significant condition by racial/ethnic group interaction effects for follow-up alcohol use. Hispanic-American students comprised almost 35% of the study sample. At baseline (and annual follow-ups) students could choose to take the surveys in English or Spanish. About 15% of the Hispanic-American students took the baseline survey in

Table 9.3
Adjusted Substance Use Prevalance Rates, 7th Grade
Students at Spring 1999 Follow-Up: Baseline Non-Users

Variable	SFA %	Control%	$p =$
Alcohol			
Lifetime	30.3	29.4	0.32
30-day	7.3	7.1	0.85
Binge Drinking	3.2	3.5	0.30
Cigarettes			
Lifetime	28.4	26.4	0.15
30-day	2.9	3.8	0.03
Marijuana			
Lifetime	9.5	11.6	0.04
30-day	4.3	5.3	0.13
Other Illicit Substances			
Lifetime	7.1	6.3	0.24
30-day	3.4	3.5	0.70

Note. Values were adjusted for baseline age, gender, race or ethincity, two-parent household, site (school district, baseline survey language, friends' drug use, and sensation seeking. Student sample size ranged from 4,104 to 5,558 depending on outcome variable. Differences between conditions are based on the $F(1,32)$ statistic, one-tailed.

Spanish (a crude proxy for degree of acculturation). When the race/ethnicity and survey language variables were combined and respecified, three group were constructed: Hispanic-American students surveyed in English, Hispanic-American students surveyed in Spanish, and non-Hispanics surveyed in English.

Additional hierarchical regression analyses showed that Hispanic students surveyed in Spanish reported significantly higher alcohol and binge drinking initiation rates at intermediate post-test than Hispanic-Americans surveyed in English and non-Hispanics (all of whom were surveyed in English), independent of treatment condition. They also confirmed the two original treatment condition by race/ethnicity interaction effects: The SFA program deterred the onset of monthly drinking and binge drinking more effectively among Hispanic-Americans who took the baseline survey in English than among Hispanics who took the survey in Spanish and among non-Hispanics; there were no differences among the ethnicity/language groups in the control programs (see Table 9.4).

For Baseline Drug Users. As expected with age, there were statistically significant increases in recent amount/frequency of use for alcohol, binge drinking, cigarettes, and marijuana reported between the sixth and seventh grades for both the SFA and control conditions. However, there

Table 9.4
Adjusted Substance Use Prevalance Rates, 7th Grade
Students, Spring 1999 Follow-Up: Baseline Non-Users,
Interaction Effects

Variable	SFA %	Control %	$p =$
Alcohol 30-day			
Hispanic-English	6.79	9.76	0.04
Hispanic-Spanish	9.56	12.23	0.18
Non-Hispanic	7.22	5.32	0.05
Binge Drinking			
Hispanic-English	2.92	6.32	0.002
Hispanic-Spanish	6.68	6.79	0.48
Non-Hispanic	2.91	1.93	0.09

Note. Values were adjusted for baseline age, gender, two-parent household, school district and baseline survey language. Student sample size ranged from 4,106 to 4,117 depending on outcome variable. Differences between ethnic/race groups are based on the $F_{(1, 32)}$ statistic, one-tailed.

were there no significant differences between SFA and control conditions at follow-up in amount/ frequency of use or in prevalence rates for any of the recent drug use indicators (not shown).

In contrast, students in SFA schools demonstrated delayed progression to use of more advanced substances (by the seventh grade) following initiation (by baseline) relative to students in control schools on three of six latent transition indicators: baseline alcohol to follow-up cigarettes; baseline alcohol to follow-up marijuana; and baseline binge drinking to follow-up marijuana (see Table 9.5). For students who reported recent alcohol use but no recent cigarette smoking and no lifetime marijuana use at baseline ($n = 325$), the progression to cigarette smoking in the previous month at follow-up was lower in SFA schools than in control schools (8.0% vs. 12.8%, $F = 4.21$, $p = .05$), as was the progression to trying (i.e., ever using) marijuana during the follow-up year (SFA = 16.8%, control = 23.5%, $F = 3.89$, $p = .059$) with salient demographic variables controlled.

Table 9.5
Adjusted Advanced Substance Use Prevalence Rates, 7th Grade Students, Spring 1999 Follow-Up: Baseline Users

Variable	SFA %	Control (%)	$p =$
To: Binge Drinking[a]			
From:			
Alcohol 30-day	16.98	20.45	0.55
To: Cigarettes 30-day[b]			
From:			
Alcohol 30-day	8.02	12.79	0.05
Binge Drinking	7.44	16.28	0.14
To: Marijuana Lifetime[c]			
From:			
Alcohol 30-day	16.81	23.52	0.06
Binge Drinking	21.11	37.57	0.02
Cigarettes 30-day	39.58	36.84	0.72

Note. Values were adjusted for baseline age, gender, race-ethnicity, and two-parent household.
[a] N=327, differences based on the $F(1,28)$ statistic.
[b] N=169, differencese based on the $F(1, 26)$ statistic.
[c] N=86, differences based on the $F(1, 23)$ statistic.

Additionally, for students who reported recent binge drinking, but no recent cigarette smoking and no lifetime marijuana use at baseline (n = 167), the transition rate to trying marijuana during the study period was significantly lower in the SFA condition (21.1% vs. 37.6%, F = 6.25, p = .019). Finally, there were no significant differences between SFA and control conditions on the 3 other transitions tested: baseline alcohol to follow-up binge drinking (n = 325); baseline binge drinking to follow-up cigarettes (n = 167); and baseline cigarettes to follow-up marijuana (n = 86) [see Table 9.4].

SUMMARY AND CONCLUSIONS

These results indicate that:

1. Exposure to a 40-session version of the SFA life skills education curriculum can help deter the initiation of regular cigarette smoking and experimental use of marijuana through the end of the seventh grade.
2. This effect held across all racial/ethnic groups studied.
3. This program can also deter the initiation of regular alcohol use and binge drinking for Hispanics.
4. This program can delay the progression to regular cigarette smoking and to experimental marijuana use among students who had initiated regular alcohol use or binge drinking but not regular cigarette smoking by the end of the sixth grade.

These findings constitute the first empirical evidence that a widely used, commercially available drug prevention curriculum produces salutary primary or secondary prevention effects on students' substance use behaviors over a 1-year postbaseline period. The results are noteworthy because they bridge an important "research to practice" gap noted earlier: Theory-based programs that include proven prevention concepts and techniques have rarely been implemented on a large scale (Botvin et al., 1990; Pentz, et al., 1989; Tobler, in press; Tobler et al., 1999), whereas widely used intuition-based programs (such as D.A.R.E. and HLAY 2000) have not been demonstrated to be effective in altering student substance use behavior (Gerstein & Green, 1993; Ennett et al., 1994; Lynam et al., 1999).

More fundamentally, these encouraging initial results support the general thrust of universal-level, life skills-based prevention programs: self-contained school interventions designed to help students translate their knowledge and attitudes into positive actions by enhancing their interpersonal skills and social competencies. SFA's short-term effects are consistent with longer-term findings from other life skills programs such as Botvin's Life Skills Training (LST) and other successful social influence-based interventions (e.g., Dent et al., 1995; Sussman et al, 1993). Based on similarities to proven intervention approaches and program elements, our early results offer hope that SFA may also continue to produce positive outcomes over time.

Our study design included a number of features that allowed a reasonable test of SFA. Random selection of metropolitan areas for initial school district recruitment and inclusion of inner city and suburban school districts and schools assured a large multiethnic sample. Random assignment of schools to study conditions from within pairs matched within their school districts helped ensure baseline comparability on major outcome indicators. A high active parent consent rate (71%) as well as a relatively high retention for in-school data collection thus far (84% of the eligible sample) should provide the basis for producing credible findings concerning longer-term effects of SFA.

Moreover, within the large Hispanic-American sample (n = 2,517) about 15% of the students complete a Spanish language survey, thus allowing us to differentiate baseline drug use prevalences between more and less acculturated Hispanics, as well as the differential impact of the SFA program on Hispanic students. Interestingly, these latter differences in SFA effectiveness may be related to the fact that the intervention program sessions are very structured, group-oriented, and highly interactive. They are intended to elicit brisk responses and discussion between teacher and students and among students. To the extent that the less acculturated Hispanic-American students were less comfortable thinking and responding quickly in English, they may not have gotten as much from SFA curriculum materials—especially those related to media literacy which were grounded in both print and television message decoding—and modes of program delivery.

In addition to the study's positives, its limitations must be considered as well. Those students whose parents failed to return the consent form or denied consent cannot be assumed to be the same as those students with more compliant parents. Attrition from sixth to seventh grade was not random, but was associated with reported sixth-grade marijuana use. Even though assignment of schools to condition was random in each district, schools self-selected into the study. Each of these factors limits the generalizability of the findings.

We are also aware that many well-designed and well-implemented school-based drug prevention interventions have shown initially encouraging behavior effects that dissipated with time (e.g., Ellickson et al., 1993). Nevertheless, given the number and range of substances initially affected by the SFA intervention at the primary and or secondary prevention level, we are cautiously optimistic regarding longer-term SFA program impact. Additional school- and student-level program implementation and exposure analyses now underway should clarify, refine, and extend these initially promising intermediate outcome results. As those analyses are completed, the eighth-grade follow-up will become available for final impact analyses.

ACKNOWLEDGEMENT

This study was supported by research grant DA 09574 from the National Institute on Drug Abuse. The views and opinions expressed herein are solely those of the author and do not represent the views or official position of either the sponsoring agency or The Urban Institute.

REFERENCES

Botvin, G., Baker, E., Dusenbury, L., Botvin E., & Diaz, T. (1995). Long-term follow-up results of a randomized drug abuse prevention trial in a white middle class population. *Journal of the American Medical Association, 273,* 1106-1112.

Botvin, G., Baker, R., Dusenbury, L., Tortu, S., & Botvin, E. (1990). Preventing adolescent drug abuse through a multimodal cognitive-behavioral approach: Results of a 3-year study. *Journal of Consulting and Clinical Psychology, 58,* 437-446.

Dent, C. W., Sussman, S., Stacy, A. W., Craig, S., Burton, D., & Flay, B. R. (1995). Two-year behavior outcomes to project towards no tobacco use. *Journal of Consulting and Clinical Psychology, 63,* 676-677.

Department of Education. (1998). *Announcement: The expert panel on safe, disciplined and drug-free schools searching for best programs.* Washington, DC: The Safe and Drug-Free Schools Program. Available online: http://www.ed.gov/offices/OESE/SDFS/programs.html

Department of Health and Human Services. (1990). *Healthy people 2000: National health promotion and disease prevention objectives.* Washington, DC: Public Health Service.

Department of Health and Human Services. (1993). *Second report to Congress on alcohol and other drug abuse prevention.* Washington, DC: Office of the Assistant Secretary for Health.

Department of Health and Human Services. (2000). *Healthy People 2010* (Conference Ed., in 2 Vols.). Washington, DC: Public Health Service.

Donaldson, S., Graham, J., & Hansen, W. (1994). Testing the generalizability of intervening mechanism theories: Understanding the effects of adolescent drug use prevention interventions. *Journal of Behavioral Medicine, 17*, 195-216.

Eisen, M., Pallitto, C., Bradner, C., & Bolshun, N. (2000). *Teen risk taking: Promising prevention programs and approaches.* Washington, DC: The Urban Institute Press.

Eisen, M., & Zellman, G. (1986). The role of health belief attitudes, sex education, and demographics in predicting adolescents' sexuality knowledge. *Health Education Quarterly, 13*, 9-22.

Ellickson, P., Bell, R., & McGuigan, K. (1993). Preventing adolescent drug use: Long-term results of a junior high program. *American Journal of Public Health, 83*, 856-61.

Ennett, S. T., Tobler, N. S., Ringwalt, C. L., & Flewelling, R. L. (1994). How effective is drug abuse resistance education? A meta-analysis of Project DARE outcome evaluations. *American Journal of Public Health, 84*, 1394-1401.

Flay, B. R., Miller, T. Q., Hedeker, D., & Siddiqui, O. (1995). The Television, School, and Family smoking prevention and cessation Project: VIII. Student outcomes and mediating variables. *Preventive Medicine, 24*, 29-40.

Flynn, B., Worden, J., Secker-Walker, R., Pirie, P., Badger, G., Carpenter, J., & Geller, B. (1994). Mass media and school interventions for cigarette smoking prevention: Effects 2 years after completion. *American Journal of Public Health, 84*, 1148-1150.

Gerstein, D., & Green, L. (1993). *Preventing drug abuse: What do we know?* Washington, DC: National Academy Press.

Hannan, P. J., & Murray, D. M. (1996). Gauss or Bernoulli? A Monte Carlo comparison of the linear mixed model and the logistic mixed model analyses in simulated community trials with a dichotomous outcome variable at the individual level. *Evaluation Review, 20*, 338-352.

Kish, L. (1965). *Survey sampling.* New York: John Wiley & Sons.

Lynam, D. R., Milich, R., Zimmerman, R., Novak, S. P., Logan, T. K., Martin, C., Leukefeld, C., & Clayton, R. (1999). Project DARE: No effects at 10-year follow-up. *Journal of Consulting and Clinical Psychology, 67*, 590-593.

Mott, F. L. & Haurin, R. J. (1988). Linkages between sexual activity and alcohol and drug use among American adolescents. *Family Planning Perspective, 20*, 128-36.

Murray, D. M. (1998). *Design and analysis of group-randomized trials.* New York: Oxford University Press.

National Institute on Drug Abuse. (1998, December). *Drug use eases among teens for second consecutive year; Secretary Shalala also announces NIDA goes to school initiative.* NIDA Media Advisory, December 28.

National Institute on Drug Abuse. (1999, December). *Drug trends in 1999 among American teens are mixed.* National Press Release, December 17.

Pentz, M. A., Dwyer, J. H., MacKinnon, D. P., Flay, B. R., Hansen, W. B., Yu, E. I., Wang, M. S., & Johnson, C. A. (1989). Multi-community trial for primary prevention of adolescent drug abuse, *JAMA, 261*, 3259-3266.

Perry, C., Kelder, S., Murray, D., & Klepp, K. (1992). Long term outcomes of the Minnesota heart health program and the class of 1989 study. *American Journal of Public Health, 82*, 1210-1216.

SAS Institute, Inc. (1997). *SAS/STAT software: changes and enhancements.* SAS Tech. Rep. P-229, Release 6.12, pp. 287-368. Cary, NC: SAS Institute, Inc.

Spoth, R., Reyes, M. L., Redmond, C., & Shin, C. (1999). Assessing a public health approach to delay onset and progression of adolescent substance use: Latent transition and log-linear analyses of longitudinal family preventive intervention outcomes. *Journal of Consulting & Clinical Psychology, 67*, 619-630.

Substance Abuse and Mental Health Services Administration, Department of Health and Human Services. (1999). *Fact Sheet: 1998 National Household Survey on Drug Abuse.* Available online: http://www.samhsa.gov/PRESS/99/990818fs.htm

Sussman, S., Dent, C. W., Stacy, A. W., Sun, P., Craig, S., Simon, T. R., Burton, D., & Flay, B. R. (1993). Project towards no tobacco use: 1-year behavior outcomes. *American Journal of Public Health, 83*, 1245-1250.

Sussman, S., Dent, C. W., Stacy, A. W., Sun, P., & Craig, S. (1998). One-year outcomes of project towards no drug abuse. *Preventive Medicine, 27*, 632-642.

Tobler, N. S. (in press). School-based adolescent drug prevention programs: 1998 meta-analysis. *Journal of Primary Prevention.*

Tobler, N. S., Lessard, T., Marshall, D., Ochshorn, P., & Roona, M. (1999). Effectiveness of school-based drug prevention programs for marijuana use. *School Psychology International, 20*, 105-137.

Warren, C. W., Kann, L., Small, M. L., Santelli, J. S., Collins, J. L., & Kolbe, L. J. (1997). Age of initiating selected health-risk behaviors among high school students in the United States. *Journal of Adolescent Health, 21*, 225-31.

Zuckerman, M. (1986). *Sensation seeking and the endogenous deficit theory of drug abuse* (Monograph 74, NIDA Research Monograph Series, 59-70). Rockville, MD: National Institute on Drug Abuse.

III

SUMMING UP

10

High-potential Mediators of
Drug-Abuse Prevention Program Effects

Stewart I. Donaldson

Claremont Graduate University

Drug prevention efforts designed by social scientists do not work.

Despite billions of dollars invested in prevention, America's drug problem is alive and well. Face it, we have lost the war on drugs.

Supply reduction approaches (law enforcement) are effective, but demand reduction (prevention) is hopeless.

The most popular drug-abuse prevention program in America today is not effective, and represents the largest waste of taxpayer resources in the history of prevention and health education.

These statements and perspectives are part of the popular discourse about drug-abuse prevention at the turn of the century. These and similar claims are commonly voiced in the mass media, by human service professionals working with youth on a day-to-day basis, in policy arenas, and in the drug-abuse prevention research literature. Given these views and your current thoughts about the effectiveness of drug-abuse prevention, please take a moment and answer the following forced-choice questions:

1. Do drug-abuse prevention interventions work?
a. Yes
b. No

2. Do drug-abuse prevention interventions work?
a. Always   c. Rarely
b. Sometimes   d. Never

If you answered *No* to question 1, or *c* or *d* to question 2, you agree with the majority of people I have asked to answer these questions. In fact, despite numerous talks and discussions about the promise of drug prevention at this conference, the majority of the audience was still skeptical about the effectiveness of social-science-based drug prevention efforts when I asked these questions during my late afternoon talk. If drug-abuse prevention programs are not effective, why do we continue to spend billions of dollars annually on them? Why is there a large federal research and demonstration project budget for drug-abuse prevention? And, why is there a burgeoning literature on the topic? The answer is that asking the common question of whether or not drug prevention programs work is much too simplistic for this complex topic. One purpose of this chapter is to convince you that whether or not an intervention works is the wrong question to ask in the drug-abuse prevention area.

TYPES OF INTERVENTION RESEARCH

Knowledge about drug-abuse prevention is generally based on three types of research: preintervention research, efficacy research, and effectiveness research (see Donaldson, 1999; Foxhall, 2000). *Preintervention research* typically focuses on theory testing and basic relationships between drug use and various psychological factors. This research is most often conducted before time and resources are invested in program development. Systematic knowledge about the correlates of drug use can be very informative for designing drug-abuse prevention programs.

Efficacy research sets out to study an actual intervention under somewhat controlled conditions. That is, a researcher designs the intervention often using social science theory and preintervention research as a guide, and then implements the program as strongly as possible. The idea is to make sure the program is delivered at full strength in a constrained setting and on a limited sample of clients, to determine if it affects drug use. The same researcher or research team usually designs and conducts the evaluation of the intervention in efficacy research. A major advantage of this type of intervention research is that the research team can maintain control of the evaluation and thus can control for extraneous variables and sort out the causal effects of the program. Disadvantages of efficacy intervention research include (a) the potential conflict of interest involved with evaluating a program one has designed, and (b) the possibility that what can be achieved under ideal conditions cannot be replicated under real world conditions (e.g., when delivered in a school, a community, or via mass media).

In contrast, *effectiveness research* investigates the effects of a program delivered in a "real-world" setting. That is, once a program is taken to scale and implemented with the intention of solving specific problems (as opposed to mainly aiding research interests and goals), the effectiveness of the intervention is evaluated. In an ideal program design scenario, an intervention is developed on the basis of preintervention research findings and tested under ideal conditions in an efficacy trial. If the results are favorable, the intervention is implemented in society and evaluated using effectiveness research procedures, including cost-effectiveness and cost/benefits analyses (Donaldson, 2000; Rossi, Freeman, & Lipsey, 1999). Interventions that demonstrate positive results across all three types of intervention research are believed to have the best chance of solving social problems such as drug-abuse, and are good candidates for future funding by local, state, and federal agencies.

It is possible that interventions judged effective by effectiveness research have not been tested in efficacy research nor based on preintervention research. The drawback of betting heavily on this "streamlined" approach is that many threats to validity often cannot be ruled out when using effectiveness research alone. For example, randomized trials are often beyond the scope of what is possible in effectiveness research; this makes ruling out threats to internal validity quite challenging. Standardization and strict control over research procedures and design are often difficult obtain, and this can introduce undesirable error variance into results. In contrast, an intervention that has shown positive results in preintervention and efficacy research but not in effectiveness research is also risky because it is often very difficult to replicate effects found in controlled studies out in society (external validity issues). The benefit of relying on all three types of intervention research (vs. just one or two) is that the strengths and weaknesses of each approach are typically offsetting. Most threats to validity can be evaluated and hopefully ruled out across the different types of studies.

One notable strength of effectiveness research is that it is more likely to be designed in a way that protects against internal evaluation biases (Scriven, 1991). There is a relatively widely held belief in the evaluation research community that internal evaluations, those evaluations done by evaluators with some stake in positive findings (e.g., evaluators whose financial compensation is in some way affected by intervention success, evaluators who designed the intervention, evaluators who developed the theory upon which the intervention is based, and the like), are less trustworthy than interventions subjected to rigorous external evaluation. In the ideal situation, external evaluators have a large stake in conducting a rigorous and objective evaluation that holds up under the scrutiny of meta-evaluation, serves the best interest of the consumer or intervention recipient, and the evaluators have no stake in whether or not the program is a smashing success or a dismal failure. This is sometimes achieved in effectiveness research by employing different teams to design, implement, and evaluate. It is important to note that this could also be achieved in efficacy research, but history suggests it is much less likely.

EXTERNAL EVALUATION PERSPECTIVE

As might be expected, external evaluators, theory developers, intervention designers, and those who serve dual roles such evaluators and intervention designers often see the world very differently. For obvious reasons, generally speaking, external evaluators are typically less enthusiastic about the potential of new interventions based on their view of the past track record of intervention research. For example, the field of intervention research has been characterized by a history of disappointing results and has been described as a "Parade of Close to Zero Effects" (see Rossi et al., 1999; Shadish, Cook, & Leviton, 1991). Rossi (1985), in a somewhat "tongue in cheek" presentation, introduced the five metallic and plastic laws of program evaluation:

1. *The Iron Law*: The expected value of any net impact assessment of any social program is zero.
2. *The Stainless Steel Law*: The better designed the impact assessment of a social program, the more likely is the net impact to be zero.
3. *The Copper Law*: The more social programs are designed to change individuals, the more likely the net impact will be zero.
4. *The Plastic Law*: Only those programs that are likely to fail are evaluated.
5. *The Plutonium Law*: Program operators will explode when exposed to typical evaluation research findings.

Although humorous on the surface, these laws capture the essence of how many external evaluators feel about the track record of social science-based programming. In short, the history of external evaluation has led many to believe that the American establishment of policymakers, agency officials, professionals, and social scientists has not been effective at designing and implementing interventions to solve social problems such as drug-abuse.

A recent example of this view in the drug-abuse prevention literature involves evaluations of Project D.A.R.E., the most popular drug-abuse prevention program in the United States. In short, Project D.A.R.E. has received record levels of government funding and has reached more than 4.5 million American children, despite a wealth of scientific evidence suggesting that it is not effective at preventing drug-abuse (Dukes, Ullman, & Stein, 1996; Ennett, Tobler, Ringwalt, & Flewelling, 1994) and may even be harmful under some conditions (Donaldson, Graham, Piccinin, & Hansen, 1995).Other external evaluators have come to a very different conclusion about the problem of null effects throughout the history of evaluation research. I have previously referred to this as the *design sensitivity problem* prevalent in evaluation practice today (Donaldson, 1999). In short, this view suggests the dismal track record produced by external evaluations of social science-based interventions is at least partly due to the quality of the evaluations, not just the effectiveness of the interventions.

Lipsey (1988) presented one of the strongest arguments for the design sensitivity position. Based on an extensive, systematic review of the program evaluation literature, Lipsey argued that conventional evaluation research:

1. Is based on constructs that substantially underrepresent the complexity of the causal processes at issue.
2. Is theoretically impoverished and yields little knowledge of practical value.
3. Is crudely operationalized and rarely meets even minimum standards for quality design and measurement.
4. Is largely insensitive to the very treatment effects it purports to study.
5. Produces results and conclusions that are largely a matter of chance and have little to do with the efficacy of the treatments under consideration.

Furthermore, Lipsey and Wilson (1993) subsequently meta-analyzed 111 meta-analyses of intervention studies across a wide range of program domains (representing evaluations of more than 10,000 programs) and reported that most of this literature was based on only crude outcome research with little attention paid to potential mediating and moderating factors.

Although most external evaluators have not been impressed with the evaluation results of social-science-based interventions, there is not general agreement as to why this phenomenon has occurred. However, regardless of whether it is the programs, the evaluations, or both that have failed us in the past, many external evaluators now seem to agree about the agenda for the next generation of intervention evaluations.

Simply stated, the question of interest should no longer be whether programs work but rather how they work and how they can be made to work better (Donaldson, 2000; Lipsey & Wilson, 1993, Rossi et al., 1999; Weiss, 1998). This approach should focus on the investigation of which program components are most effective, the mediating causal processes through which they work, and the characteristics of the participants, service providers, settings, and the like that moderate the relationships between an intervention and its outcomes.

HIGH-POTENTIAL MEDIATORS

Traditional program conceptualization and evaluation (as described earlier) focused on determining the direct effects of undifferentiated "black box" interventions and on answering the question of whether or not interventions worked (see Figure 10.1). Again, a main drawback of this approach is that very little is typically learned when no effect is found. The evaluation researcher is not able to disentangle the success or failure of implementation from the validity of the conceptual model or program theory on which the intervention is based (Crano & Brewer, in press). There is also no way to sort out which intervention components are effective, ineffective, or counterproductive. Furthermore, Hansen and McNeal (1996) argued that behavioral interventions such as drug-abuse prevention programs can only have indirect effects. They called this the Law of Indirect Effect:

> This law dictates that direct effects of a program on behavior are not possible. The expression or suppression of a behavior is controlled by neural and situational processes over which the interventionist has no direct control. To achieve their effects, programs must alter processes that have the potential to indirectly influence the behavior of interest. Simply stated, programs do not attempt to change behavior directly. Instead they attempt to change the way people think about the behavior, the way they perceive the social environment that influences the behavior, the skills they bring to bear on situation that augment risk for the occurrence of the behavior, or the structure of the environment in which the behavior will eventually emerge or be suppressed. The essence of health education is changing predisposing and enabling factors that lead to behavior, not the behavior itself. (Hansen & McNeal, 1996, p. 503)

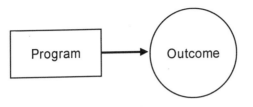

FIGURE 10.1 A direct effect model.

The new agenda for evaluation begins by recognizing that interventions like drugabuse prevention programs are often complex and multidimensional, and aspire for indirect effects on drug use behavior.

In its simple form, an indirect effect conceptualization involves an intervention (e.g., drug prevention video program) affecting a mediator variable (e.g., drug-abuse knowledge), which in turn affects an outcome (e.g., drug use; see Figure 10.2). In this example, the intervention must be effective at increasing knowledge, and increased knowledge must lead to reduced drug use for the intervention to be viewed as effective. Therefore, the link between an intervention and a behavioral outcome is highly dependent on the nature of the mediator/behavioral outcome relationship. Hansen and McNeal (1996) called this the Law of Maximum Expected Potential Effect:

> The magnitude of change in a behavioral outcome that a program can produce is directly limited by the strength of relationships that exist between mediators and targeted behaviors. The existence of this law is based on the mathematical formulae used in estimating the strength of mediating variable relationships, not from empirical observation, although we believe that empirical observations will generally corroborate its existence. An understanding of this law should allow intervention researchers a mathematical grounding in the selection of mediating processes for intervention. An added benefit may ultimately be the ability to predict with some accuracy the a priori maximum potential of programs to have an effect on targeted behavioral outcomes, although this may be beyond the current state-of-the-science to achieve. (Hansen & McNeal, 1996, p. 502)

Therefore, within the specific context of an intervention, if the mediator variable can be adequately affected by the intervention, and the mediator has an adequately strong causal effect on the behavioral outcome, I refer to this variable as a *high-potential mediator*. That is, a high-potential

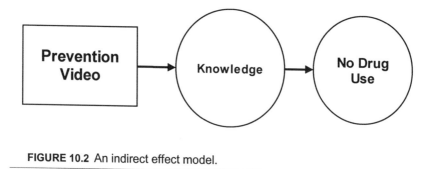

FIGURE 10.2 An indirect effect model.

mediator is a variable that has a strong probability of being affected by an intervention, *and* subsequently affecting a behavioral outcome at a desired level (i.e., has a practically significant effect size; see Donaldson, Street, Sussman, & Tobler, 2000). Based on the preceding discussion, I now argue that a major challenge for the field of drug-abuse prevention is making sure interventions are aimed at the right targets, high-potential mediators.

ADOLESCENT DRUG-ABUSE PREVENTION

The field of drug-abuse prevention is vast and consists of many different prevention approaches (e.g., primary, secondary, and tertiary prevention), types of interventions (e.g., school, work site, community, and mass media), target populations (e.g., children, adolescents, and young adults), and behavioral outcomes (e.g., marijuana use, cocaine use, binge drinking, etc.). The pursuit of high-potential mediators must begin by specifying the particulars of the prevention intervention context. Obviously, high-potential mediators in one prevention context may be worthless in another. To illustrate how one goes about identifying high-potential mediators of drug-abuse prevention interventions, I focus the subsequent discussion on one of the popular and challenging drug prevention problems, the primary prevention of the onset of adolescent substance use.

A recommended first step in the process of selecting high-potential mediators is to isolate the behavioral outcomes of interest. The "gateway drugs" of cigarettes, alcohol, and marijuana use are often the main focus of primary prevention interventions targeted at adolescents. It is very important to have realistic expectations for how a prevention intervention may influence these behavioral outcomes. For example, it is not uncommon to think that the goal of a drug-abuse prevention intervention is to prevent adolescents from ever using or abusing drugs. This would be ideal but is well beyond what can be realistically expected from most primary prevention efforts. A more realistic expectation for a primary prevention intervention is to delay the onset of drug use and/or the prevalence of use among at least a subgroup of a target population. It is important to underscore the point that many drug-abuse prevention interventions are ultimately judged as failures because initial behavioral objectives are unrealistic. Interventions that deter the onset of substance use are believed to be important because they prevent school failure and other problem behaviors during the formative years of adolescents, and the earlier adolescents begin using drugs, the more likely they are to abuse drugs as young adults (Hawkins et al., 1997).

Once realistic behavioral outcomes are selected, theory and prior research can be a good starting point for isolating high-potential mediator variables that are likely to be strongly related to the behavioral outcomes of interest. For example, Petraitis, Flay, and Miller (1995) reviewed 14 multivariate theories of experimental substance use among adolescents and proposed a framework that organizes their central constructs into three types of influence (social, attitudinal, and intrapersonal) and three distinct levels of influence (proximal, distal, and ultimate). Each theoretical approach described suggests specific mediators, which vary in effectiveness across the various time frames (e.g., proximal versus distal behavioral outcomes).

Even more specific to this illustration, Hawkins, Catalano, and Miller (1992) conducted a thorough review of the literature and isolated 17 risk and protective factors for the onset of drug use (see Table 10.1). Interventions designed to prevent these risk factors are presumed to lower rates of adolescent drug-abuse. However, it is clear to see from this table that some risk/protective factors are much more likely to be influenced by primary prevention interventions (e.g., attitudes, peer associations, family practices) than others (e.g., neighborhood disorganization, some physiological factors). It is important to underscore that high-potential mediators must be both strongly causally related to the behavioral outcome of interest, and amenable to practically significant change by the intervention of interest. Therefore, in a given prevention context, one must make sure both that the set of targeted mediators are powerful enough to affect the behavioral outcomes and that it is feasible to change them in the target population.

There now is a large body of literature describing efforts to prevent adolescent substance use. Hansen (1992, 1993) summarized the 12 most popular substance-abuse prevention strategies and identified their

Table 10.1
Seventeen Risk and Protective Factors
for the Onset of Drug Abuse

Factor #	Factor
1	Laws and norms
2	Availability
3	Extreme economic deprivation
4	Neighborhood disorganization
5	Physiological factors
6	Family drug use
7	Family management practices
8	Family conflict
9	Low bonding to family
10	Early and persistent problem behaviors
11	Academic failure
12	Low commitment to school
13	Peer rejection in elementary grades
14	Association with drug-using peers
15	Alienation and rebelliousness
16	Attitudes favorable to drug use
17	Early onset of drug use

Note. Abstracted from Catalano and Miller (1992).

presumed theoretical program or mediating mechanisms (see Table 10.2). Although all three of these frameworks (Hansen, 1992, 1993; Hawkins et al., 1992; Petraitis et al., 1995) and others (Newcomb & Early-wine, 1996; Wills, Pierce, & Evans, 1996) can be very useful for narrowing down the range of possibilities, it often is difficult to find evidence that reveals which combination of mediators will produce the largest effects on the behaviors of interest.

Fortunately, relatively recent mediation analyses in this area have begun to isolate some of the strongest mechanisms at work in adolescent drug-abuse prevention. This work has suggested that social-influence-based prevention programming is one of the most effective approaches for preventing drug-abuse among young adolescents from general populations (see Donaldson et al., 1996). For example, MacKinnon et al. (1991) found that social norms, especially among friends, and beliefs about the positive consequences of drug use appeared to be important mediators of program effects in project STAR (Students Taught Aware-

TABLE 10.2
Twelve Popular Substance-Abuse Prevention Strategies

Item	Strategy
1	Normative education: Ddecreases perceptions about prevalence and acceptability beliefs; establishes conservative norms.
2	Refusal assertion training: Increases the perception that one can deal effectively with pressure to use drugs if offered; increases self-efficacy.
3	Information about consequences of use: Increases perceptions of personal vulnerability to common consequences of drugs.
4	Personal commitment pledges: Increases personal commitment and intentions not to use drugs
5	Values: Increases perception that drug use is incongruent with lifestyle
6	Alternatives: Increases awareness of enjoying life without drugs.
7	Goal-setting skills: Increases ability to set and achieve goals; increases achievement orientation
8	Decision-making skills: Increases ability to make reasoned decisions.
9	Self-esteem: Increases feeling of self-worth.
10	Stress skills: Increases perceptions of coping skills; reduces reported level of stress.
11	Assistance skills: Increases availability of help
12	Life skills: Increases ability to maintain positive social relations

Note: Adapted from Hansen (1992, 1993).

ness and Resistance). The program did not appear to have effects through resistance skills (refusal training). The notion that social norms are a potent aspect of prevention programming was subsequently found in a randomized prevention trial, the Adolescent Alcohol Prevention Trial (Donaldson, Graham, & Hansen, 1994; Donaldson et al., 1995).Continuing with the example, we might decide that a set of high-potential mediators, broadly conceived as social norms variables, are what we will try to influence with a mass media drug-abuse prevention strategy. A careful examination of how these variables are currently operating in the target population is needed to determine what types of communication and data

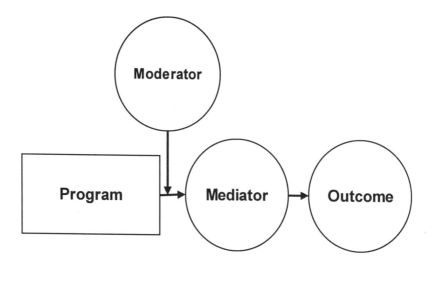

FIGURE 10.3 A moderator effect model.

are most appropriate. It is important to note that it is possible that for some prevention problems, the variables most likely to affect the behavioral outcomes are not likely to be affected by the available prevention strategy options. However, in this example, mass media prevention approaches seem particularly well suited for influencing the social norm variables identified in the adolescent drug-abuse prevention literature (e.g., Donohew, Sypher, & Bukoski, 1991).

Once a set of high-potential mediators has been selected, it is important to consider potential moderators of the links in a mediation model of drug-abuse prevention (see Donaldson, 2000). A moderator is a qualitative (e.g., gender, ethnicity, viewing setting) or quantitative (e.g., amount of viewing prevention message, length of prevention message) variable that affects the direction and/or strength of the relationships between the intervention and mediator, or the mediator and the outcome (see Baron & Kenny, 1986). Figure 10.3 illustrates that the moderator variable conditions or influences the path between the intervention and the mediator. This means that the strength and/or the direction of the relationship between the intervention and the mediator is significantly affected by the moderator variable. This type of moderator relationship is of primary importance in drug-abuse prevention programming. Intervention designers can benefit greatly from considering whether or not potential moderator variables such as participant characteristics, message characteristics, characteristics of the viewing setting, and the like influence the intervention's ability to affect target mediators.

A series of evaluations is sometimes needed to fully understand mediating and moderating effects of drug-abuse prevention interventions. This is because many drug-abuse prevention interventions are complex, context dependent, and delivered to target populations with diverse characteristics. A summary of findings from social-influence-based prevention mediation studies mentioned previously provides a nice illustration of this complexity. Following is a summary of key findings from evaluations of the Adolescent Alcohol Prevention Trial:

1. A school culture change program (normative education) lowered beliefs about drug use acceptability and prevalence estimates (in seventh grade), which predicted cigarette, marijuana, and cigarette use (in eighth grade). This pattern of results was virtually the same across potential moderators of gender, ethnicity, context (public vs. private school), drugs and levels of risk and was durable across time (see Hansen & Graham, 1991; Donaldson et al, 1994).
2. Resistance skills training did improve refusal skills, but refusal skills did not predict subsequent drug use (Donaldson et al., 1994).
3. Those who received only resistance skills in public schools actually had higher prevalence estimates (a harmful effect; type of school is shown as the moderator; Donaldson et al., 1995).
4. Refusal skills did predict lower alcohol use for those students who had negative intentions to drink alcohol (negative intention to drink is the moderator; Donaldson et al., 1995).
5. The effects of normative education were subsequently verified using reciprocal best friend reports of drug use, in addition to traditional self-report drug use measures (Donaldson, Thomas, Graham, Au, & Hansen, 2000.

SUMMARY AND CONCLUSIONS

There remains considerable skepticism about our ability to use social science knowledge to prevent or solve social problems such as drug-abuse. Although there often are promising early findings from preintervention research and efficacy studies, the history of external evaluations of effectiveness research has been rather disappointing. Whether one interprets the prevalence of null effects as the result of ineffective interventions or insensitive external evaluations, most agree that modern evaluation research needs to move beyond just asking whether or not interventions work. A new focus on high-potential mediators promises to help us understand how interventions work and how to design them to work better.

The field of drug-abuse prevention seems ahead of the curve in identifying high-potential mediators of intervention effects. In this chapter, I summarized some of the recent literature on the primary prevention of adolescent drug use to illustrate the value of this approach. This literature suggests that social-influence-based strategies have been quite effective under some conditions, but can be counterproductive under other conditions. This example underscores the value of identifying and evaluating mediator and moderators variables in the drug-abuse prevention area. It is important to note that the example was limited to just one of the many domains of drug-abuse prevention, but the process of high-potential mediator and moderator analysis may be just as relevant across different domains.

The recognition that drug-abuse prevention interventions often need to be complex and multidimensional to address a specific prevention problem, and may vary in effectiveness across participant characteristics, contexts, and behavioral outcomes, should be helpful for the conceptualization and evaluation of future prevention efforts. It is my belief that a careful investigation of the scientific literature in most prevention domains will turn up at least some information helpful for identifying high-potential mediators. Finally, future systematic external evaluations that involve mediation and moderator analysis of intervention efforts promise to increase our cumulative wisdom about how drug prevention interventions work—and how to make them work better.

REFERENCES

Baron, R. M., & Kenny D. A. (1986). The moderator-mediator variable distinction in social psychological research: Conceptual, strategic, and statistical considerations. *Journal of Personality and Social Psychology, 51*, 1173-1182.

Crano, W. D., & Brewer, M. B. (in press). *Principles and methods of social research* (2nd Ed.). Mahwah, NJ: Lawrence Erlbaum Associates.

Donaldson, S. I. (1999). The territory ahead for theory-driven program and organizational evaluation. *Mechanisms, 3*, 3-5.

Donaldson, S. I. (2000). Mediator and moderator analysis in program development. In S. Sussman (Ed.), *Handbook of program development for health behavior research* (pp. 470-496). Newbury Park, CA: Sage.

Donaldson, S. I., Graham, J. W., & Hansen, W. B. (1994). Testing the generalizability of intervening mechanism theories: Understanding the effects of school-based substance use prevention interventions. *Journal of Behavioral Medicine, 17,* 195-216.

Donaldson, S. I., Graham, J. W., Piccinin, A. M., & Hansen, W. B. (1995). Resistance-skills training and onset of alcohol use: Evidence for beneficial and potentially harmful effects in public schools and in private catholic schools. *Health Psychology, 14,* 291-300.

Donaldson, S. I., Street, G., Sussman, S., & Tobler, N. (2000). Using meta-analyses to improve the design of interventions. In S. Sussman (Ed.), *Handbook of program development for health behavior research* (pp. 449-466). Newbury Park, CA: Sage.

Donaldson, S. I., Sussman, S., MacKinnon, D. P., Severson, H. H., Glyn, T., Murray, D. M., & Stone, E. J. (1996). Drug-abuse prevention programming: Do we know what content works? *American Behavioral Scientist, 39,* 868-883.

Donaldson, S. I., Thomas, C. W., Graham, J. W., Au, J., & Hansen, W. B. (2000). Verifying drug prevention program effects using reciprocal best friend reports. *Journal of Behavioral Medicine, 23,* 221-234.

Donohew, L., Sypher, H. E., & Bukoski, W. J. (1991). *Persuasive communication and drug-abuse prevention.* Hillsdale, NJ: Erlbaum.

Dukes, R., Ullman, J., & Stein, J. (1996). Three-year follow-up of drug abuse resistance education (DARE). *Evaluation Review, 20,* 49-66.

Ennett, S. T., Tobler, N. S., Ringwalt, C. L., & Flewelling, R. L. (1994). How effective is drug abuse resistance education? A meta-analysis of Project DARE outcome evaluations. *American Journal of Public Health, 84,* 1394-1401.

Foxhall, K. (2000). Research for the real world: NIMH is pumping big money into effectiveness research to move promising treatments into practice. *APA Monitor, 31,* 28-36.

Hansen, W. B. (1992). School-based substance abuse prevention: A review of the state of the art in curriculum, 1980-1990. *Health Education Research: Theory and Practice, 7,* 403-430.

Hansen, W. B. (1993). School-based alcohol prevention programs. *Alcohol Health and Research World, 17,* 54-60.

Hansen, W. B., & Graham, J. W. (1991). Preventing adolescent alcohol, marijuana, and cigarette use among adolescents: Peer pressure resistance training versus establishing conservative norms. *Preventive Medicine, 20,* 414-430.

Hansen, W. B., & McNeal, Jr., R. B. (1996). The law of maximum expected potential effect: Constraints placed on program effectiveness by mediator relationships. *Health Education Research, 11,* 501-507.

Hawkins, J. D., Catalano, R. F., & Miller, J. M. (1992). Risk and protective factors for alcohol and other drug problems in adolescence and early adulthood: Implications for substance abuse prevention. *Psychological Bulletin, 112,* 64-105.

Hawkins, J. D., Graham, J. W., Maguin, B., Abbot, R., Hill, K. G., & Catalano, R. (1997). Exploring the effects of age of alcohol use initiation and psychosocial risk factors on subsequent alcohol misuse. *Journal of Studies on Alcohol, 58,* 280-290.

Lipsey, M. W. (1988). Practice and malpractice in evaluation research. *Evaluation Practice, 9,* 5-24.

Lipsey, M. W., & Wilson, D. B. (1993). The efficacy of psychological, educational, and behavioral treatment: Confirmation from meta-analysis. *American Psychologist, 48,* 1181-1209.

MacKinnon, D. P., Johnson, C. A., Pentz, M. A., Dwyer, J. H., Hansen, W. B., Flay, B. R., & Wang, E. Y. (1991). Mediating mechanisms in a school-based drug prevention program: First-year effects of the Midwestern prevention project. *Health Psychology, 10,* 164-172.

Newcomb, M., & Earlywine, M. (1996). Intrapersonal contributors to drug use: The willing host. *American Behavioral Scientist, 39,* 823-837.

Petraitis, J., Flay, B. R., & Miller, T. Q. (1995). Reviewing theories of adolescent substance abuse: Organizing pieces of the puzzle. *Psychological Bulletin, 117,* 67-86.

Rossi, P. H. (1985, April). *The iron law of evaluation and other metallic rules.* Paper presented at State University of New York, Albany, Rockefeller College.

Rossi, P. H., Freeman, H. E., & Lipsey, M. W. (1999). *Evaluation: A systematic approach* (6th edition). Thousand Oaks, CA: Sage.

Scriven, M. (1991). *Evaluation thesaurus* (4th Ed.). Newbury Park, CA: Sage.

Shadish, W. R., Cook, T. D., & Leviton, L. C. (1991). *Foundations of program evaluation: Theories of practice.* Newbury Park, CA: Sage.

Weiss, C. H. (1998). *Evaluation* (2nd Ed.). Upper Saddle River, NJ: Prentice Hall.

Wills, T. A., Pierce, J. P., & Evans, R. I. (1996). Large-scale environmentl risk factors for substance use. *American Behavioral Scientist, 39,* 808-822.

11

A Meta-analysis of the Effectiveness of Mass-Communication for Changing Substance-use Knowledge, Attitudes, and Behavior

James H. Derzon
Pacific Institutes for Research and Evaluation

Mark W. Lipsey
Vanderbilt University

Recent data show that within a given 30-day period, 37% of 12th graders used tobacco, 53% used alcohol, 24% used marijuana, and 11% used one or more other illegal drugs (*Monitoring the Future*, 1998). The personal, social, and economic costs of the abuse of these substances dictates that steps be taken to minimize their impact on young persons' lives. In 1997, in response to this community need, the Office of National Drug Control Policy began an unprecedented 5-year mass-media campaign to educate and enable America's youth to reject illegal drugs.

One facet of the National Youth Antidrug Media Campaign is directed at youth ages 9-19 years and is designed to enhance awareness that (a) most youth do not use drugs, (b) most youth disapprove of drug use, (c) drug use is a poor choice, and also to (d) enhance refusal skills, (e) reinforce acceptable alternatives to drug use, and (f) encourage public pledges not to use drugs. The second facet of the campaign is directed at parents, caregivers, and other youth-influential adults. On this front the objectives are to (g) heighten negative perceptions of drug use, (h) encourage discussions of the negatives of drug use, (i) improve parenting skills, particularly management and communication, (j) promote community involvement, especially around prevention programming, and (k) enhance skills to recognize drug use in children and seek services to aid these children.

The implementation of this initiative makes a synthesis of the state of current knowledge on the capability of media interventions to reduce youth substance-use particularly timely. Prior reviews of the research on this issue have reached mixed conclusions, as the summary that follows shows. Given this ambiguity, meta-analysis offers distinct advantages by applying a systematic quantitative approach to the task of describing study findings and integrating the results, to the extent possible, into a coherent depiction of the current state of knowledge. Meta-analysis techniques, therefore, were applied to a selection of relevant studies of the effects of media messages directed to youth audiences. Study coding and analysis were organized around a set of themes drawn from these studies and conventional reviews, as summarized later.

MEDIA INTERVENTIONS TO REDUCE YOUTH SUBSTANCE USE

After reviewing over 400 articles, books, reports, and reviews about the relationships between mass media, its audiences, and the images and messages mass media contain regarding alcohol, Dorn and South (1985) came to "inconclusive conclusions" regarding the effect of media messages on increasing or decreasing the amounts individuals drink. Considering media specifically designed to influence alcohol and tobacco use, Saffer (1995) found that advertising could be linked to increases in alcohol and tobacco use but the evidence was not consistent. Perhaps the best general characterization of the effectiveness of the media for producing behavior change comes from Mendelson (1968), who described "mass communication as a sort of an aerosol spray. As you spray it on the surface, some of it hits the target; most of it drifts away; and very little of it penetrates" (p. 132).

Research on the effects of media messages specifically directed at reducing substance-use has yielded similarly mixed results with regard to behavioral outcomes, but has produced more positive results for awareness, knowledge, and attitude change. McAlister's (1981) review of the effectiveness of several large-scale antismoking campaigns, for instance, found that these campaigns had not been very successful in getting people to stop smoking, but had worked well in making them aware of the dangers of smoking and the health benefits of stopping. A somewhat more favorable review of 56 mass-media programs to reduce adult cigarette smoking by Flay (1987a) concluded that such programs could produce small but meaningful differences in smoking behavior as well as larger changes in knowledge and attitudes. When media messages are combined with supporting programs at the school and community-level, they are associated with more significant reductions in both short- and long-term smoking prevalence (Pierce, Macaskill, & Hill, 1990). Carefully designed evaluations of public service announcement (PSA) campaigns targeting substance-use have shown only small effects. For example, a study of an antidrug abuse campaign found little impact, even at the informational level (Schmeling & Wotring, 1980). PSAs to decrease cigarette use appear to be similarly ineffectual (e.g., Warner, 1977; Murphy, 1980). Despite the evidence of weak effects, however, confidence in the value of PSAs runs high (Brawley, 1983; Sprafkin, Swift, & Hess, 1983). Much of the ineffectiveness of earlier programs has been attributed to low recall of the announcements (e.g., Goodstadt, 1977; O'Keefe, 1971), which to a large extent may have been a function of the timing and targeting of the broadcasts. Hanneman and McEwen's (1973) content analysis of 2 weeks of drug-abuse appeals found that only 15 of 85 were directed at youth, nearly half were broadcast between 10:00 a.m. and 3:00 p.m., and another third were broadcast between 10:30 p.m. and 10:00a.m. None were shown during prime time and none were directed toward, or specific to, the needs of any identifiable subpopulation.

Flay (1987a) concluded that media campaigns work best when they are accompanied by interpersonal or community support components. One of the most highly cited examples of a successful media intervention is the Stanford Three Community Study, which tested the impact of a 2-year campaign to reduce cardiovascular disease among adults living in a small California city (Farquhar, Maccoby, & Solomon, 1984; Farquhar, Maccoby, & Wood, 1977; Stern, Farquhar, Maccoby, & Russell, 1976). The first community in this study was exposed to television and radio spots, newspaper columns and advertisements, billboards, posters, and mailed materials to create problem awareness and teach cardiovascular risk reduction techniques. A second, similar community received all of these plus face-to-face instruction for a subset of high-risk individuals; a third community served as a control. The general finding was that the media campaign was effective at stimulating health-related behaviors, such as better diet, that were based on new knowledge (Flora, Maccoby, & Farquhar, 1989), but alteration of ingrained behaviors such as smoking or sedentary lifestyle occurred only when the media messages were supplemented with more intensive instruction (Alcalay, 1983).

The Stanford project and others like it (e.g., Finland's North Karelia project) have explored the role of various supplementary components in facilitating the effects of media messages on behavior change. Supporting activities, such as school programs, group discussions, face-to-face discussions, community organization, and the like, have been demonstrated to increase the effectiveness of media messages for inducing behavioral change (e.g., Flay, 1987a, 1987b; Katz, 1988; Lewin, 1997; Lewin & Gold, 1999).

These conclusions are consistent with McAlister, Ramirez, Galavotti, and Gallion's (1989) observation that campaigns designed to reduce smoking must fulfill three functions. First, audiences must be informed about problematic behaviors and their potential consequences. Second, they must be persuaded to stop or avoid those behaviors. And third, they must be trained in the skills needed to make changes. These authors noted the importance of social learning or modeling for achieving this last function and the contribution of an adequate support network. Thus, although mass media can provide many of the components of an effective intervention, there are indications that campaigns must rely, in part, on the availability of personal and community support to be successful in changing behavior.

Wallack and DeJong argued that by themselves, PSAs primarily fulfill political and commercial functions and should not be expected to be effective tools for improving public health (Atkin, DeJong, & Wallack, 1992; DeJong, Atkin, & Wallack, 1992; Wallack, 1990; Wallack & DeJong, 1995). Politically, PSAs give the impression of concern while maintaining the status quo (Wallack, 1990). Commercially, they may be used to shift attention from one concern to another (e.g., Partnership for a Drug-Free America is partially funded by alcohol and tobacco producers and focuses attention on marijuana and cocaine) or to improve public perceptions of an industry (e.g., beer industry sponsored "moderation" campaigns). From this somewhat cynical perspective, PSAs are ineffectual because they are largely irrelevant– at best they address symptoms, and at worst they blame the victims of social inequality (Ryan, 1971).

A less pessimistic view is that individual change is an appropriate target for public health media campaigns, but such campaigns often are unsuccessful because their effects depend heavily on the characteristics of the message (e.g., Hale & Dillard, 1995; Leventhal, 1970) and various intra-personal (Fazio, Chen, McDonel, & Sherman, 1982; Kahneman, Slovac, & Tversky, 1984) and interpersonal processes (e.g., Cartwright, 1949; Katz, 1957; Katz & Lazarsfeld, 1955; Wallack, 1990). Following McGuire (1966, 1978, 1980, 1985), the various factors related to the effectiveness of media campaigns can be depicted as an input-output array with the manipulable independent variables from which persuasive messages are constructed constituting the input column. The output column, in turn, consists of the dependent variables the message may be expected to affect, for example, the substance-using behaviors of adolescents, and the attitudes, awareness, and knowledge relating to those behaviors. Thus, much of the variation in study findings on the effect of media interventions for reducing youth substance-use may be explained by knowing the characteristics of the campaign (input), what outcome was assessed (output), and which substance the campaign targeted.

Input variables. The input dimension of media campaigns is described by the characteristics of the source, message, dissemination, and supplementation. The *source* refers to the channel or type(s) of media used (e.g., TV, print, radio) to disseminate the message. Because these media require different amounts of recipient involvement, the channel used may influence the impact of a message (Maibach & Flora, 1993; Petty, Baker, & Gleicher, 1991). In discussions of persuasive communication, source variables typically also include characteristics of the spokesperson. There is evidence that spokespersons who are credible (Hass, 1981), attractive (Chaiken, 1979; Janis, 1983), and male (Robinson & McArthur, 1982) are more persuasive.

The *message* itself is critical. Communication is most effective when the message is tailored to the social and psychographic profiles of the target audience (Flynn et al. 1994; Maibach, & Cotton, 1995; Palmgreen, Donohew, & Lorch, 1995). For example, messages with high sensation value have been shown to be effective in attracting the attention and interest of certain youth at risk for drug use (Lorch et al. 1994). Similarly, fear appeals may be effective in combination with messages that heighten vulnerability to the threat and offer a solution that is easy and effective (Hale & Dillard, 1995). Ads may also be designed to change prevailing attitudes, such as those relating to the perceived risks of substance-use or social disapproval, which are expected to lead to changes in substance-use prevalence (Bachman, Johnston, & O'Malley, 1990; Bachman, Johnston, O'Malley, & Humphrey, 1988). Messages directed at improving knowledge also can be tailored to youthful audiences. Adolescents tend to overestimate the prevalence of drug use and rarely discuss it with each other (Dusenbury & Falco, 1997). Correcting these misperceptions has been found effective in reducing substance-use (Botvin et al. 1995; Ellickson & Bell, 1990; Graham, Marks, & Hansen, 1991; Hansen, 1992). Similarly, messages aimed at enhancing social desirability, health appeals, improving decision-making skills, and promoting resistance skills also are believed to have the potential to reduce youth substance-use.

For media messages to be effective, they must be noticed by their intended audience (Flay & Sobel, 1983). *Dissemination* refers to when and how often a message is delivered (e.g., the time of day the message airs and how often it is broadcast), how long the message runs (i.e., the period of implementation), and the length of the message. Each of these items has the potential to influence whether the communication is noticed by the intended audience (Goodstadt, 1977; Rappeport, Labow, & Williams, 1975) and may influence the effects of the message on substance-use (Field, Deitrick, Hersey, Probst, & Theologus, 1983; Hanneman, McEwen, & Coyne, 1973). A more relevant formulation may be in terms of the perceptions of the audience, as assessed by measures of message recall and accuracy.

Another way of improving dissemination is through *supplementation* with additional community resources that are used to reinforce, provide depth, and extend the salience and generalizability of messages provided by a media campaign. For instance, a media campaign may enlist the support of parents, teachers, or other youth-influential adults to support the message in face-to-face or group settings (Goldberg et al., 1996; Hafstad, Aarø, & Langmark, 1996; Katz & Lazarsfeld, 1955). Or, community organizations, schools, clubs or other naturally occurring youth groups may provide supportive programs (Field et al., 1983; Murray, Prokhorov, & Harty, 1994; Perry, Klepp, & Sillers, 1989; Worden et al., 1996). It is important to note that supplementation in this sense is defined in terms of using local advocates to reinforce the message, and is thus distinguished from mass-communication interventions of the "talk with your child" type in which the behaviors, attitudes, and knowledge of parents and other youth-influential adults are the target of the media campaign itself.

In addition to characteristics of the campaign, characteristics of the *recipient* will likely influence how the message is encoded, interpreted, stored, and recalled. For example, youth will react differently if they are at high risk for substance-use than if they are low risk (Flynn et al., 1997). Similarly, age and gender may affect the response to a media message. Targeting media messages to specific groups and designing them to appeal to such groups, therefore, constitute important features of the input function. Each input variable represents choices that can be made by the designers or distributors of a media campaign, and each likely will influence which message is received and attended to by those whose behavior the campaign seeks to change.

Output Variables. The output side of a media campaign consists of the potential effects of the media messages on various audiences. The literature on media campaigns to reduce substance-use generally reports findings on some mix of outcome variables representing awareness of the messages and knowledge, attitudes, and behaviors related to use of the substance(s) at issue. Youth substance-use behaviors, and the attitudes and knowledge that presumably precede that use, often are the primary focus of media campaigns. However, parents and other adults with influence on youth also may be targeted for messages aimed at affecting their knowledge, attitudes, and behavior in ways that will, in turn, influence youth.

Media messages have been used in attempts to enhance the perceptions of harm associated with the adolescent use of gateway drugs (Kandel, Yamaguchi, & Chen, 1992), make parents aware that their children are at risk for using drugs and vulnerable to their negative consequences (Black, 1991), strengthen perceptions of personal efficacy in preventing youth drug use (Newcomb & Felix-Ortiz, 1992; Resnick et al., 1997), improve parenting skills such as communication with youth or applying consistent rules (Block, Block, & Keyes, 1988; Coombs, Paulson, & Richardson, 1991; Dishion, Andrews, Kavanaugh, & Soberman, 1996; Moschis, 1987; Williams, 1994), and increase parental supervision and monitoring (Biglan, Duncan, Ary, & Smolkowski, 1995; Wu & Kandel, 1995).

For policy purposes, the important outcome variables relate to substance-use by the youth targeted in media campaigns (e.g., as indicated by prevalence rates, age of initial use, frequency of use, and the like). However, media interventions cannot reduce substance-use directly (e.g., through incapacitation or reduction in supply), but rather, must work by changing the knowledge and attitudes of their audience with the expectation that these changes will, in turn, produce the desired changes in behavior. Although this knowledge-attitude-behaviors (KAB) model may not be the most effective approach to behavior change (Wallack, 1980; Winett, 1993), and other conceptions abound (e.g., Bandura, 1986, p. 252; Wicker, 1969), it is nonetheless central to the logic of media campaigns for reducing substance-use. From this perspective, positive changes in knowledge and attitudes are proximal outcomes necessary to the success of the intervention; they demonstrate transfer of the information contained in the communication. Changes in substance-use behaviors are the distal outcomes of the intervention and are presumed to follow from the psychological effects of the messages. That is, knowledge and attitudes are presumed to be the mediator variables in a causal chain connecting receipt of the message (awareness) with behavior change. If this logic is faulty, then success by a media campaign in changing knowledge and attitudes will not necessarily lead to changes in substance-use behavior.

Thus, in examining media-based programs for substance-use, it is appropriate to attend both to input and output variables. Among output variables, effects on putative mediators must be distinguished from substance-use behaviors themselves. These various outcomes, in turn, should be investigated in relation to the input characteristics of the media messages and their distribution to the target audience. This framework, and the specific variables and features described earlier, guided the design of our meta-analysis.

METHODS

Meta-analysis revolves around effect sizes computed to represent the key findings of the studies under investigation. A critical step in meta-analysis is to determine which effect size statistic provides the most appropriate representation of the relationships of interest in a body of research (Lipsey & Wilson, 2001). Because media interventions are often delivered to a community, school, or other aggregate unit, few studies involve random assignment of such units to intervention and control conditions. Research on the effects of media interventions for substance-use among youth consists largely of one-group pre-to-post designs, nonequivalent comparison-group designs, and comparisons of one intervention with another. Despite the inherent weaknesses of such designs, this research provides the best information currently available about media effects under realistic conditions. To capture the range of findings presented in studies of such diverse design, we chose to use the standardized pre-to-post gain effect size statistic (Becker, 1988) for the meta-analysis. This effect size statistic is defined for a given sample and a given dependent variable as the post-test mean minus the pretest mean divided by the pooled standard deviations of posttest and pretest. Thus, the effect size represents the change from pretest to posttest in standard deviation units. By convention, changes on a dependent variable in the direction the intervention is intended to produce are coded as positive values and those in the contrary direction are coded as negative values, irrespective of the sign of the arithmetic difference between the respective means. Reduced substance-use, for instance, would yield a positive pre-to-post gain effect size, as would an increase in favorable attitudes toward abstinence.

For a one-group pre-to-post design, the standardized gain effect size is computed straightforwardly using the means and standard deviations of the pretests and posttests for each dependent variable of interest from the single subject sample used in the study. For group comparison designs (i.e., those with nonrandomly assigned control groups or comparisons between groups receiving different interventions), the separate arms of the comparison were separated and pre-to-post standardized gain effect sizes computed for each distinct respondent sample on each dependent variable of interest. Thus in a design in which a media intervention was applied to one school with a neighboring school used as a control, pre-to-post effect sizes were computed separately for the students in each school.

It is important to emphasize that the effect sizes that result from this approach cannot be interpreted directly as estimates of intervention effects. The difference between pretest and posttest measures reflects the amount of change due to the intervention, if any, plus that stemming from all factors that have influence during the measurement interval. The change reflected in these effect sizes, therefore, confounds the effect of the treatment with such other factors as changes in the cost or availability of drugs (Warner, 1986), attention-focusing events such as the death of comedian Chris Farley from a drug overdose (Jeter, 1998), changes in policy such as those introduced by the 1971 ban on radio and television advertising of cigarettes (Hamilton, 1972; Teel, Teel, & Bearden, 1979), and various secular and population trends associated with substance-use. These effect sizes are interpretable (cautiously) only in relation to others in a set with which they are compared. For instance, if the pre-to-post changes for media interventions with supplementary components are significantly larger than for similar interventions without supplements, this provides evidence that supplements enhance the intervention effects. Evidence of this form is not definitive but, given the weak research designs typical of media research, it provides some systematic indication of the factors that appear most effective in that research. The inclusion of pre-to-post effect sizes from untreated control groups in these comparisons allows estimation of the magnitude of change that occurs without intervention and thus supplies an approximate baseline for assessing relative effects.

Studies Summarized. Research studies were identified and selected for this meta-analysis if they met the following criteria:

1. They assessed the effects of a media intervention designed to prevent or reduce youth substance-use. Eligible media interventions included messages designed for dissemination to a specific audience or the general public and delivered via print, audio, video, or electronic media, or some combination thereof.
2. The research was conducted in a community, field, or research setting (e.g., university), and the message content and outcomes measured involved the relevant areas of substance-use.
3. The intervention studied was directed toward prevention or reduced use of (a) illicit drugs (or any specific illicit drug, e.g., marijuana), (b) tobacco, or (c) alcohol.
4. The intervention focused primarily on youth substance-use and targeted youth audiences. However, interventions intended to change

parents' or other youth-influential adults' knowledge, attitudes, behaviors, and so on, were also eligible if the theme of the message was to encourage attention to the youth problem.

5. The study presented quantitative data from which preintervention to postintervention change could be derived for one or more dependent variables related to substance-use. The study design could be either a one-group pre-to-post design, a non-equivalent multi-group comparison, or a randomized experiment. Case studies, one group post-test only designs, and other such approaches that did not permit pre-to-post effect size estimation were excluded.

6. The study was reported in English and carried out in a developed, Western country. Both published and unpublished reports were included.

The data assembled for this meta-analysis represent the findings presented in 110 reports from 72 distinct studies (a bibliography of these reports is available from the first author on request). These reports were identified from computer searches in such bibliographic databases as ERIC, Social SciSearch, PsycINFO, NCJRS, Dissertation Abstracts Online, Mental Health Abstracts, and MEDLINE. Additional articles were identified from the citations in reports and reviews that were screened during the course of the search. Journals specific to the media industry were also examined to ensure completeness. The 72 studies of the effects of media interventions for substance-use that qualified for the meta-analysis yielded 1,288 pre-to-post effect size values for 90 distinct subject samples that received media messages and 33 control samples that did not.

To keep any one subject sample from contributing multiple effect sizes to any analysis, effect size values for different operationalizations of the dependent variable involved in the analysis were averaged within the study to produce a single mean value for each independent sample. This procedure ensured that no subject sample contributed more than one effect size to any analysis so that the effect sizes in each analysis were statistically independent. In all computations with effect sizes from different samples, each was weighted by its inverse variance to reflect the greater statistical precision of estimates based on larger samples (Becker, 1988; Hedges & Olkin, 1983; Shadish & Haddock, 1994).

FINDINGS

The majority of the studies contributing to this meta-analysis were conducted in the United States in urban or suburban settings using a quasi-experimental design. Of the 72 studies, 48 reported outcomes on substance-use behavior. Among these, tobacco was the substance most often addressed by the media messages, followed by illicit drugs and alcohol in about equal numbers. Most studies involved print and/or TV media, and all targeted youth or youth-influential adults. A majority of the campaigns used multiple, repetitive messages and broadcast to a general audience.

There were 39 studies that reported effects on substance-use attitudes. Nearly all of these used TV as the media source, with print and radio also frequent (often in combination with TV). Most of the campaigns targeted youth and used multiple, different messages with repetition broadcast to a general audience. Only 24 studies reported intervention effects on substance-use knowledge. These studies showed distributions of print, TV, and radio media similar to those already described. They also mainly targeted youth audiences but addressed alcohol use as commonly as tobacco. As in the other groups of studies, nearly all the campaigns in these studies used multiple, different messages, with repetition, that were broadcast to the general public.

The distributions of audience and media intervention characteristics with comparisons of the mean pre-to-post effect sizes for each are shown in Figures 11.1-11.3. Because these graphical displays are somewhat unusual, it is worthwhile taking a moment to explain the information displayed. Each figure shows a different output variable—effects on substance-use behavior, attitudes, and knowledge, respectively. To the left of each figure the categories of input features are displayed in bold. Within each category are different features of the subject sample, media message, and so forth on which study findings can be contrasted. Immediately to the right of each feature, in parentheses, is the number of effect sizes from samples receiving interventions that have that feature followed by the number that did not have that feature. The first line in each figure (labeled *Exposed to Media Intervention*) presents the contrast between all the intervention groups and all the control groups for which the respective outcome variable was measured (behavior, attitude, or knowledge).

The mean pre-to-post standardized gain effect sizes are charted on the right of each figure. The hollow circles represent the mean pre-to-post effect sizes for those intervention samples for which the features were not present. The solid circles represent the mean pre-to-post effect sizes for intervention samples for which the features were present. The distance between these two means for a given feature indicates the extent to which the outcomes were better (or worse) when the feature was present than when it was absent. Thus when the solid circle is to the right of the hollow circle, the corresponding intervention feature is associated with better outcomes than occur in the interventions that do not have that feature. Finally, note that the order of media features within each category changes from figure to figure. Within each category, features are sorted according to the amount of change associated with each feature.

EFFECTS ON SUBSTANCE-USE BEHAVIORS

The mean pre-to-post change in substance-use behavior found for the 48 subject samples exposed to a mass media intervention can be compared with the mean change in such behavior for the 18 samples in control groups that did not receive media intervention. The first line in Figure 11.1 shows that, on average, samples exposed and not exposed to media interventions both increased their substance-use between pre- and post-testing (both mean effect sizes were negative). Those receiving the media interventions, however, exhibited smaller increases than those in the control groups (the difference between the mean pre-to-post effect sizes, Δ = .04 standard deviations).

The various features of the media campaign and target audience shown in Figure 11.1 (and Figures 11.2 and 11.3) were coded as present or absent but are not necessarily mutually exclusive. Thus, media source (radio, video, etc.) indicates whether, for instance, radio was used in the campaign but does not exclude the possibility that television or other sources were also used in combination with radio. Figure 11.1 shows that reduced substance-use was associated with exposure to all the media sources, but interventions using radio exhibited the greatest relative effects (Δ = .10) and print, the least (Δ = .04).

Messages targeting youth were associated with greater increases in substance-use behaviors than those targeting other groups (Δ = -.14), but the behaviors at issue are different for the different groups. The messages for youth typically relate to abstaining from substance-use; those for parents and others may call only for talking with youth about substance-use. The message characteristics associated with the largest relative effects on substance-use behaviors were themes involving alternatives to use (Δ = .09), what to say to others about use (Δ = .07), and positive attitudes to nonuse (Δ = .05).

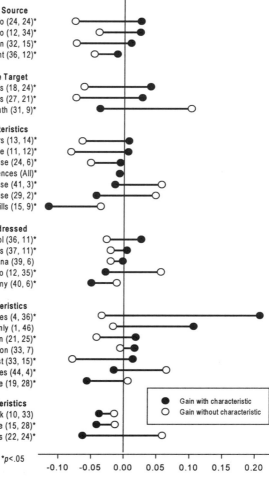

Mean Pre-Post Standardized Gain Effect Sizes

FIGURE 11.1 Relative effects of media features on substance use behaviors.

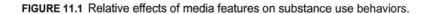

Messages that addressed tobacco were associated with effects on behavior that were negative relative to those addressing other substances (Δ = -.09). However, this may represent an age-graded difference related to greater experimentation with tobacco than other substances among youth. The media interventions addressing alcohol, marijuana, and other illicit substances all showed positive relative effects on relevant behaviors, with the greatest difference associated with media messages addressing alcohol use.

Interpretation of the relative effects of different intervention characteristics is compromised in some instances by small numbers of samples exposed to those characteristics. The largest relative effect on substance-use behavior was associated with use of a series of messages or sequenced messages in the media campaign. Only four studies reported using such messages, however. Similarly, only one study used a one-time-only message, and the large effect relative to use of more than one message is not significant and probably is not meaningful. There were sufficient numbers of studies for stable estimates of the relative effects of other intervention characteristics. Media messages supplemented with other program components, which were repeated, and which were broadcast to general audiences, were each associated with positive relative effects.

Finally, and not surprisingly, each of the recipient characteristics examined appear to be important. Samples that were primarily female, were considered at-risk for substance-use, or were under 22 years of age showed greater increases in substance-use behavior relative to other message recipients, although, on average, all recipients except those age 22 and over tended to increase their use. These results do not necessarily mean that mass-media interventions do not deter vulnerable youth, but rather that their effects, not surprisingly, are smaller than for their less vulnerable counterparts.

EFFECTS ON SUBSTANCE-USE ATTITUDES

In striking contrast to the relative effects of media interventions on substance-use behavior, the pre-to-post changes in substance-use attitudes were almost universally positive, irrespective of the specific characteristics of the intervention or even of whether participants were exposed to one of the interventions studied. This is demonstrated in Figure 11.2 by the very high proportion of mean pre-to-post effect sizes with positive values, indicating more favorable attitudes at posttest than at pretest. The first line of Figure 11.2 shows that samples exposed to media intervention

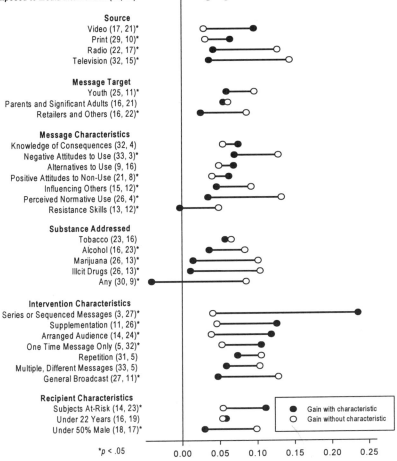

Mean Pre-Post Standardized Gain Effect Sizes

FIGURE 11.2 Relative effects of media features on substance-use attitudes.

and control groups not exposed both improved in their substance-use attitudes. The participants in the 39 samples exposed to media interventions, however, exhibited somewhat greater improvement than those in the 12 control samples ($\Delta = .02$).

Although attitudes improved, on average, for nearly all respondents, the relative effects were greater for those exposed to video and print messages rather than other sources. Messages aimed at parents and other youth-influential adults, and those aimed at youth themselves, showed smaller relative effects than those directed toward other audiences. Indeed, messages targeted on any of these specific audiences showed smaller relative effects than those not so targeted. This reflects generally smaller attitude changes for all targeted audiences than for recipients of media messages that do not target any specific audience or that target multiple audiences.

None of the message characteristics shown in Figure 11.2 were associated with especially large relative effects on substance-use attitudes. Messages with content relating to knowledge of consequences, alternatives to use, and positive attitudes to nonuse were each associated with somewhat greater attitude change than messages without that respective content. Messages addressing specific substances were all associated with less attitude change than those not so targeted, that is, those that did not identify specific substances. This may reflect weaker effects for more narrowly focused media messages than for those that address multiple substances, but it could also relate to the more specific attitudes about substance-use that are measured in the former case relative to the latter. In any event, the smallest differential was observed for media campaigns addressing tobacco.

The greatest measured improvement in substance-use attitudes was observed for studies in which the media intervention used a series or a sequence of messages, but only three studies had this characteristic. The use of supplementary program components, arranged audiences, and one-time-only messages also were associated with positive relative effects on substance-use attitudes. Finally, at-risk samples showed large relative effects on attitude change whereas those with a minority of males showed the opposite pattern. Differences in gain between younger and older samples were minimal, although both showed positive attitude change.

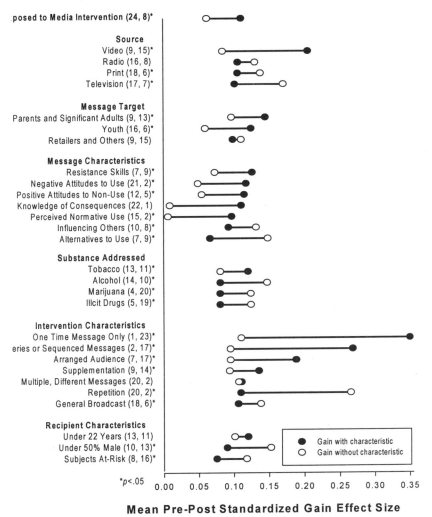

Media Feature (N with, N without)

posed to Media Intervention (24, 8)*

Source
Video (9, 15)*
Radio (16, 8)
Print (18, 6)*
Television (17, 7)*

Message Target
Parents and Significant Adults (9, 13)*
Youth (16, 6)*
Retailers and Others (9, 15)

Message Characteristics
Resistance Skills (7, 9)*
Negative Attitudes to Use (21, 2)*
Positive Attitudes to Non-Use (12, 5)*
Knowledge of Consequences (22, 1)
Perceived Normative Use (15, 2)*
Influencing Others (10, 8)*
Alternatives to Use (7, 9)*

Substance Addressed
Tobacco (13, 11)*
Alcohol (14, 10)*
Marijuana (4, 20)*
Illcit Drugs (5, 19)*

Intervention Characteristics
One Time Message Only (1, 23)*
eries or Sequenced Messages (2, 17)*
Arranged Audience (7, 17)*
Supplementation (9, 14)*
Multiple, Different Messages (20, 2)
Repetition (20, 2)*
General Broadcast (18, 6)*

Recipient Characteristics
Under 22 Years (13, 11)
Under 50% Male (10, 13)*
Subjects At-Risk (8, 16)*

● Gain with characteristic
○ Gain without characteristic

*p<.05   0.00   0.05   0.10   0.15   0.20   0.25   0.30   0.35

Mean Pre-Post Standardized Gain Effect Size

FIGURE 11.3 Relative effects of media features on substance-use knowledge.

EFFECTS ON SUBSTANCE-USE KNOWLEDGE

Substance-use knowledge outcomes showed universal improvement across all categories and options (Figure 11.3). Thus all the different subsets of subject samples broken out in the meta-analysis displayed increased knowledge between pre- and posttesting about such topics as the prevalence of substance-use and the consequences of use. Although knowledge was the least frequently reported outcome among the studies contributing to this meta-analysis, the 24 studies reporting knowledge measures before and after media intervention showed larger gains than control groups not receiving intervention (Δ = .05). Although this is the largest pre-to-post change observed for any outcome, its effect is reduced because control groups themselves showed positive gains despite the absence of intervention.

Among the media sources, video was associated with particularly large relative effects on substance-use knowledge. Messages targeting parents and other youth-influential adults, and those targeting youth themselves, showed positive relative effects. Relative effects associated with the characteristics of the message, however, were difficult to assess because only a small number of studies involved some of the characteristics of interest. Among the characteristics with reasonable numbers, the largest relative effects on substance-use knowledge were associated with messages involving resistance skills or positive attitudes to nonuse.

Media interventions specifically addressing tobacco use showed large positive relative effects on knowledge, whereas those targeting alcohol displayed large negative relative effects. Small numbers of studies with some of the coded intervention characteristics made their relative effects difficult to interpret. Among those with sufficient data points, media interventions using arranged audiences and supplementary program components were associated with the largest positive relative effects on knowledge. Turning to recipient characteristics, audiences that were under age 22 showed the largest relative knowledge gains, whereas at-risk subject samples demonstrated less gain in knowledge than those samples not considered at-risk for substance-use. Also, samples that were under 50% male showed smaller knowledge gains than those with a majority of males.

DISCUSSION

This chapter represents a first step in an attempt to use meta-analysis techniques to assess the effects of media interventions on the substance-use behaviors, attitudes, and knowledge of youth. This is a difficult topic area for any research synthesis technique. Media interventions are typically delivered to geographic areas or aggregate audiences that cannot easily be randomly assigned to treatment and control conditions and studied in field experiments. When control groups are employed, they usually represent neighboring areas or convenience samples that are not necessarily similar to the intervention samples on critical variables and thus, at best, yield nonequivalent comparison designs of questionable internal validity (Cook & Campbell, 1979). As a result, we have chosen to examine media intervention research in terms of pre-to-post change on measures of substance-use behavior, attitudes, and knowledge for samples exposed to a range of different configurations of media interventions. Although not definitive with regard to the nature and magnitude of the effects specifically attributable to the intervention, this approach offers some potential for identifying more and less effective forms of intervention. The inclusion of pre-to-post effect size measures for the available control samples that did not receive intervention provides some baseline against which to compare intervention effects, although the control samples are not necessarily well-matched to the intervention samples and therefore may differ for reasons other than intervention effects.

Despite the design limitations inherent in the available research, the analysis of pre-to-post effect sizes yields some useful findings. First, there are measurable differences between pretest and posttest for all three categories of outcome variables. On average, for attitudes and knowledge measures, posttest scores are better than pretest scores, that is, are less favorable to substance-use. For substance-use behavior, however, the mean pre-to-post effect sizes are generally negative, indicating more substance-use and related behaviors at posttest than at pretest. The critical finding, however, is that the pre-to-post changes for samples receiving media interventions are more favorable than those for untreated control groups on all three categories of outcome variables. Thus, participant samples exposed to media interventions show more positive change on attitudes and knowledge, and less negative change on behavior, than those not exposed to the interventions. Because of the potentially poor matching of control groups to intervention groups already described, this finding cannot be taken as convincing evidence that media interventions are effective, but it is consistent with that possibility.

If we take at face value for a moment the differential change between the intervention and control samples as an estimate of the effect of the media interventions, we can raise the question of the magnitude of that effect. The first paragraph of this chapter reported 30-day use rates among high school seniors of 53% for alcohol, 37% for tobacco, 24% for marijuana, and 11% for other illegal drugs (Monitoring the Future, 1998). If we take these as base rates, we can calculate the reductions represented by the Δ = .04 standard deviation mean differential change between intervention and control groups found for substance-use behavior (Figure 11.1). This is done by applying the procedure from Cohen (1988) for converting proportions to effect sizes via the arcsine transformation. The results shows that, in round figures, a .04 standard deviation difference would reduce the alcohol use figure from 53% to 51%, tobacco use from 37% to 35%, marijuana use from 24% to 22.5%, and other drug use from 11% to 10%. In short, these effects, if produced by media intervention, would reduce substance abuse among youth by 1 to 2 percentage points.

Although these effects are small by most standards, they cannot be dismissed as trivial in this context. Mass media interventions can be widely disseminated at modest cost so that even small effects may involve a significant number of individuals with a high degree of cost-effectiveness. Although the goals and aims of advertising differ from those of health education, commercial advertisers are likely to be satisfied with a ½ to 1% change in behavior as a result of an advertising campaign (Dorn & South, 1985). Moreover, for tobacco use, the SimSmoke computer simulation model (Levy, Cummings, & Hyland, 2000) permits estimation of the cumulative effects of a 2% annual reduction in smoking rates. According to this model, such a reduction would result in 5.5 million fewer smokers by the year 2010. In this light, mass media interventions may achieve small wins (Weick, 1984) that yield significant cumulative reductions in substance-use. Although the estimates of media intervention effects on substance-use we have used here are admittedly poor, their implications reveal the importance of conducting better research that can yield more definitive estimates.

Assuming some effects of media interventions on substance-use behavior, attitudes, and knowledge, however modest, the relative effect size comparisons in Figures 11.1 to 11.3 help identify those characteristics of the messages, interventions, and audiences that may yield the largest effects. Interpreting these relative effect size comparisons is not straightforward, however. Many of these characteristics are combined and confounded in various ways in the source studies, and thus their independent influence is difficult to assess. A further limitation is that some of the more interesting characteristics are represented in too few studies to provide a good estimate of their relative effects. Any attempt to identify the characteristics of more effective media interventions, therefore, must be done very cautiously.

Even with these limitations in mind, however, there are some rather robust patterns in the differential effect sizes presented in Figures 11.1 to 11.3 that warrant discussion as clues to potentially important features of effective media interventions. We consider, first, those features represented in at least five studies across all the outcome domains (behavior, attitudes, and knowledge) as a hedge against overinterpreting findings involving only a few atypical studies. Among these, some show relative effects that are consistent across all three outcome domains. If attitude and knowledge change mediate behavioral change, as assumed in the conventional logic for mass media campaigns, then features that make a media intervention more effective should make it more effective for all these outcomes.

The pre-to-post effect size contrasts summarized in Figures 11.1 to 11.3 reveal five characteristics consistently associated with greater gain and represented in at least five studies. With regard to the media source, messages communicated via video are associated with larger pre-to-post gains in substance-use attitudes, knowledge, and behavior than those that do not use video. Video presentations are typically made to students in school settings or other such arranged audiences and tend to involve longer and more multifaceted messages than those communicated via television, radio, or print.

Among the message targets, more pre-to-post change in all three outcome domains was found for communications directed toward parents and other youth-influential adults than for those not directed at these groups. That it is easier to change attitudes, knowledge, and behavior related to youth substance abuse among parents than among the youth themselves, however, is hardly surprising. This is especially so in media campaigns that aim to reduce youth substance-use. The behaviors, attitudes, and knowledge these campaigns attempt to induce from parents are those related to their influence on children's substance-use and are thus different, and likely more amenable to persuasion, than those that the campaigns attempt to influence in the youth themselves. In any event, the only specific characteristic of the media message consistently associated with positive relative effects was content involving positive attitudes toward nonuse of substances.

There were no robust patterns in the relative effect sizes for the substance addressed in the media interventions, which is interesting in its own right. It does not appear that messages targeted on any specific substance are uniformly more or less effective than those targeted on another. One characteristic of the intervention itself, however, was consistently associated with greater pre-to-post change in the three outcome domains—supplementary components with the media message, such as group discussion, role play, or supportive services. Such supplementation cannot be easily arranged for community-wide media campaigns, however, and is generally restricted to school-based programs and others of restricted scope.

Finally, recipient samples for media interventions that were less than 50% male were associated with smaller relative effects on substance-use attitudes, knowledge, and behavior. Put in positive terms, of course, this finding shows that samples with a majority of males show greater positive pre-to-post change in all three outcome domains than majority female samples.

Relative pre-to-post change provides a limited and fallible form of evidence for the effects of media interventions for youth substance-use, but the nature of research on this topic is such that it is the best that is available for a representative range of these interventions. That evidence indicates that media interventions may well have small effects on substance-use behaviors, attitudes, and knowledge, which, when multiplied by the large audiences media can reach, could affect significant numbers of youth and their families. It also appears that some configurations of these interventions are more effective than others, but, to large extent, those variants involve such characteristics as video media and supplementary programs that are more suitable for school-based programs and other special circumstances than for mass audiences.

REFERENCES

Alcalay, R., (1983). The impact of mass communication campaigns in the health field. *Social Science and Medicine, 17,* 87-94.

Atkin, C. K., DeJong, W., & Wallack, L. (1992). *The influence of responsible drinking TV spots and automobile commercials on young drivers.* Washington, DC: AAA Foundation for Traffic Safety.

Bachman, J. G., Johnston, L. D., & O'Malley, P. M. (1990). Explaining the recent decline in cocaine use among young adults: Further evidence that perceived risks and disapproval lead to reduced drug use. *Journal of Health and Social Behavior, 31,* 173-184.

Bachman, J. G., Johnston, L. D., O'Malley, P. M., Humphrey, R. H. (1988). Explaining the recent decline in marijuana use. Differentiating the effects of perceived risks, disapproval, and general lifestyle factors. *Journal of Health and Social Behavior, 29,* 92-112.

Bandura, A. (1986). *Social foundations of thought and action: A social cognitive theory.* Englewood Cliffs, NJ: Prentice Hall.

Becker, B. J. (1988). Synthesizing standardized mean-change measures. *British Journal of Mathematical and Statistical Psychology , 41,* 257-278.

Biglan, A., Duncan, T. E., Ary, D. V., & Smolkowski, K. (1995). Peer and parental influences on adolescent tobacco use. *Journal of Behavioral Medicine, 18,* 315-330.

Black, G. S. (1991). Changing attitudes toward drug use: The effects of advertising. In L. Donohew, H. E. Sypher, & W. J. Bukoski (Eds.), *Persuasive communication and drug abuse prevention* (pp. 157-191). Hillsdale, NJ: Lawrence Erlbaum Associates.

Block, J., Block, J. H., & Keyes, S. (1988). Longitudinally foretelling drug usage in adolescence: Early childhood personality and environmental precursors. *Child Development, 59,* 336-355.

Botvin, G. J., Schinke, S. P., Epstein, J. A., Diaz, T., & Botvin, E. M. (1995). Effectiveness of culturally focused and generic skills training approaches to alcohol and drug abuse prevention among minority adolescents: Two-year follow-up results. *Psychology of Addictive Behaviors, 9,* 183-194.

Brawley, E. A. (1983). *Mass media and human services.* Beverly Hills, CA: Sage.

Cartwright, D. (1949). Some principles of mass persuasion: selected findings of research in the sale of United States War Bonds. *Human Relations, 2,* 253-268.

Chaiken, S. (1979). Communicator physical attractiveness and persuasion. *Journal of Personality and Social Psychology, 37,* 1387-1397.

Cohen, J. (1988). *Statistical power analysis for the behavioral sciences* (2nd ed.). Hillsdale, NJ: Lawrence Erlbaum Associates.

Cook, T. D., & Campbell, D. T. (1979). *Quasi-experimentation: Design and analysis issues for field settings.* Boston: Houghton Mifflin.

Coombs, R. H., Paulson, M. J., & Richardson, M. A. (1991). Peer vs. parental influence in substance-use among Hispanic and Anglo children and adolescents. *Journal of Youth and Adolescence, 20,* 73-88.

DeJong, W., Atkin, C. K., & Wallack, L. (1992). A critical analysis of "moderation" advertising sponsored by the beer industry: Are "responsible drinking" commercials done responsibly? *Milbank Quarterly, 70,* 661-678.

Dishion, T. J., Andrews, D. W., Kavanagh, K., & Soberman, L. H. (1996). Preventive interventions for high-risk youth: The Adolescent Transitions Program. In R. DeV. Peters & R. J. McMahon (Eds.), *Preventing childhood disorders, substance abuse, and delinquency. Banff international behavioral science series* (Vol. 3, pp. 184-214). Thousand Oaks, CA: Sage.

Dorn, N., & South, N. (1985). *Message in a bottle: Theoretical overview and annotated bibliography on the mass media and alcohol.* Aldershot, UK: Gower.

Dusenbury, L., & Falco, M. (1997). School-based drug abuse prevention strategies: From research to policy and practice. In R. P. Weissberg, T. P. Gullotta, & R. Hampton (Eds.), *Enhancing children's wellness: Issues in children's and families' lives* (Vol. 8, pp. 47-75). Thousand Oaks, CA: Sage.

Ellickson, P. L., & Bell, R. M. (1990). Drug prevention in junior high: A multi-site longitudinal test. *Science, 247,* 1299-1305.

Farquhar, J. W., Maccoby, N., & Solomon, D. (1984). Community applications of behavioral medicine. In W. D. Gentry (Ed.), *Handbook of behavioral medicine* (pp. 437-478). New York: Guilford Press.

Farquhar, J. W., Maccoby, N., & Wood, P. D. (1977). Community education for cardiovascular health. *Lancet, 1*, 1192-1195.

Fazio, R. H., Chen, J., McDonel, E. C., & Sherman, S. J. (1982) Attitude accessibility, attitude-behavior consistency and the strength of the object-evaluation association. *Journal of Experimental Social Psychology, 18*, 339-357.

Field, T., Deitrick, S., Hersey, J. C., Probst, J. C., & Theologus, G. C. (1983). *Implementing public education campaigns: Lessons from alcohol abuse prevention.* Summary report to NIAAA. Washington, DC: Kappa Systems.

Flay, B. R. (1987a). *Selling the smokeless society: Fifty-six evaluated mass media programs and campaigns worldwide.* Washington DC: American Public Health Association.

Flay, B. R. (1987b). Mass media and smoking cessation: A critical review. *American Journal of Public Health, 77*, 153-160.

Flay, B. R. & Sobel, J. L. (1983). The role of mass media in preventing adolescent substance abuse. In T. J. E. Glynn, C. G. Lukefeld, & J. P. Ludford (Eds.), *Preventing adolescent drug abuse: Intervention strategies* (pp. 5-35). NIDA Research Monograph 47. Rockville, MD: National Institute on Drug Abuse.

Flora, J., Maccoby, N., & Farquhar, J. (1989). Communication campaigns to prevent cardiovascular disease: The Stanford community studies. In R. E. Rice & C. K. Atkin, (Eds.), *Public communication campaigns* (2nd ed., pp. 233-252). Newbury Park, CA: Sage.

Flynn, B. S., Worden, J. K., Secker-Walker, R. H., Pirie, P. L., Badger, G. J., Carpenter, J. H., & Geller, B. M. (1994). Mass media and school interventions for cigarette smoking prevention: Effects 2 years after completion. *American Journal of Public Health, 84*, 1148-1150.

Flynn, B. S., Worden, J. K., Secker-Walker, R. H., Pirie, P. L., Badger, G. J., & Carpenter, J. H. (1997). Long-term responses of higher and lower risk youths to smoking prevention interventions. *Preventive Medicine, 26*, 389-394.

Goldberg, L., Elliot, D., Clarke, G. N., MacKinnon, D. P., Moe, E., Zoref, L., Green, C., Wolf, S. L., Greffrath, E., Miller, D. J., & Lapin, A. (1996). Effects of a multidimensional anabolic-steroid prevention intervention: The adolescents training and learning to avoid steroids (ATLAS) program. *Journal of the American Medical Association, 276*, 1555-1562.

Goodstadt, M. S. (1977). *An evaluation of the Ontario (1975-1976) Alcohol Education Program: TV and radio exposure and initial impact* (Substudy No. 847). Toronto: Addiction Research Foundation.

Graham, J. W. Marks, G., & Hansen, W. B. (1991). Social influence processes affecting adolescent substance-use. *Journal of Applied Psychology, 76*, 291-298.

Hafstad, A., Aarø, L. E., & Langmark, F. (1996). Evaluation of an anti-smoking mass-media campaign targeting adolescents: The role of affective responses and interpersonal-communication. *Health Education Research, 11*, 29-38.

Hale, J., & Dillard, J. (1995). Fear appeals in health promotion campaigns. In E. Maibach & R. Parrott (Eds.), *Designing health messages* (pp. 65-80). Thousand Oaks, CA: Sage

Hamilton, J. R. (1972). The demand for cigarettes: Advertising, the health scare, and the cigarette advertising ban. *Review of Economics and Statistics, 54,* 401-411.

Hanneman, G. J., & McEwen, W. J. (1973). Televised drug abuse appeals: A content analysis. *Journalism Quarterly, 50,* 329-333.

Hanneman, G. J., McEwen, W. J., & Coyne, S. A. (1973). Public service advertising on television. *Journal of Broadcasting, 17,* 387-404.

Hansen, W. B. (1992). School-based substance abuse prevention: A review of the state of the art in curriculum, 1980-1990. *Health Education Research, 7,* 403-430.

Hass, R. G., (1981). Effects of source characteristics on cognitive responses and persuasion. In R. E. Petty, T. M. Ostrom, & T. C. Brock (Eds.), *Cognitive responses to persuasion* (pp. 141-172). Hillsdale, NJ: Lawrence Erlbaum Associates.

Hedges, L. V., Olkin, I.(1983). Clustering estimates of effect magnitude from independent studies. *Psychological Bulletin, 93,* 563-573.

Janis, I. L. (1983). The role of social support in adherence to stressful decisions. *American Psychologist, 38,* 143-160.

Jeter, J. (1998, January 3). Chris Farley died of drug overdose: Comedian joins the list of celebrities who lived fast, died young. *Washington Post,* p. A1.

Kahneman, D., Slovac, P., & Tversky, A. (1984). *Judgment under uncertainty: Heuristics and biases.* Cambridge: Cambridge University Press.

Kandel, D. B., Yamaguchi, K., & Chen, K. (1992). Stages of progression in drug involvement from adolescence to adulthood: Further evidence for the gateway theory. *Journal of Studies on Alcoholism, 53,* 447-457.

Katz, E. (1957). The two-step flow of communication: An up-to-date report on an hypothesis. *Public Opinion Quarterly, 21,* 61-78.

Katz, E. (1988). On conceptualizaing media effects: Another look. In S. Oskamp (Ed.), *Television as a social issue. Applied social psychology annual* (Vol. 8, pp. 361-374). Beverly Hills, CA: Sage.

Katz, E., & Lazarsfeld, P. F. (1955) *Personal influence.* New York: Free Press.

Leventhal, H. (1970). Findings and theory in the study of fear communications. In L. Berkowitz (Ed.), *Advances in experimental social psychology* (Vol. V., pp. 119-186). New York: Academic Press.

Levy, D., Cummings, K. M., & Hyland, A. (2000). A Simulation of the Effects of Youth Initiation Policies on Overall Cigarette Usage. *American Journal of Public Health, 90,* 1311-14.

Lewin, K. (1997). *Resolving social conflicts; and, Field theory in social science.* Washington, DC: American Psychological Association.

Lewin, K., & Gold, M. (Eds). *The complete social scientist: A Kurt Lewin reader.* Washington, DC: American Psychological Association. 1999,

Lipsey, M. W., & Wilson, D. B. (2001). *Practical meta-analysis.* Thousand Oaks, CA: Sage.

Lorch, E. P., Palmgreen, P., Donohew, L., Helm, D., Baer, S. A., & Dsilva, M. U. (1994). Program context, sensation-seeking, and attention to televised antidrug public service announcements. *Human Communication Research, 20,* 390-412.

Maibach, E., & Cotton, D. (1995). Motivating people to change: A staged social cognitive approach. In E. Maibach & R. Parrott (Eds.). *Designing health messages* (pp. 41-64). Thousand Oaks, CA: Sage

Maibach, E., & Flora, J. (1993). Symbolic modeling and cognitive rehearsal. *Communications Research, 20,* 517-545.

McAlister, A. L., (1981). Anti-smoking campaigns: Progress in developing effective communications. In R. E. Rice & W. J. Paisley (Eds.), *Public communication campaigns* (pp. 91-103). Newbury Park, CA: Sage.

McAlister, A. L., Ramirez, A. G., Galavotti, C., & Gallion, K. J. (1989). Anti-smoking campaigns: Progress in the application of social learning theory. In R. E. Rice & C. K. Atkin (Eds.), *Public communication campaigns* (2nd ed., pp. 291-308). Newbury Park, CA: Sage.

McGuire, W. J. (1966). Attitudes and opinions. *Annual Review of Psychology, 17,* 475-514.

McGuire, W. J. (1978). The communication/persuasion matrix. In B. Lipstein & W. J. McGuire (Eds.), *Evaluating advertising: A bibliography of the communication process* (pp. xxvii—xxxv). New York: Advertising Research Foundation.

McGuire, W. J. (1980). The communication-persuasion model and health risk labeling. In L. A. Morris, M. B. Mazis, & I. Barofsky (Eds.), *Product labeling and health risks* (pp. 99-122). New York: Banbury.

McGuire, W. J. (1985). Attitudes and attitude change. In G. Lindzey & E. Aronson (eds.) *The handbook of social psychology* (Vol. II, 3rd ed., pp. 233-346). New York: Random House.

Mendelson, H. (1968). Which shall it be: Mass education or mass persuasion for health. *American Journal of Public Health, 58,* 131-137.

Monitoring the Future (1998). *Table 1b: Trends in annual and 30-day prevalence of use of various drugs for eighth, tenth, and twelfth graders* [On line]. Available at http://www.isr.umich.edu/src/mtf/mtfdat97.html.

Moschis, G. (1987). *Consumer socialization: A life-cycle perspective.* Lexington, KY: Lexington Books.

Murphy, R. D. (1980). Consumer responses to cigarette health warnings. In L. A. Morris, M. B. Mazis, & I. Barofsky (Eds.), *Product labeling and health risks* (pp. 13-21). Cold Spring Harbor Laboratory, NY: Banbury Report.

Murray, D. M., Prokhorov, A. V. & Harty, K. C. (1994). Effects of a statewide anti-smoking campaign on mass media messages and smoking beliefs. *Preventive Medicine, 23,* 54-60.

Newcomb, M. D., & Felix-Ortiz, M. (1992). Multiple protective and risk factors for drug use and abuse: Cross-sectional and prospective findings. *Journal of Personality and Social Psychology, 63,* 280-296.

O'Keefe, M. T. (1971). The anti-smoking commercials: A study of television's impact on behavior. *Public Opinion Quarterly, 35,* 245-248.

Palmgreen, P., Donohew, L., & Lorch, E. (1995). Reaching at-risk populations in a mass media drug abuse prevention campaign: Sensation seeking as a target variable. *Drugs and Society, 8,* 27-45.

Perry, C. L., Klepp, K. I., & Sillers, C. (1989). Community-wide strategies for car-diovascular health: The Minnesota Heart Health Program youth program. *Health Education Research, 4,* 87-101.

Petty, R., Baker, S., & Gleicher, F. (1991). Attitudes and drug abuse prevention: Implications fo the Elaboration Likelihood Model of persuasion. In L. Dono-hew, H. E. Sypher, & W. J. Bukoski (Eds.), *Persuasive communication and drug abuse prevention* (pp. 71-90). Hillsdale, NJ: Lawrence Erlbaum Associates.

Pierce, J. P., Macaskill, P., & Hill, D. (1990). Long-term effectiveness of mass media led antismoking campaigns in Australia. *American Journal of Public Health, 80,* 565-569.

Rappeport, M., Labow, P., & Williams, J. (1975). *The public evaluates the NIAAA Public Education Campaign: A study for the U.S. DHEW, PHS, ADAMHA.* Princeton, NJ: Opinion Research Corporation.

Resnick, M. D., Bearman, P. S., Blum, R. W., Bauman, K. E., Harris, K. M., Jones, J., Tabor, J., Beuhring, T., Sieving, R. E., Shew, M., Ireland, M., Bearinger, L H., & Udry, J. R. (1997). Protecting adolescents from harm: Findings from the National Longitudinal Study on Adolescent Health. *Jama: Journal of the American Medical Association, 278,* 823-832.

Robinson, J. & McArthur, L. Z. (1982). Impact of salient vocal qualities on causal attribution for a speaker's behavior. *Journal of Personality and Social Psychology, 43,* 236-247.

Ryan, W. (1971). *Blaming the victim.* New York: Random House.

Saffer, H. (1995). Alcohol advertising and alcohol consumption: Econometric stud-ies. In S. E. Martin & C. P. Mail (Eds.), *Effects of the mass media on the use and abuse of alcohol* (pp. 83-100). NIAAA. Research Monograph No. 28. Bethesda, MD: NIAAA.

Schmeling, D. G., & Wotring, C. E. (1980). Making antidrug abuse advertising work. *Journal of Advertising Research, 20,* 33-37.

Sprafkin, J., Swift, C., & Hess, R. (Eds.). (1983). *Rx television: Enhancing the pre-ventive impact of TV.* New York: Hawthorn.

Stern, M. P., Farquhar, J. W., Maccoby, N., & Russell, S. H. (1976). Results of a two-year health education campaign on dietary behavior: The Stanford Three Community Study. *Circulation, 54,* 826-833.

Teel, S. J., Teel, J. E., & Bearden, W. O. (1979). Lessons learned from the broad-cast advertising ban. *Journal of Marketing, 43,* 45-50.

Wallack, L. (1980). Assessing effects of mass media campaigns: An alternative perspective. *Alcohol and Health Research World, 5,* 17-27.

Wallack, L. (1990). Improving health promotion: Media advocacy and social mar-keting approaches. In C. Atkin & L. Wallack (Eds.), *Mass communication and public health: Complexities and conflicts* (pp. 147-163). Newbury Park, CA: Sage.

Wallack, L., & DeJong, W. (1995). Mass media and public health: Moving the focus from the individual to the environment. In S. E. Martin & C. P. Mail (Eds.) *Effects of the mass media on the use and abuse of alcohol* (pp. 253-268). NIAAA Research Monograph No. 28. Bethesda, MD: NIAAA.

Warner, K. E. (1977). The effect of the anti-smoking campaign on cigarette consumption. *American Journal of Public Health, 67,* 645-650.

Warner, K. E. (1986). Smoking and health implications of a change in the federal cigarette excise tax. *Journal of the American Medical Association, 255,* 1028-1032.

Weick, K. E. (1984). Small wins: Redefining the scale of social problems. *American Psychologist, 39,* 40-49.

Wicker, A. (1969). Altitudes versus actions: The relationship of verbal and overt behavioral responses to attitude objects. *Journal of Social Issues, 45,* 41-78.

Williams, J. H. (1994). Understanding substance-use, delinquency involvement, and juvenile justice system involvement among African American and European American adolescents (Doctoral dissertation, University of Washington). *Dissertation Abstracts International, 56(04-A),* 1530. (University Microfilms No. 95-23776)

Winett, R. (1993). Media-based behavior change: Approaches to prevention. In D. S. Glenwick & L. A. Jason (Eds.), *Promoting health and mental health in children, youth, and families. Springer series on behavior therapy and behavioral medicine* (Vol 27, pp. 181-204). New York: Springer.

Worden, J. K., Flynn, B. S., Solomon, L. J., Secker-Walker, R. H., Badger, G. J., & Carpenter, J. H. (1996). Using mass-media to prevent cigarette-smoking among adolescent girls. *Health Education Quarterly, 23,* 453-468.

Wu, P., & Kandel, D. B. (1995). The role of mothers and fathers in inter-generational behavioral transmission: The case of smoking and delinquency. In H. B. Kaplan (Ed.), *Drugs, crime, and other deviant adaptations: Longitudinal studies* (pp. 49-81). New York: Plenum Press.

12

The Media and Drug Prevention Programs

Gary W. Selnow

San Francisco State University

Social scientists and prevention specialists by their training, and probably by their natures, like to control their own agendas, and that's where they run into trouble with the media. The media defy control. Publishers are covered by the bulletproof First Amendment, and broadcasters are comfortably shielded by case law and administrative rules. These protections grant the media broad control of what they carry and what they reject. If newspapers or broadcasters don't have time or space, if they earn more profit from other messages, if they don't like the tone of a message, they can simply reject it. Even for commercial advertisers, a media snub is possible—although the media don't often turn away paying customers.

Not that it would matter much to prevention programs, because most of them are shallow in the pocket and can't afford to buy their way into the media anyway. Few have the largesse of a recent program run by the ONDCP, the Office of National Drug Control Policy, which touts a $1 billion media budget, most earmarked for television.[1] By contrast, university and organization-based programs rely heavily on handouts of time and space, which drives them, hat-in-hand, to the media for a little airtime or a few column inches. Consequently, without much purchasing power, most

---

[1] "In late 1997, Congress approved an immense, five-year, $1 billion ad buy for anti-drug advertising as long as the networks sold ad time to the government at half price—a two-for-one deal that provided over $2 billion worth of ads for a $1 billion allocation." Daniel Forbes, *Salon*, January 13, 2000. From www.Salon.com.

public-arena prevention programs are obliged first to persuade the media to lend a hand before they can persuade their audiences to do much of anything.

That brings us to the important question: What do media decision-makers think about their own roles in drug prevention programs, and what advice would they give organizers to improve their chances of getting their messages into print and on the air? Using a convenience sample, we talked with media professionals from various segments of the industry in wide-ranging, free-wheeling interviews.

To start the discussions, we began with this question: If you were standing before a group of academics who were working on media-based drug prevention messages and strategies, and they asked for your thoughts about how the media fit into drug prevention efforts, what would you tell them?

This chapter reports the findings for three forms of media exposure: entertainment programming, public service messages and news.[2]

ENTERTAINMENT PROGRAMMING

Background

Broadcasters were quick to report that outside pressure sometimes works and sometimes backfires—and that holds for non-profit groups and government agencies. Outside influence on the content of television programs is nothing new. Antismoking and antialcohol organizations successfully pressured the networks and Hollywood during the 1970s and 1980s to embed antiusage messages, or at least to avoid showing drug and alcohol use as attractive behaviors. Citing the power of the media to persuade, groups such as Mothers against Drunk Driving, the American Cancer Society, and the American Lung Association argued that for little financial or artistic costs, television depictions could favorably impact the attitudes of vulnerable young viewers. The industry agreed, and over time drug use was rarely glamorized, and smoking and drinking were seen less often. The lesson is that the industry sometimes will yield to logical arguments offered by organized pressure groups, especially if it comes at no cost.

---

[2] Paid-for time and space were not included because the bearers of cash have a lot of leverage.

Sometimes, however, the networks need more pressure, as they did to change their views of drugs as humor. That change took place during the 1980s after an incident related by Maurie Goodman, an NBC Standards and Practices executive at NBC during this period.[3] Goodman told of an event that helped steer the networks away from light-hearted references to drugs.

In a national broadcast in the early 1980s, entertainer Billy Crystal used the line, "When it snows in California, half the population are snorting their driveways." According to Goodman, Paul Newman and his wife, JoAnn Woodward—who had established the Scott Newman Foundation for Drug and Alcohol Abuse Education, in memory of their son who died from an overdose—were incensed at the reference. Newman and Woodward contacted NBC and invited the network to send an NBC Standards representative to visit their foundation in California. NBC's Marcy Kelly took the trip, and after a day at the treatment facility came away convinced that the network should ban drug humor. She reported that view to Goodman, who took it up the administrative line.

Not long after that incident, Bob Hope taped a 20-min monologue that included a few drug jokes. NBC president Grant Tinker got wind of the sketch and sent Goodman to California to talk with Hope about the drug references and the network's evolving views on the matter. Hope was apparently moved by Goodman's arguments, because the next day, he declared that "drugs are no longer funny," and he pulled all drug references from his monologue. After that, Goodman said, NBC and the other networks avoided humorous drug references.

Network policy on drugs evolved slowly from the moral arguments made by organizations, influential industry leaders, and concerned viewers. As former NBC Standards executive Richard Gilbert put it, "It was an education for the networks to see that the use of drugs was not humorous, nor were drugs helpful as a crutch for plot lines. It was our moral decision to avoid drugs in our programming, and if we referenced them at all, it was almost always in a negative light."[4]

Network positions on drugs in programming evolved further when, at the end of the 1990s, the White House Office of National Drug Control Policy (ONDCP) used its billion-dollar media budget to leverage antidrug content on prime-time shows. Here's the story. In 1997, the U.S. Congress approved the purchase of $1 billion worth of antidrug advertising

---

[3] Maurie Goodman interview with the author on February 22, 2000.

[4] Richard Gilbert interview with the author on February 23, 2000.

with the provision that the networks sell the air time for one-half the going rate. The networks accepted the deal, but reluctantly. They loved the regular placement of spots, but hated the reduced rate, which increasingly ate into revenues. Finally, the expanding economy and the increasing need for commercial air time drove the networks to withdraw their original agreement. They cried over lost opportunities to earn top dollar for each second of air time.

Apparently without much arm-twisting, the ONDCP consented to a new arrangement: it would trade advertising slots for the placement of antidrug messages directly into network programming. That worked for the network green eyeshades, who were free to sell the ad time to commercial sponsors while still collecting revenues from the ONDCP. (What a sweet deal. It worked for the government because it successfully bought ONDCP influence over potentially the most powerful antidrug vehicle, network programming. Instead of preaching in sound bites, the message could be woven directly into the fabric of prime-time content with a significantly greater impact on network audiences.)

Popping the bubble of the network-government deal, however, were critics who challenged the arrangement on several levels. They charged that ONDCP officials were allowed to review and alter program scripts, which granted the government an unprecedented level of access to network shows. Several groups, including the Media Access Project and the Nieman Foundation, immediately condemned the practice as anti-First Amendment. Jay Schwartzman, president of the Media Access Project, said: "This is the most craven thing I've heard of yet. To turn over content control to the federal government for a modest price is an outrageous abandonment of the First Amendment. . . The broadcasters scream about the First Amendment until McCaffrey opens his checkbook."[5]

The charge of hypocrisy struck a nerve because broadcasters have always longed for the same freedom enjoyed by print media. Historically, broadcast and print have been treated differently when it comes to the control of content. Broadcasters' use of the public airwaves incurs a public responsibility to carry or to avoid certain material. They must serve the public good (e.g., with public service programming), and they must avoid strong language and lurid content (although those restrictions have been watered down with the advent of cable). Thus, Congress and the courts have treated broadcasting and print differently, placing print comfortably

---

[5] Daniel Forbes, "Prime-time propaganda: How the White House secretly hooked network TV on its anti-drug message." *Salon*, January 13, 2000. From Website: www.salon.com.

within First Amendment safeguards, allowing television and radio less autonomy. Nonetheless, broadcasters have fought bitterly against the slippery slope of outside influence of their programs, and they have particularly resisted government intervention, challenging even the Fairness Doctrine and Equal Time Provisions.[6] Representing the state, the Federal Communications Commission (FCC) has repeatedly said that it does not determine program content, only public responsibility in general terms.

And so the deal with the ONDCP set off alarms among watch groups because here were the networks in bed with their devil. The offense was selling out principle for profit, by some estimates to the tune of $25 million.[7] The networks shielded their content until money was at stake, and then they sold out. The critics cried foul at the cozy relationship and fretted about the impact of this precedent-breaking arrangement on future programming, dealing not only in drug topics but all topics.

Critics also attacked the secrecy of the deal. How could the networks and the government keep these multi-million-dollar deals from the public? Did Congress know? It took a 6-month investigation by Internet-based *Salon News* to reveal the arrangement, because both parties worked quietly behind the scenes.

In addition, the networks may have broken payola laws that require public disclosure of direct or indirect financial support for programming. The premise for these rules is that viewers have a right to know who is behind the shows they watch, and that use of the public airwaves obliges the networks to tell them. Not much has been made of the payola issue, but the matter remains open at this writing, and the brass have some explaining to do.

PROGRAMMING AND PREVENTION

Influencing the content of network programming has never been a cinch, but thanks to the ONDCP episode, it will be exceedingly difficult for orga-

---

[6] The Equal Time Provision compelled licensed station operators to provide an even-handed treatment of controversial topics, and the Fairness Doctrine required them to provide equity in the coverage of political candidates.

[7] This is according to Alan Levitt, the drug-policy official running the ONDCP campaign during the Clinton administration. Reported by Daniel Forbes, D. "Prime-time propaganda: How the White House secretly hooked network TV on its anti-drug message." *Salon,* January 13, 2000. From Website: www.salon.com.

nizations now to influence the networks. Chastened for their lapses, the networks are gun-shy of suggestions from outside groups, and at least for a while, they are likely to turn a deaf ear to requests.

The networks are hypersensitive because watch groups and news hounds are spring-loaded to find fault. Nina Thorsen, a producer for programs aired on Public Radio, said the ONDCP deal disturbed everyone in the industry, not so much because scripts were government edited and approved but because everything was done behind closed doors. "What they've done by sneaking messages past the gatekeepers is to incur a tremendous loss of credibility. Everything the White House does now with respect to drug messages will be suspect and all their activities will be examined in great detail."[8]

"The fact is," Maurie Goodman said, "the ONDCP didn't need these back-room deals because the networks had long ago settled on the drug issue in programming." As Goodman described it, the broadcasters don't glamorize drug usage, they don't depict it as attractive, they don't offer it as humorous. There isn't much more they could do without becoming morbidly moralistic about drugs and that would chase off audiences and tamper with revenues—something the networks guard more tenaciously than their scripts.

The point is, drug prevention researchers and antidrug organizations can expect little assistance from the entertainment side of network operations. The government exploited the network's weakness and went too far with its purchase of content. In the process, it frightened off the industry that can deliver the most potent antidrug messages. The outcome is that networks will continue their traditional policies toward the depiction of drugs. For prevention specialists, even that is not a bad deal.

PUBLIC SERVICE MESSAGES

The Communications Act of 1934, altered and updated over the years, has required broadcast stations to serve the public good in exchange for use of the public airwaves. Out of these obligations grew public service programming, including the 30-sec spots (public service announcements or PSAs) and sometimes longer shows, which typically air during the least popular times of the day. Networks are not licenced directly by the federal government, except through their owned and operated stations, so they are under no obligation to demonstrate or perform public service.

---

[8] Nina Thorsen interview with the author on February 24, 2000.

Public service programming offered by the networks is, therefore, offered as a benefit to their affiliates and as a public relations tool. As such, it is reasonable that such services would not be viewed by the networks as central to their mission. It has been a running joke that public service programming often is scheduled in place of a test pattern—and with the same effect.

Federal expectations for public service have always been deliberately vague, and historically, even the lamest programming with a public bent would qualify as serving the public. Further weakening the public service obligations, major revisions of the Communication Act in 1996 and alterations of administrative rules have all but eliminated a station's need to run public service material. Without the government leverage, media access by prevention programs has become a tougher sell. The fact is, stations just don't need to run your messages.

Given that the odds are stacked against public-interest groups, what can they do to increase their slim chances for free air time? The best strategy is the personal appeal. Organizers increase their chances of success when they approach station management personally and when they understand management's driving self interests. That being true, a few guidelines are in order.

Provide a Complete, Ready-to-Air Package. Broadcasters are not eager to give away air time, but they are even less excited about spending money to produce programs or ads that earn no income. They will respond more favorably to requests for public service time when organizations offer ready-to-run, air-quality spots. Come with well-produced videos edited to the proper running time, in a format compatible with the station's equipment.

Be Noncontroversial and Noncommercial. Radio and television stations, like all businesses, try to minimize risk. Groups seeking PSA time must be prepared to demonstrate that their messages are without legal risk and are unlikely to bring about negative public reaction. Any smell of controversy will kill the deal.

The media are unlikely to give free air time to an organization that promotes a product or service, even indirectly. Steer clear of anything with a commercial angle and advocate ideas, not goods and services.

Demonstrate Audience Appeal. Broadcast stations are in the public relations business as they strive to cultivate loyal, dependable audiences that sustain the advertising base. Accordingly, groups should appeal to the stations' self-interests by demonstrating a public relations kick from their messages. Show that the public will think more highly of the station for carrying these messages and thereby fortify its perceived good-citizen status. It's a matter of perspective: where sponsors see a prevention message, the stations should see a public image opportunity.

Illustrate the Integration of the Spots with Current Issues and News. Following the logic of the previous point, stations will reject outdated or irrelevant issues because they can damage the broadcaster's image. Groups therefore should describe the mainstream qualities of their messages. Their success can bring about several benefits.

First, and most obviously, they will increase their chances of getting their spots on the air. In addition, a demonstration that this issue has public appeal may promote it as a story for a local news program. This can extend the reach of prevention efforts beyond the quick PSA spots and convert an isolated message into a campaign.

As with any sales pitch, selling a PSA must appeal to the self-interest of the buyer; in this case, the buyer is focused on the bottom line. Broadcasters today minimize costs and maximize audience appeal to converge on the profit margin. Appeals to these interests stand the best chance of success.

NEWS: PRINT AND BROADCAST

Getting prevention messages into programming and public service slots may be easier than getting them into news stories if for no other reason than that reporters and editors steadfastly reject outside influence on their product. They are often pitched by public relations flacks, and yes, occasionally they report on an item because someone sells it to them, but it isn't in their natures to buy a story from someone with a vested interest. Maybe it's their fear of becoming a pushover for every pitch in the business, or maybe it's a perceived obligation to guard the gates of the fifth estate. Journalism schools preach a hard line when it comes to deciding what is news and what is hype, and that catechism has taken hold within the press corps. The degree of resistance, moreover, is proportional to the size of the news organization, so calibrate your goals accordingly and, without losing heart, realize what you're up against.

Every journalist who participated in our nonrandom survey made clear that he or she would not be pushed around when it came to choosing a story. A 30-year wire-service veteran minced no words: "I am a reporter. It's not the job of a newspaper to preach, but to report. Don't ask us to persuade readers, that's not what we do. We get out the news." Think Jason Robards in *All the President's Men*.

Resistant or not, the news media cover the prevention message, and their coverage offers several benefits. For one, with stories appearing in print, on air and online, reporting can be ubiquitous. It can be hard for audiences to escape, and that's the dream of prevention organizations (see Wartella & Stout, chap. 2, this volume). Moreover, the multimedia coverage reinforces the message, increases its salience, and elevates its ranking on the public agenda. News coverage can have a greater impact than PSAs.

News media coverage is also free, and given the valuable time and space it can offer, that's not a bad deal. Organizational budgets are always tight, but even if they were flush with cash, they would be hard pressed to buy the kind of exposure they can receive on an evening newscast or in a daily paper.

The news media also can add new dimensions to the prevention story. They can tie substance abuse to other current issues, say, poverty, crime, and illness, that demonstrate the widespread, societal depredations of drugs. Further, their analyses can personalize the message and target the calculated interests of audiences gathered around any given medium. PSAs and small print ads generally hit a single issue, and their targeting often is poor. News coverage can provide a broad context and demonstrate the many aspects of the problem while pinpointing specific groups of readers and viewers.

For lots of reasons, then, it's a good idea to get the prevention message into the newspapers and onto television and radio, and well worth the effort to convince the media to help in doing so. However, be aware of a caution offered by several reporters and editors: "Watch what you wish for, you might get it." When you convince the media to cover an issue, you set in motion a process that escapes your control.

Consider the thoughts of an editor for Public Radio. "If you convince me to do a story about antidrug education, I'd find it hard to confine my piece to the five ills of substance use, or whatever. I'd also have to talk about the consequences of antidrug policies that send lots of people to prison."

She explained that she would have to find a coordinated strategy that placed the prevention message in the larger context of society's approach to drugs. "How do you cover the setup issues without getting into the whole package? For a one-minute story, you might get away with it, but for a longer piece, you would have to look at the larger basket of issues. We would have to find a way of saying that we're trying to put an emphasis on prevention, but does this mean less emphasis on enforcement of drug offenses? Is this prevention plus?"

A television news producer also took a hard line. When asked how she would work with prevention organizations, she said, "I think it's important for the media to look at what's being done to curtail drug problems, but also to measure the effectiveness of those programs. If millions of dollars are going into a campaign that hasn't made any measurable difference, then it's also the reporter's job to look into that. . . In other words, hold them [the prevention organizations] to the same amount of accountability they want from the drug addict."

Planting a prevention story in a wider landscape, often called "contextual reporting," was shared by other news professionals. All agreed they would refuse to be trapped into covering a single feature of any story. Several people said they would also bring into their stories more balanced positions than are typically advanced by advocacy groups. One newspaper reporter, for instance, said that when he reports on the dangers of smoking, he also feels obligated to express probabilities rather than an absolutist view.

"In reporting the facts, I have to give the reader a sense for the likelihood of the outcomes of smoking. Not every smoker gets cancer or emphysema, although smoking increases the probability of it." He said that the press loses credibility when it reports an absolutist's view; people know the correlation of usage and its consequences are not 100%. The point for prevention groups is that the press will temper the intensity of your message as it transplants your issue within its own beds of concern.

Those points are understood by politicians, businesses, and government organizations that routinely work with the press. It's a Pandora's box because you unleash the whimsy of reporters and editors who have minds of their own and who will take a story where their research and their instincts lead them. As we noted earlier, the instincts of many in the business warn them against becoming a pawn for any group or cause. Their aim is to "get out the news." Some have been known to prove their independence defiantly by sticking it to one cause or another. At best, prevention organizations can flag an issue, make the case for their point of view, and hope that the media take their lead.

APPROACHING THE PRESS

After respondents laid out the cautions about working with the press, we warily asked them for advice about approaching newsrooms to pitch a prevention story. It was like asking officials at Fort Knox for a combination to the vault. In fact, we weren't looking for secrets, only for a workable formula that would allow news professionals and prevention organizations to meet over development of a story.

Their responses focused on three items:

1. Develop an organizational structure that feeds the press.

2. Take into account the chaotic nature of the news business when pitching a story.
3. Be prepared to answer key questions about your proposal.

Develop an Organizational Structure that Feeds the Press. A television reporter said that many advocacy organizations fail to develop an organizational structure that systematically serves the press. The problem may stem from an organization's view of information as a product rather than a process—as an isolated message rather than a system by which that message reaches the public. To make the point, he told this story:

> I was running my daily round of calls to police stations, city hall offices, and hospitals when the receptionist at the hospital mentioned there was a sharp increase in the number of heroin overdoses in the emergency room. I asked how long was this going on, and she said, "a few weeks."
>
> I called the public health department to find out what was happening, and I got the bureaucratic run-around. Nobody knew anything, nobody wanted to talk. Finally, I found a researcher who said, "Yes, we've measured this increase, and we know about it, sure."
>
> "'And you didn't' tell us," I asked? "A matter of such public importance, and you didn't tell us?"
>
> He said it wasn't his responsibility to tell anyone but his supervisor. So, I called his supervisor.
>
> The supervisor said that it wasn't his responsibility to tell the press, and so the information died on his desk. The fact is, this outfit had no mechanism in place to get out this important news, so it was hidden from public view.
>
> Do I think they were trying to conceal anything? No, it just wasn't in their blueprints to pass along information to the press or to other interested constituencies. It demonstrated poor management and a general misunderstanding of how the press should figure in organizational plans.

The public health department of a medium-size city is not the same as a prevention organization, of course, but the reporter's story is relevant just the same. Academics, nonprofit organizations, and advocacy groups should view their interactions with the press as an ongoing, two-way relationship. The press may come to the organization for quotations, expert opinions, and perspectives on related stories in the news. Reporters often need to flesh out a story, and they rely on a stable of professionals for fast background information and observations of events. In turn, these organizations are in a better position to approach the media when they need public exposure.

How do organizations set this process in motion? Begin by assigning someone to establish contact with the press and to examine organizational activities routinely for possible press interest. What issues have public relevance or interest, what items ultimately will impact public policy? Any group whose work has relevance to the community should keep the press in the organizational loop.

Two benefits result: The organization will cultivate better relations and strengthen its credibility with the press. Reporters will see the organization as a regular source of information and not just as a beggar seeking favors when it needs publicity. This will result in the increased likelihood—but no guarantee—that the media will smile on the organization's occasional requests for news coverage and public service time. It's a matter of familiarity and credibility and of having an advocate that can grease the skids.

Take into Account the Chaotic Nature of the News Business when Pitching a Story. Contracting lead times, increased competition, and a tightening definition of "instant" have ratcheted up the pressures on journalists who every day face the daunting task of filling a gaping news hole. Just as television has impacted radio and newspapers, the Internet is now changing the role and operations of traditional media.

One of the changes is the around-the-clock news operation, which means always-open, always current, always ready to handle the breaking news the moment something newsworthy occurs. The Net is ideal for the instant release of news and this instant-turnaround puts enormous pressure on all media to monitor news sources, and to rush a story into the market as quickly as possible, where a few minutes late is a lifetime and relevance is measured by the hour. For all media, this breakneck delivery can create problems with accuracy, depth, and scope, but that's another discussion, and it doesn't change the fact that what is new and what is news today are changing the character and conduct of news reporting.

The Internet, with its unlimited capacity, has pushed the other media to include more information, more stories, more coverage of local, regional, and global events. This has become the most information-drenched period in human history, with greater opportunity for more people to get more information about more places and topics than ever before. Whether or not people are accessing this information and using it for productive ends is another matter, but today the potential for a well-informed populace is extraordinary.

Respondents reminded us of these increased pressures. A radio reporter said,

> It never stops, you never fill the hole, because just as soon as you complete one story, one newscast, you face yet another deadline for the next story, the next newscast. And every day is the same. In this business, you can't plan much in advance or get ahead the way you can in other businesses, especially now that people are concerned about what happened only in the last hour, and, of course, you can't plan ahead for that.

The frenetic pace of newsgathering has affected the way reporters interact with news sources. As this reporter suggested, the heightened demands make it more difficult to ease into a report or to spend much time with someone who has a newsworthy story to tell.

It also changes how sources approach the media. For better or worse, sources bearing ready-to-run stories have a greater chance at getting the attention they seek. Those with press releases, interesting quotations, photos, and other items that enrich a story sharpen the appeal for a stressed reporter. It's human nature to take the most convenient route, especially when schedules are tight and the story is a good one to begin with.

What's the lesson? Don't call reporters with a great idea and expect then to set aside a few days to research it. Come with a package under your arm that lays out the details, explains the importance of your program, offers quotations, has visual material where appropriate, and lists sources, phone numbers, and e-mail addresses for further inquiries. Reporters will use this information as a basis on which to determine their interest in the story, and, if they like it, for a quick start at their own research and inquiry. Bear in mind an earlier caveat that once you evoke a reporter's interest, you lose control of where the reporter ultimately goes with it. A story about drug prevention could easily morph into an account of sentencing laws, border control, national budget priorities, and a dozen other areas of little concern to you. Don't just brace for this, anticipate it. Be prepared to answer these key questions about your proposal.

Why is Your Story "News?" Along with traditional newsmakers, millions of people everyday engage in millions of activities that are expressed as anecdotes at the dinner table. With proper treatment, a good number of them could make an interesting, if not entirely newsworthy, item in the morning paper or on an evening newscast. What elements of your story make it soar above all the other things happening to people that day? Why should the media cover your prevention issue rather than someone else's story? What is news about your issue?

Give the media reasons to single you out. Draft a list of features that ratchet up the salience of your story. Show its relevance to people's lives, its political, economic, cultural significance. List the qualities that make it interesting to readers and viewers and show editors how covering this particular story will educate the audience and leave consumers of news with a positive view of the medium that carried it.

Even though we urge organizations to prove the newsworthiness of a story, we know that the media today, and particularly local television, are drawn to the bells and whistles, to the ambulance chasers, to the cats in the trees and other trivia that could not possibly be confused with news of substance. Call it infotainment, soft news, or just amusement, the media often are attracted to what draws a large--and accordingly profitable— audience, journalistic content be damned. Paraphrasing an old saying, the business of the news business is business.

In our interviews, the journalists talked about news in terms you would expect to hear in a journalism class. They were, no doubt, sincere, and in the best of all worlds, that is how they would like to see the news-room run. The evidence suggests, however, that there is room for the human interest argument—along side the news argument--in presenting a prevention story. Maybe it's just a definition of news, but don't be afraid to make the point that a story can stimulate audience interest simply because it appeals to curiosities and something called human interest.

Why Is Your Story News Today? The accelerating pace of the news business puts added pressure on journalists to demonstrate not only the currency of a story, but its immediacy as well. Several professionals said that the chances for taking on a story increase when organizations can show that the story should be run *today*. "If someone pitching a story says it could just as easily be covered next week, then we'll probably bag it. If it can be done next week, we won't cover it today, we'll say, come back next week."

This concern for immediacy suggests that prevention organizations should pin their story on an event that will command attention. For instance, link a research finding to a presentation at a conference. The conference taking place today or tomorrow marks a place on the calendar, and the research finding comes along for the ride. A similar timed event can be the publication of a journal ("This month's edition of *The Journal of the American Medical Association*," just reported that..."). For groundbreaking or genuinely significant matters, a press conference serves the same purpose: It's an event with a fixed place in time, and reporting on that event opens the door for the contents. The bottom line is that journalists look out for today, and they judge the value of a proposed story, in part, on how firmly it ties to the moment.

Does that mean feature stories with less of a time lock become more difficult to sell as news items? Yes. The human-interest elements of less time-bound features may be enough to draw in the media, but they are sold differently, and they are often sold to different divisions of the organization—entertainment or feature rather than news. Here, the pitch is purely human interest, and promoters must rely on that element. This leads to the final question.

Why Is Your Story Important to My Audience? Editors and producers size up a story by its appeal to certain audiences. Anyone pitching a story must demonstrate why the readers, listeners, viewers of *this particular medium* will look at this particular topic. Stories about technology may sell better in some parts of the country than in others. Prevention stories may have greater appeal to young audiences gathered around MTV, unless the story is about elders addicted to prescription drugs, which would attract seniors. For many media, a story with specific audience draw will trump a story with general human interest every time.

This argues for audience research, if only informal, and for a presentation that includes a roster of reasons demonstrating the likely attraction of this story to this editor's readers. How do you make the case? Examine the target medium's previous articles and news clips. Radio and television pieces often are archived on the web these days, so a review of broadcast stories is not as difficult as it once was.

Read letters to the editor, op-ed pieces, and editorials to discover interests generated by people outside the news staff. Argue that recent letters about drug use in schools suggest an audience concern for prevention stories about youth. Incidentally, letters to the editor are high in reader interest, and most papers accept letters written by organizational representatives.

Examine polls, attend public meetings, visit local websites, look at other media to uncover community concerns. A hot item within the reading/viewing area can argue for media coverage of related issues. This can demonstrate the relevance of a topic to a local community and earn the medium wider audiences.

Ultimately, the editors/producers will determine what is of interest to their audiences. Many resent an outsider telling them they have systematically missed a topic, and thus deprived their readers. Presentation is everything. Offer the story as an opportunity to expand the agenda and attract an audience.

Whether pitching a news story or a feature piece, it is essential to demonstrate audience relevance, and it is always better to arrive with hard evidence. Before pitching the story, do the research. Moreover, think like a media professional: Start with the audience and adapt the idea and style to that target.

Several news professionals reminded us that stories must be pitched with two related audiences in mind: first the gatekeepers—the editors and producers—and second the readers and viewers. The media gatekeepers will apply their own values and interests even as they anticipate the values and interests of their audience. For prevention stories, this has a special relevance.

"Most of the people in their thirties, forties, and fifties have probably tried drugs themselves," said a thirty-something producer. "They may associate that period of their lives with fun and pleasure and see it as a time of experimentation, the days of passage. Besides, they may now offer their own professional success as evidence that a little drug use does not always end in tragedy and death."

So, the hard sell to people whose own experiences may refute tough claims about the evils of drugs may not be all that easy; moreover, it may invite the kind of point-counterpoint and contextual reporting we discussed earlier. Prevention organizations will have to anticipate the values of the gatekeepers if they are to expect success in placing their news story. They must do this, of course, without compromising the message to their primary audience. A national radio producer said, "That makes it a tougher sell. You must double-package your pitch, once for the assignment editors, once for the listeners."

In light of all this advice, we asked the pros to describe what they think are successful pitches. Four items surfaced in our discussions:

Offer Hope. There is always a need for stories about hope," a TV producer told us. "A rehabilitated addict who is willing to share his or her story would be something that could potentially hit home for parents and addicts." People have come to expect the problem-statement, problem-resolution formula found on television dramas, and a news story that fits this model is an easier sell. A drug abuser may have hit bottom, but because of some remarkable intervention or grim determination, he or she has beaten the problem and rejoined the unaddicted. That offers hope for everyone in the audience that drug addiction is not always a terminal condition, and that makes a good story.

Offer Visuals. Another element that helps the sale, at least for television, is visuals. TV needs pictures, action, people doing things. That's one explanation for the overdose of ambulance stories and police activities on the evening news. They offer action, people in motion, something that tells the story without a lot of words. This medium is best when its cameras, rather than its reporters, grab audiences, so producers are naturally drawn to offers of visuals. To a lesser extent this is true for newspapers, even though they, too, favor stories with a visual angle, particularly now that most papers have moved to the graphics-oriented, *USA Today* layout, which itself was inspired by television.

Offer the Local Community Perspective. Start from the perspective of a recognized community problem and show how your program or approach to prevention specifically addresses it. The community angle is something the producer/editor will look for in telling your story, so increase your chances of success by pitching the story from that point of view.

A newspaper reporter offered similar advice: "No reporter wants to put his byline on a story that tells readers to stop using drugs. That's too much like being a stooge for the antidrug industry. We are more comfortable using the paper to help solve a particular problem, or to show people solving a particular problem. The word gets out, but it's not preachy because it's focused on a specific community concern."

Offer Concrete Examples for Statistics. When you're selling statistics and research findings to the press, come armed with data that are reliable, easy to understand, and translated into concrete examples that a layman can understand. "I'm always amazed when academics come with charts and graphs and expect us to understand what they mean, and then to build a story around them," said a political reporter, who himself understands survey data. Even trained technical writers don't want to hassle with difficult statistics, because interpreting them can be time-consuming and dangerous if they draw erroneous conclusions.

The answer is to strip research findings to their bare essentials. Come up with a few—and only a few—key conclusions, even if it means you must sacrifice some of the gems you've worked so hard to collect. Be prepared to discuss methodology only so far as to demonstrate that the process used sound scientific procedures and that the findings are reliable. Good technical reporters know the dangers of bad research; show them you played by the rules.

Pin every statistic to a flesh-and-blood example. Discuss trends and patterns within the population, yes, but offer anecdotes and case studies that nail the numbers to a specific instance. Remember the final audience isn't a classroom of experts but living rooms with average people who are uncomfortable with the math needed to balance a checkbook.

Ronald Reagan and Bill Clinton knew the value of anecdotes to exemplify the effects of complex federal regulations and policies. Both presidents would tell stories of people in the heartland to demonstrate the flesh-and-blood consequences of public policy. They did not do this whimsically, but, one might argue, as a calculated method of political persuasion. Such anecdotes make the point and stick -- they convey the point without the qualifications that often are so necessary when promoting a position.[9] Audiences remember something about a tax cut when they see a woman from Nebraska who benefited from it, and they are more likely to remember a prevention study if they know about a 16-year-old whose life was turned-around by the new program. At the same time, the downsides of the new program -- increased costs, potential threats to civil liberties, etc., can be conveniently avoided.

The news business today is filled with ironies. Reporters operate around the clock to meet unforgiving deadlines and to beat the competition by a few minutes, and yet they are reluctant to accept much help from someone offering a story. Journalists treasure their independence and guard their access. Despite the resulting frustrations, this arm's-length relationship remains a necessary safeguard for the fifth estate. The integrity of journalism depends on it. Competitive pressures should never force reporters to adopt packaged stories rather than to research the facts themselves.

Another irony concerns the nature of news. Is news the presentation of hard facts, the five W's, the dispassionate analysis of events and policies, or is it the soothing appeals to human interest that entertain, pacify, and attract unthinking audiences? Most analysts would agree that recent trends are toward the latter, the "infotainment" brand of news that preoccupies local television programs and now even the serous print media. Reporters present a hard front, saying they will track a story wherever their research leads them for the sake of truth and balance, but the evidence suggests otherwise. Shouts from money crunchers in news organizations all too often are heeded in the newsrooms, where stories many times are selected for their capacity to attract rather than their insights to inform an audience. Front pages of leading newspapers resemble the style sections of papers published years ago. The operational definition of news today is an irony.

This dual personality of the news media poses challenges to organizations interested in getting their story into the papers and onto the newscasts. Organizations have to provide helpful information, but not too much, and they can't expect their lead to be followed. They must demonstrate the newsworthiness of their stories, but they must also show the

---

[9] Reagan was known to make up convenient anecdotes when he needed a good example. Reporters often discovered these fabrications, but somehow it hardly dented Reagan's credibility. No one other than Reagan should count on such forgiveness. Al Gore tried it during the 2000 presidential campaign and the media nailed him every time.

story's appeal to audiences. They have to serve as an information source—or their story would never see the light of day—but they can't appear to be so self-absorbed in good works as to be blind to the realities of the news game.

CONCLUSION

In the final analysis, the relationship between prevention programs and the media represents an opportunity and a challenge for both players. For professionals devoted to prevention, the media are an essential tool. They are ubiquitous, and they blanket the country with so many formats, with so much repetition, that only the most isolated people escape their reach. Moreover, it is simply impossible today to reach large segments of the population except through the media. In time, with growth of the Internet, that may change, but for now the traditional media remain the only link to wholesale audiences. Prevention specialists know the media are a great opportunity.

Media access is the specialists' great challenge. Anyone who needs the reach and power of the media is forced, often on bended knee, to plead for time and space. Unless prevention programs are flush with cash, like the ONDCP effort, they must appeal to the better instincts of the media gatekeepers who allot precious resources among all supplicants. In the best of all worlds, the users of public airwaves would freely run messages that serve the public good, but sadly, that is not the case today, if indeed it ever was. Getting media attention and slivers of time and space are the prevention specialists' challenge.

Media find that prevention stories have an opportunity to generate human interest and, along with interest, audience good will. Audiences everywhere would warm to community newspapers and local broadcast stations that fight the devils of addiction. Telling the righteous story is a sure ticket to good corporate citizenship.

The media are challenged to maintain autonomy and prevent outside control, or at least the appearance of it. In TV programming, media must safeguard artistic freedoms and avoid telling stories that preach morality. No audience wants to suffer through a prevention infomercial, and no programmer wants his name on a show that fronts for the thought police. The networks' deal with the ONDCP appeared to some to come awfully close to that line.

In news, there's the challenge of journalistic standards, of outside influence, of prepackaged stories that are so easy to slip into the lineup of news. Taking the easy way out looks more appealing in the face of time pressures, staff limitations and increasing competition that make matters so much worse for 21st-century journalists.

The media are racked by contradictions, and in the end, it comes down to a shifting balance of purpose. Prevention specialists should be aware of that. They should know that the media strive for accuracy of information, responsibility to audiences, fairness to newsmakers and respect to journalists and the producers of entertainment. But increasingly, competition and a preoccupation with the bottom line drive the media to sensationalism, specious efficiencies, pandering to base audience interests. Within this changing balance of principles and profits, organizations seeking access must contend their case by showing they understand the vagaries of this business and they have a story that is just what the media need.

About the Authors

The Editors:

William D. Crano (Ph.D., Northwestern University) is Professor of Psychology at Claremont Graduate University. He has served as the Program Director in Social Psychology for the National Science Foundation, as Liaison Scientist for the Office of Naval Research, London, as NATO Senior Scientist, University of Southampton, and was a Fulbright Fellow to the Federal University-Rio Grande do Sul, Porto Alegre, Brazil. He was founder/director of the Center for Evaluation and Assessment, Michigan State University, and directed the Public Policy Resources Laboratory of Texas A&M University. Crano has written 10 books, more than 20 book chapters, and more than 200 scholarly articles and scientific presentations. He is the past president of the Society for Experimental Social Psychology, and is a Fellow of the American Psychological Association, the American Psychological Society, and the Society for Personality and Social Psychology.

Michael Burgoon (Ph.D., Michigan State University) is the Head, Communication Research Section, Cancer Prevention and Control Program, in the University of Arizona's Cancer Center. He is Professor of Medicine, Public Health, Family and Community Medicine, and Communication at the University of Arizona. Dr. Burgoon founded the communication outreach section of the Arizona Cancer Center, and serves as its director. He has written extensively on persuasion in general, and on prevention and health relevant communication in particular. He is a Fellow of the International Communication Association, and a member of the Society for Experimental Social Psychology.

The Contributors:

R. Kirkland Ahern (M.A., University of Pennsylvania) is a doctoral student at the University of Pennsylvania's Annenberg School for Communication. Her research interests are the neurological and psychological processes of cognition and affect that give rise to message effects, such as how health messages are processed and how the Internet affects information perception.

Eusebio M. Alvaro (Ph.D., MPH, University of Arizona) is Director of the Health Communication Research Office at the Arizona Cancer Center, at the University of Arizona. He has published on fundamental aspects of persuasion, including personality correlates of healthy behavior, and on minority group influence. His current research focuses on assessing the relative efficacy of drug prevention campaign messages on adolescent drug use. His most recently completed research assesses effectiveness of different forms of counseling intervention for youth tobacco cessation.

Charles Atkin (Ph.D., University of Wisconsin) is University Distinguished Professor and Chair of the Department of Communication at Michigan State University. Dr. Atkin's work focuses on the role of the mass media in health promotion; he has published the books *Public Communication Campaigns* and *Mass Communication and Public Health,* and has served as a campaign design consultant or evaluation researcher on a number of national public information and education programs, including drunk driving and safety belts, and alcohol and drug abuse. He has authored more than 125 journal articles and book chapters.

Katherine Broneck, (M.A., University of Arizona) is a Graduate Research Associate in the University of Arizona's Health Communication Research Office. Her research is concerned with issues of credibility and the new media.

Judee Burgoon (Ed. D., West Virginia University) is Professor of Communication and Director for Human Communication Research, Center for the Management of Information, at the University of Arizona. Her published research spans interpersonal and nonverbal interaction, media and new communication technologies, and influence processes. Her work, which has been funded by private and government sources, including the Research and Advanced Concepts Office of the U. S. Army Research

Institute, has earned her several awards from national and international associations. In 1992, she was named the most prolific female scholar in communication, 1915-1990, and five years later was given the B. Aubrey Fisher Mentorship Award of the National Communication Association. She is a fellow of the International Communication Association, and was elected to the Society for Experimental Social Psychology.

Joseph N. Cappella (Ph.D., Michigan State University) is Professor of Communication and holds the Gerald R. Miller Chair at the Annenberg School for Communication at the University of Pennsylvania. His research has focused on social interaction, interpersonal communication, political communication, nonverbal behavior, media effects, and statistical methods. He is author of *Spiral of Cynicism*, *Multivariate Techniques in Human Communication Research*, and *Sequence and Pattern in Communicative Behavior*. He is a Fellow of the ICA, recipient of the B. Aubrey Fisher Mentorship Award, and a past President of the International Communication Association

James Derzon (Ph.D., Claremont Graduate University) is the Director of Knowledge Synthesis and Computer Modeling at the Pacific Institutes for Research and Evaluation. Before moving to PIRE, Dr. Derzon was Associate Director for Research at the Hamilton Fish Institute on School and Community Violence at George Washington University. His research has concentrated on developing and using meta-analytic techniques and methods to improve prevention science, particularly in the policy relevant areas of predicting and preventing antisocial behavior, delinquency, and substance use. Dr. Derzon has used meta-analytic techniques to examine the quality of evidence for predicting criminal and substance using outcomes. He has also conducted meta-analytic studies on the effectiveness of school-based programs to reduce violence and the effectiveness of mass-media interventions to reduce youth substance use.

Stewart I. Donaldson, (Ph.D., Claremont Graduate University), is Professor of Psychology, Chair of the Organizational Behavior Doctoral Program, and Director of the Institute of Organizational and Program Evaluation Research at Claremont Graduate University. Dr. Donaldson currently serves as co-chair of the Program Theory and Theory-Driven Evaluation Division of the American Evaluation Association. His research interests include theory-driven program design and evaluation, substance abuse prevention, workplace health promotion, and organizational development. Dr. Donaldson has received numerous research grants on these topics from agencies such as the National Institute on Alcohol Abuse and

Alcoholism, National Institute of Mental Health, and the California Wellness Foundation. In 1996, he was a recipient of the American Evaluation Association's Marcia Guttentag Early Career Achievement Award, in recognition of his work on theory and method and for accomplishments in teaching and practice of program evaluation.

Lewis Donohew (Ph.D., University of Iowa) until recently held an appointment as Professor in the Department of Communication, College of Communications and Information Studies, and an adjunct appointment as Professor in the Department of Behavioral Science, College of Medicine, both at the University of Kentucky. He has written extensively on theory development and construction and on health communication, and has been principal investigator on eight major grants from agencies of the National Institutes of Health. He currently holds a post-retirement appointment in his home department and continues to be active on funded research projects.

Marvin Eisen (Ph.D., Ohio State University) is a Principal Research Associate at The Urban Institute in Washington, D.C. He is a developmental psychologist with 30 years of research and evaluation project experience in the areas of adolescent and youth sexual behavior, substance use, and mental health services. His major interest is in primary prevention of high-risk sexual behaviors and substance use, and measurement of health-related behavior change through interviews and surveys. These interests have led to a focus on development, implementation, and outcome evaluation of sexuality, drug education, HIV/AIDS prevention, and family planning programs for high-risk adolescents and young adults. Dr. Eisen has held project and evaluation leadership roles in several national, multi-site, collaborative research projects and outcome and impact evaluations of community- and school-based health and mental health intervention programs. He is the author or co-author of numerous journal articles, monographs, book chapters, and technical research reports on primary prevention, program evaluation, and child development. He has held teaching and research positions at Michigan State, Yale, RAND, Texas, and Sociometrics Corporation. Currently, he is Principal Investigator of the multi-site, multi-year project to evaluate the effectiveness of the Lions-Quest *"Skills for Adolescence (SFA)"* program [described here]. He has recently completed a RWJ Foundation study identifying promising problem behavior prevention programs, including drug education, suitable for use in schools and school-based health centers.

Martin Fishbein (Ph.D., UCLA) is the Harry C. Coles Jr. Distinguished Professor of Communication and Director of the Health Communication Area in the Public Policy Center of the Annenberg School for Communication at the University of Pennsylvania. Developer of the Theory of Reasoned Action, he has published over 200 articles and chapters and has authored or edited six books. He has been President of the Interamerican Psychological Society and the Society for Consumer Psychology.

Cynthia A. Frank (M.A., University of Arizona) is a Support Systems Analyst Sr. in the Biomedical Communications Division of the Arizona Health Sciences Center, where she assists in the development of multimedia interventions for prevention and clinical applications.

Joseph R. Grandpre (Ph.D., MPH, University of Arizona) is a Research Specialists, Principal, in the Arizona Cancer Center. His research has been concerned with smoking prevention, and with the development of techniques to enhance the effectiveness of the mass media anti-drug campaign directed at early adolescents.

John Hall (Ph.D., University of Arizona) is Associate Director of the Biomedical Communications Division at the Arizona Health Sciences Center. His research has focused on a broad range of preventive behaviors in the service of health promotion, including tobacco cessation, drug prevention, and HIV/AIDS avoidance.

Nancy Grant Harrington (Ph.D., University of Kentucky) is Associate Professor and Chair of the Department of Communication at the University of Kentucky. She is principal investigator or co-principal investigator on three major research projects dealing with drug abuse prevention. Her primary areas of interest are in interpersonal communication and in health communication.

Robert Hornik (Ph.D., Stanford University) is Professor of Communication and holds the Wilbur Schramm Chair in Communication and Health Policy in the Annenberg School for Communication at the University of Pennsylvania. He has just completed two evaluations of domestic violence prevention projects and is currently co-principal investigator and scientific director for the evaluation of the National Youth Anti-Drug Media Campaign. He has recently completed editing, *Public Health Communication: Evidence for Behavior Change.*

Alan I. Leshner (Ph.D., Rutgers University) is Director of the National Institute on Drug Abuse. Prior to this appointment, Dr. Leshner served as Deputy Director and Acting Director of the National Institute of Mental Health, and in various senior positions in the National Science Foundation, where he held a variety of senior positions focused on basic research in the biological, behavioral and social sciences, and on science education. Before his government service, Dr. Leshner was Professor of Psychology at Bucknell University. While on Bucknell's faculty, he also held appointments at the Postgraduate Medical School in Budapest, Hungary, at the Wisconsin Regional Primate Research Center, and as a Fulbright Scholar at the Weizmann Institute of Science in Israel. Dr. Leshner's research has focused on the biological bases of behavior. He is the author of a major textbook on the relationship between hormones and behavior, and numerous book chapters and papers in professional journals. He also has published extensively in the areas of science and technology policy and education. Dr. Leshner received the Presidential Distinguished Executive Rank Award, and is a member of the Institute of Medicine of the National Academy of Sciences.

Mark W. Lipsey (Ph.D., Johns Hopkins University) is Professor of Public Policy at Vanderbilt University, and Co-Director of the Center for Evaluation Research and Methodology at the Vanderbilt Institute for Public Policy Studies. Dr. Lipsey received the American Evaluation Association's Paul Lazarsfeld Award for evaluation theory, and has served on the editorial boards of numerous journals, including *Evaluation Review*, the *American Journal of Community Psychology*, and *New Directions for Program Evaluation*, among others. He has published widely on applied research methods, evaluation and meta-analysis. His *Evaluation, A systematic approach* is in its sixth edition, and his *Toolkit for practical meta-analysis* remains an outstanding contribution to the practice of this important research technique

Elizabeth Lorch (Ph.D., University of Massachusetts) is Professor of Psychology at the University of Kentucky whose specialty is developmental psychology. She has been studying young people and television throughout her career.

Claude Miller (Ph.D., University of Arizona) is an Assistant Professor at Wake Forest University. His research focuses on the utilization of affective appeals in prevention research. He also has researched characteristics of tobacco prevention campaign messages.

Philip Palmgreen (Ph.D., University of Michigan) is Professor of Communication at the University of Kentucky and currently serves on the behavior change expert panel for the Office of National Drug Control Policy's national media campaign on drug abuse prevention. He currently is principal investigator on one of the two cities projects described in this volume.

Joseph R. Priester (Ph.D., Ohio State University) is Assistant Professor of Marketing at the University of Michigan. His research is concerned with the psychological processes underlying social and consumer behavior, especially as related to attitudes and persuasion, ambivalence, expectancies, and source perceptions. He has co-authored a book on the *Social Psychology of Consumption*, and numerous book chapters and journal articles. He has served on the editorial boards of three major journals in social psychology and consumer behavior.

Sarah Sayeed (Ph.D., University of Pennsylvania) is an Assistant Professor in the School of Public Affairs at Baruch College in the City University of New York. She is engaged in research about anti-drug media campaigns, especially on the interplay of interpersonal and mass communication processes in determining health outcomes.

Gary Selnow (Ph.D., Michigan State University) is Professor of Communication at San Francisco State University, and Director of WiRED (World Internet Resources for Education and Development), a nonprofit corporation. Selnow is the author/co-author of seven books including *Society's Impact on Television, High Tech Campaigns, Electronic Whistle-Stops: The Impact of the Internet on American Politics*, and most recently, *The People, Press and Politics of Croatia*. He is currently writing a book about the Internet's effects on American politics; it is titled *Through Washington's Back Door*. Selnow was a Fulbright Senior Scholar in Austria and most recently at the University of Zagreb in Croatia. He has lectured at the London School of Economics, the University of Warsaw, the Free University of Amsterdam and other universities in Europe. Selnow coordinated a national communication program for a White House task force and served as a research methodologist for the U.S. Information Agency. He is a consultant with the U.S. Department of State and consulted for NBC Television and the National Academy of Sciences. Selnow was a pilot and information officer for the U.S. Air Force. He occasionally airs commentaries on Public Radio International's Marketplace program.

Jason T. Siegel (M.A., University of Arizona) is a Research Associate for the Health Communication
Research Office at the Arizona Cancer Center, and a PhD candidate in the University of Arizona's Department of Educational Psychology. He is the co-author of *Breaking Into Television*, and has worked as a FOX-TV producer, a consultant for UPN, and has contributed essays to both the *Encyclopedia of Advertising* and the *Encyclopedia of Radio*.

Patricia Stout (Ph.D., University of Illinois) is Professor and Associate Dean of the College of Communication, The University of Texas at Austin. Dr. Stout's main research interests include viewer response to advertising, with particular emphasis on emotional response. She is interested in health-promotion messages and social marketing issues. Her publications include articles in *Journal of Advertising, Psychology and Marketing, Journalism Quarterly, Journal of Media Planning*, and various book chapters and conference proceedings. Dr. Stout has been a visiting research professor at the U.S. Centers for Disease Control and Prevention in Atlanta, with the AIDS Information and Education Program, and a visiting professor at the University of Auckland, New Zealand. She has served as President of the American Academy of Advertising and on the Accreditation Council for Education in Journalism and Mass Communication.

Ellen Wartella (Ph.D., University of Minnesota) is Dean of the College of Communication, Walter Cronkite Regents Chair in Communication and Mrs. Mary Gibbs Jones Centennial Chair in Communication at The University of Texas at Austin. She serves on the editorial board of seven journals and book series, including *Communication Theory* and *Human Communication Research*. She is co-author or editor of nine books and dozens of book chapters and articles on mass media effects on children and other audiences. As consultant to the Federal Communications Commission, Federal Trade Commission and Congressional investigations of children and television issues, she has been an advocate for better programming for children. Furthermore, she has been an advisor to producers of educational television programs for children, such as the Sesame Workshop, the producers of Sesame Street, Learning Designs, Inc., the producers of Behind the Scenes, and Scholastic Inc., producers of The Magic School Bus. She has been a fellow at the Gannett Center for Media Studies at Columbia University a visiting professor at the University of Munich. She was named Beckman Fellow at the University of Illinois, and has received the Kreighbaum Award from the Association for Education in Journalism and Mass Communication. She is a fellow of the International Communication Association, and served as President of that organization. She serves on the Advisory Boards of the Children's Advertising Review Unit of the Council of Better Business Bureaus and the American Children's Television Center. She is a member of the Board of Trustees of the Sesame Workshop, a member of the Board of Directors of the Center for Media Education, and a member of the National Advisory Board of the Hogg Foundation.

Marco Yzer (Ph.D., University of Groningen) is a post-doctoral fellow in the Public Policy Center of the Annenberg School for Communication at the University of Pennsylvania. His research has focused on the evaluation of mass-media campaigns, experimental tests of message effectiveness, and tests of the validity of theories of behavioral prediction and change.

Rick S. Zimmerman (Ph.D., University of Wisconsin) is Associate Professor of Communication in the Department of Communication, with an adjunct appointment in the Department of Behavioral Science in the College of Medicine, both at the University of Kentucky. He is the developer of the Impulsive Decision Making Scale and currently holds three major grants on prevention of sexual risk taking in relation to alcohol use and HIV.

Author Index

Subject Index